Balzac's Lives

PETER BROOKS

nyrb **New York Review Books** New York

This is a New York Review Book

published by The New York Review of Books

435 Hudson Street, New York, NY 10014

www.nyrb.com

Library of Congress Cataloging-in-Publication Data
Names: Brooks, Peter, 1938– author.
Title: Balzac's lives / by Peter Brooks.
Description: New York : New York Review Books, [2020] | Includes
    bibliographical references and index.
Identifiers: LCCN 2020016060 (print) | LCCN 2020016061 (ebook) |
    ISBN 9781681374499 (paperback) | ISBN 9781681374505 (ebook)
Subjects: LCSH: Balzac, Honoré de, 1799–1850—Characters. | Balzac,
    Honoré de, 1799–1850—Criticism and interpretation.
Classification: LCC PQ2184.C5 B76 2020 (print) | LCC PQ2184.C5
    (ebook) | DDC 843/.7—dc23
LC record available at https://lccn.loc.gov/2020016060
LC ebook record available at https://lccn.loc.gov/2020016061

ISBN 978-1-68137-449-9
Available as an electronic book; ISBN 978-1-68137-450-5

Printed in the United States of America on acid-free paper.

1 2 3 4 5 6 7 8 9 10

As for his eyes, there was never anything like them. They had inconceivable light, life, magnetism. . . . They were eyes to make an eagle blink, eyes to read through walls and rib cages, eyes to stop a wild beast in its tracks, eyes of a sovereign, of a seer, of a lion tamer.

—Théophile Gautier, on Balzac

Contents

Introduction: Why Balzac? 1

1. Eugène de Rastignac 11

2. Jean-Esther van Gobseck 38

3. Antoinette de Langeais 55

4. Raphaël de Valentin 78

5. Lucien Chardon de Rubempré 104

6. Jacques Collin 131

7. Henriette de Mortsauf 155

8. Colonel Chabert 179

9. Marco Facino Cane and Friend 195

10. Living in Fictional Lives 215

Acknowledgments 237

Notes 239

Selected Bibliography 251

Chronology: France from the Revolution to 1850 255

Index 259

Introduction
Why Balzac?

THIS IS NOT A BIOGRAPHY—IT'S an antibiography or maybe more accurately an oblique biography of the great novelist Honoré de Balzac. Balzac's life has often been told, but it's less compelling than Balzac's *lives*, the extraordinary, extravagant, profligate creation of the well over two thousand fictional beings who people his novels. That's where we find the truth of his time and of his imaginative life.

Oscar Wilde noted in one of his truest paradoxes that the nineteenth century as we know it is largely Balzac's invention.[1] The invention takes the form of a remarkable set of life stories that marshal the dynamic forces of a new era, its entrepreneurs, bankers, inventors, industrialists, poets, artists, bohemians of both sexes, journalists, aristocrats, politicians, doctors, musicians, detectives, actors and actresses, moneylenders, peasants, professors, prostitutes—the list extends to cover all social spheres and all careers in a world where the assigned identities of the ancien régime have given way to an uncertain new order where everything seems to be up for grabs, if you can find some way to get the money you need to acquire things, name, reputation, fortune. There are group portraits in Balzac: the Princesse de Cadignan leafing through the album of her past lovers, for instance, or the party following the large soiree given by the novelist Félicité des Touches when an elite of his characters gathers to exchange worldly wisdom in the form of stories. At such moments the reader has an almost vertiginous sense of the richness and completeness of Balzac's fictional world. There has really never been anything quite like it before or since. The *Index of Fictional Characters* in *The Human Comedy*, the who's who of his world, lists some 2,472 beings invented by the novelist.[2]

It's notable that nearly every time one of these characters enters one of the many tales that make up *The Human Comedy*, he or she is given a biography, sometimes a few lines, in the case of the minor figures, but often several paragraphs or even pages. Balzac needs to situate his people; showing how their personal histories are related to the history of the nation at a given moment is crucial. At times, it is astonishing to find the movement of the narrative arrested for the backstory of a new character; we may even be annoyed at the delay, until we come to realize that the new character's story is indispensable to the narrative as a whole. As in collections of interconnected tales such as *The Decameron* and *The Arabian Nights* (the latter being one of Balzac's touchstones) each new person is defined as the bearer of a story—they are people-narratives.[3] Balzac can't conceive of representing the world other than through these people-narratives: to understand contemporary France is to tell the story of all its inhabitants, to rival, as he put it, the "civil registry." *The Human Comedy* resembles the office of the census. But much more fun.

Balzac proclaimed himself a political conservative in reaction to an era of unregulated change, in which the individual ego seemed to have become the sole measure of things. His nostalgia for a past organic society where people knew their place and social rank was evident in dress and manner is matched by his fascination with the new possibilities for each individual to forge a unique destiny. The growing city of Paris, the increase in social mobility, and the ambitions unleashed by capitalism and nascent democracy all called for a new semiotics of modern life, new ways to read who people are, what their clothes and accessories and ways of walking and speaking say about where they come from and where they are going. The sum of those invented destinies is *The Human Comedy*.

He was born in 1799—the year Napoleon Bonaparte seized power to put an end to the French Revolution—as Honoré Balzac to a family only one generation removed from peasant farmers named Balssa. The pseudo-aristocratic "de" was added later. His father rose to a middling rank in the postrevolutionary bureaucracy, and that took the family from its native Tours to Paris in 1814. Honoré studied law but yearned for literature. He wheedled his family to grant him two years to succeed as a writer. His first efforts were failures. During the 1820s, though, he managed to publish a number of Gothic and adventure novels, signed with pseudonyms since he knew they were not what he wanted to be known for (he later called them literary slop, yet also republished them to make money). The first novel signed with his name came in 1829. Then during the 1830s he became the Balzac that we know; he published a series of powerful novels and then conceived of making them the building blocks of a larger ensemble not yet known as *The Human Comedy*. The July Revolution of 1830, which sent the last Bourbon monarch, Charles X, into exile and enthroned the "Citizen King" Louis-Philippe (from the younger branch of the royal family), confirmed Balzac in the view that he was living in at a moment of social chaos, with authority and traditional social roles in deplorable decline. Most of his work was composed during the 1830s and 1840s but is set during the 1820s, during the Restoration following the fall of Napoleon. In other words, he is writing about a period that has already ended—in the July Revolution that brought the bourgeois monarchy to power.

This retrospective view of society allowed him to become the first writer truly to seize the meaning of the emergent modern world, its nascent capitalism, its valuation of money above all else, its competition for social and political prominence, promoting the individual above social cohesion. He saw also the new importance of the city as provincials streamed to it, either to work in bottom-level jobs and become the urban proletariat or, like his ambitious young men (and some women also), to seek to conquer and to dominate the social order. Balzac became a successful writer, read throughout Europe, though the more he wrote and published, and lived the Parisian existence he dreamt of, the more he went into debt. He traveled, had a number of liaisons (and at least one child we can be sure of), and eventually married Evelina Hanska, the Polish countess who nearly twenty years earlier had sent him a fan letter. He died in 1850, just after he returned with her to his new house in Paris. His uncompleted literary monument contained some ninety novels and tales.

Henry James called Balzac the "father of us all," the writer one must study if the novel is to recover "its wasted heritage."[4] When after his many years of exile James toured the United States in 1904 and 1905, he delivered his lecture "The Lesson of Balzac" not only in Boston and New York but also in Cincinnati and St. Louis and San Francisco. The choice of subject might seem odd—but the cultivated American family most likely had Balzac on the bookshelf, possibly a complete edition of *The Human Comedy* as translated by Katharine Prescott Wormeley, who lived in Newport, Rhode Island, and spent summers not far from William James in Jackson, New Hampshire, and worked her way through all of Balzac's novels and tales, published in forty volumes from 1883 to 1897. By the start of the twentieth century, Balzac was a global author, translated and read in all the dominant languages, a commanding figure in the history of the novel.

In France, he still holds this eminence, his work available in a number of complete editions and many paperbacks, popular with readers of all sorts, studied in school and at university, a reference for historians—who claim him as the best of all witnesses to his time. Marcel Proust, as well as James, recognized Balzac as his master, the novelist he had to know in order to forge his own style and create his novelistic world. With postmodernism, Balzac seems even to have gained a new ascendancy: if high modernism, in literature as in architecture, preferred a certain pared-down formalism, the reaction against such austerity brought a new appreciation for the excessive and melodramatic dimensions of Balzac's mode of representation.

Outside of France, however—maybe especially in the English-speaking world—Balzac has lost his primacy, perhaps because it's hard to come by much of his work in decent contemporary translations. Publishers may suspect that contemporary life doesn't provide the leisure needed for *The Human Comedy*. And yet: the television serial is nothing if not Balzacian. It is a medium he would have loved to master given the chance. And indeed adaptations of Balzac for both film and television are myriad.

I have chosen to approach my initial question—why Balzac?—by way of the lives of his characters. A traditional form of literary biography attempted to present "the man and his works." This usually meant a chronological presentation of the life interspersed with commentary on the writings. That format seems to me to draw a misleading connection between life and work. In contrast, starting with fictional lives and moving outward to their implications for authorship opens up richer and subtler contexts for reading the work. To talk about fictional characters as if they were "real" is of course delusional—and yet when we read we do give them a provisional substantiality. And Balzac himself confounded life and storytelling. A famous anecdote describes a terminally ill Balzac calling for the care of Dr. Horace Bianchon—his own fictional creation. The story may be apocryphal, but it suggests the deep truth that Balzac lived in the world he invented. To understand the dimensions and applications of this invented world is what matters. That may be the way into Balzac's inner world, which often seems to escape traditional biographies.

There are already a number of fine biographies of Balzac (I'll give my own sketch of his life in the final chapter), and in any case his life, though spectacular in its financial speculations, bankruptcies, flights from creditors, as well as get-rich-quick schemes, was in large part what James called "the long prison of his labor," the nights of writing dressed in a monk's robe, fueled by endless cups of coffee, in order to meet the next deadline.[5] Those ninety-odd novels and tales were mainly produced in a span of twenty years, in an extravagant act of creation (Shakespeare may be the only parallel). Patient scholars later compiled the stories of the fictional lives that interweave in his novels into dictionaries that re-create a normalized chronology for this novelistic world more densely and fully peopled than any other. Those people demand our attention.

I intend, then, to look over the novelist's shoulder as he creates his fictional beings, to revel in them and to talk about what he does with them—who they are and what they are for: what he creates with the plots he weaves them into, often over several different novels. The use of characters who reappear from one novel to the next as well as the fragmented form in which the works were published indicate that the point of reference is not the single novel but rather the entire *Human Comedy*, which individual readers reconstruct anew, to the best of their ability, usually with a sense of wonder at its crisscrossing paths and ever receding horizons. I can only present a small selection of the 2,472 figures who enter this imagined world, of course, but chosen carefully they open onto the whole Balzacian universe. They serve as optics on the world: they offer what Proust called the only true adventure—to see the world through another's eyes.

In what follows I retrace the stories of nine Balzacian lives—along, at times, with the lives of friends and lovers when they are hardly to be detached. Writing about each of them seemed to beg for more, given *The Human Comedy*'s webs of interconnection and the way one encounters, it seems, old acquaintances at every new turn. As he revised his work—and the creation of *The Human Comedy* was a process of constant revision—Balzac tended to eliminate mentions of "real" people in favor of his invented ones: the real poet Alphonse de Lamartine, for instance, over time is erased and replaced by the invented poet Melchior de Canalis. Balzac's possible world becomes increasingly self-sufficient and self-referential. It mimics the social world in which we live but allows interventions, experimentations, and dramatic heightenings that are unavailable to us in reality. There was a time when "the Balzacian character" was scorned by avant-garde critics and novelists as the incarnation of nineteenth-century bourgeois ideology of the coherent and upholstered individual. That was quite wrong—as avant-garde novelist, critic, and Balzac lover Michel Butor always maintained.[6] The Balzacian character is on the contrary extraordinarily mobile, unfinished, known through actions that are hardly predictable. James said that Balzac gives his created beings "the long rope," so they can act themselves out. He grants them the freedom to be what they can be. He respects the life in them.

Through Balzac's fictional lives we see into his inner world, its obsessions and fantasies, all that drove him in his writing. His many get-rich-quick schemes suggest more than the usual desire for riches. His plan to reopen ancient abandoned Roman silver mines in Sardinia, which involved a trip to the island in disguise, takes on the allure of a dream or Gothic romance, with Balzac as his own novelistic hero. His frustrated pursuit of aristocratic women such as the Marquise (later Duchesse) de Castries suggests a fixation on the impossible, while his close friendships with young men such as Jules Sandeau may have given him greater emotional satisfaction. Yet in the end he did marry a countess. A story such as *A Passion in the Desert* imagines woman in the guise of panther, an object of fear as well as fascination. Balzac's inner life, it seems clear, was driven by fantasies of conquest and power that largely find their outlet in fiction, not fact. The monomaniacs in his novels—for instance, the chemist/alchemist of *The Search for the Absolute* (*La Recherche de l'Absolu*)—tend to seek a sphere of absolute intelligibility and power, leaving the earth behind. So too does the principal philosopher of *The Human Comedy*, Louis Lambert, who goes mad from his attempt to understand all of human existence. The "dream of an intenser experience" (that is James again, acknowledging his debt to Balzac) pressures reality until it yields a hidden drama that displays the basic forces of existence.[7] Balzac's imagination is deeply melodramatic, as are psychoanalytic conflict and dreamwork. One of the subcategories of *The Human Comedy* is the "philosophical works," in which social life is only a veneer under which other drives, only partly expressible in novelistic terms, are at work. At the heart of Balzacian creation is the fear that what is most important may not be representable—or, like the unconscious, emerge only in oblique and distorted fashion. The philosopher Louis Lambert succumbs to aphasia; the painter Frenhofer commits pictorial suicide.

The novels and tales of *The Human Comedy* intertwine; one leads to another, as characters migrate from text to text, and as the massive ongoing unfinished work obsessively ponders the nature of the modern world and the needs of the modern novel. More and more, Balzac appears an indispensable master of the novel, Balzac who at one point bought a printshop and a type foundry in order to control the means of production of his written work. Another bankruptcy followed, but the ambition to control the creation of the novel from beginning to end is telling. Balzac's vast novel is not just a mirror of his time—it's about the very making of that mirror.

1. Eugène de Rastignac
(1799–after 1846)

A Young Man Comes to Conquer Paris

A YOUNG MAN ARRIVES in Paris to study law, but quickly discovers the allure of beautiful women and high society, and how rich one must be to live the good life. Eugène de Rastignac is handsome and well-connected but penniless; he dreams of worldly success but lives in the sordid premises of the Pension Vauquer. His name will become proverbial—not only in the novel but in the real world; to call someone a Rastignac in France still today suggests unbridled and possibly unscrupulous ambition. But when we meet him in *Père Goriot* (*Le Père Goriot*) he is on the threshold of life. He faces difficult moral and practical choices that are represented in the form of father figures: the King Lear–like Old Goriot who has sacrificed everything for his two daughters, and the disguised ex-con Vautrin who speaks the language of cynical worldliness and proposes a pact that will guarantee success. Vautrin puts the issue starkly. If Rastignac rejects the proposed pact on grounds of "morality" he will be doubly a dupe: missing his chance to make his fortune, he will be sure to do something much worse in pursuit of his dream. But love also beckons to Rastignac, and maybe it can be a stepping-stone to fortune. The stakes are high, Rastignac is a quick learner, and Paris is a hieroglyph he must manage to read. *Père Goriot*, published in 1834–1835 when Balzac was reaching the height of his powers, is the most popular of his novels, and in it he creates high drama from the basic desires and choices of life.

Rastignac's story speaks to an age of revolution and counterrevolution, of blurred and reasserted class boundaries, a turbulent age in which the pursuit of wealth has taken on stark new importance. Success requires learning to read subtle distinctions of class and the meanings embodied in the Paris cityscape. In this bourgeois century where everyone looks alike you are going to have to find out for yourself who's who. If you are ambitious and if you are out for love, you will need to choose wisely to advance your career. You need to understand both the social hierarchy and the economic substratum that lies hidden beneath it.

Rastignac's name suggests his Gascon origins, from the south of France where names ending in *ac* derive from the langue d'oc. His original name, in Balzac's first draft, was in fact Massiac. Balzac crossed that out and in its place wrote the name of a character from an earlier novel, *The Fatal Skin* (*La Peau de chagrin*), where we meet a somewhat older Rastignac. This small change speaks of a momentous decision: from now on Balzac will recycle the same characters from novel to novel, slowly building up the rich impasto of *The Human Comedy* as a whole. Standing at the very end of Balzac's oeuvre, we see the unfolding of Rastignac's career, how he makes his fortune, how he eventually attains fame and influence as a government minister and peer of the realm. Vautrin, like a phrenologist, reads ambition writ large on Rastignac's forehead: "Succeed, succeed at any cost!"[1] But that's only Vautrin's version of a young man he wants to claim as a disciple, to make his very own. At the start of *Père Goriot*, Rastignac is very much up for grabs—the book's intricate, interweaving plots forge his future.

The novel begins by dwelling on the poverty apparent in the place where Rastignac is obliged to live, the Pension Vauquer. We approach the place in a long traveling shot (Balzac often anticipates the cinema), passing through the "valley of plaster" and the "gutters full of mud" to arrive at a "frame of bronze" that might take you down to the catacombs—or else into the boardinghouse. The pension stinks of grease and sweat, its furniture resembles rejects from a hospice for incurables, and we meet a collection of characters who, unlike the fresh and untried Eugène, have pasts that have brought them low. The character of Madame Vauquer is "fetid" like the atmosphere of her boardinghouse, and the appearance of such inhabitants as Mlle Michonneau and Monsieur Poiret prompt the narrator/ observer to wonder how such beings are to be explained. Then there is Vautrin with his dyed mustache, later in the novel revealed to be the escaped convict and convicts' underground banker Jacques Collin. The virginal Victorine Taillefer, with her lady companion, has been relegated to the pension by an unjust father who doubts her legitimacy and wants to give his immense fortune entirely to his son. Her presence allows for the plot, a marriage accompanied by murder, that Vautrin will soon conceive for Eugène.

As for Eugène, when we first meet him he has just returned to the Pension Vauquer from summer vacation following the first year of his law studies; he is returning also, at two o'clock in the morning, from a ball given by the Vicomtesse Claire de Beauséant, a distant cousin who occupies the summit of Faubourg Saint-Germain society—the old aristocracy whose social preeminence has returned with the Restoration. Here as throughout the novel, critical moments of decision are structured by Rastignac's returns from the heights of society to the lower depths of the Pension Vauquer—a sinister contrast that forces him to compare and react. This night, he plans to sit up and study his law books, but soon he slips into a reverie on high society and two beautiful women he's seen there, the Vicomtesse de Beauséant and the Comtesse Anastasie de Restaud. (Anastasie will turn out to be Old Goriot's daughter, though as yet neither he nor the reader knows this.) "To be young, to have a thirst for the world and hunger for a woman, and to see two houses open before you!" (SC 38/P 3:77–78) Eugène's desires are primal and oral, to ingest society and its women—or in another image: "to have your foot in the Faubourg Saint-Germain at the Vicomtesse de Beauséant's, your knee in the Chausée d'Antin at the Comtesse de Restaud's!" (The Chausée d'Antin is a newer luxury address, the dwelling place of bankers as well as aristocrats.) The passage continues: "to plunge with one's gaze through the salons of Paris aligned before one, and to believe yourself good-looking enough to find aid and protection in a woman's heart! To feel oneself ambitious enough to make a fine leap on the high wire on which you need to walk with the confidence of the acrobat who will not fall, and to have found in a charming woman the best of balancing poles!"

Rastignac has looks and charm, and from the outset he makes the calculation that the road to fortune lies through a beautiful and prominent woman. After Madame de Beauséant's ball, law books forgotten, he decides that he must pay a call on Anastasie de Restaud. But now the simple form of the ambition plot becomes complicated.

While he dreams of future glory in his shabby bedroom, a groan comes from the next room. He tiptoes across the corridor to peep through the keyhole, and there is Old Goriot engaged in twisting and kneading a silver tea set into an ingot, while uttering the phrase "poor child!" And now the front door opens—though it was supposed to be bolted from inside—and Eugène hears Vautrin come in, as well as the clink of money. The story of social ambition begun with Eugène's discovery of high society now is complicated by mysteries that will need to be penetrated. And though these plotlines at first seem unrelated, by the next morning they will collide. At the breakfast table Eugène reports his astonishment at having glimpsed the divine Madame de Restaud at nine o'clock in the morning in the nearby rue de Grès. Vautrin provides an explanation: "She was certainly going to see Papa Gobseck, the moneylender. Reach deep enough into the Parisian woman's heart, you find the moneylender even before the lover. Your comtesse is named Anastasie de Restaud, and she lives in the rue du Helder." (SC 47–48/P 3:86) Goriot's reaction is also telling: Eugène detects that there must be some sort of a connection—money, maybe exploitation?—between the old man and the Comtesse de Restaud. Vautrin uses the occasion to draw a lesson: "Yesterday at the top of the wheel at a Duchesse's . . . this morning at the bottom of the ladder, at a moneylender's, that's Parisian women for you. If their husbands can't support their insane need for luxury, they sell themselves. . . . I've seen it all."

Here and throughout the novel Vautrin's restatement of Eugène's discoveries in the form of a general social law raises the stakes of the young man's social adventures, for the reader as for Eugène himself. On the one hand, Vautrin's analysis gives Rastignac a fierce desire to learn the truth about Anastasie and how she is connected to

Gobseck and Goriot: Could the old man be the keeper of this beautiful society woman? On the other, he is disgusted by the links between love and money that Vautrin posits as essential. "Your Paris is only a mudhole." To which Vautrin responds with a new generalization: "And a very strange mudhole," he says. "Those whose carriage gets muddy in its streets are respectable, those who get muddy on foot are crooks. Have the misfortune to snatch some trifle and you are put on display in the law courts. Steal a million, you're noted in the drawing rooms as a man of honor. You pay thirty million a year for the police and the judges to maintain that kind of morality. Charming!" Vautrin, the ex-convict disguised as a businessman, offers a kind of proto-Marxist denunciation of emergent bourgeois capitalist society—echoing Balzac's right-wing Catholic and royalist indictment of contemporary France from the left. Both extremes reject the cash nexus of the new order.

"You make me desperate to know the truth!" Rastignac says to Vautrin, and off he goes to call on Anastasie de Restaud. He isn't quite the ingénu he claims to be: Vautrin has planted a seed of suspicion within his understanding of social relations. On his way to the Hôtel de Restaud on foot he gets his boots and trousers muddy, and must stop to have them brushed and polished. Paris is not just a metaphorical mudhole; the need to ride in a carriage is not a mere figure of speech. When he reaches his destination, he tries to play the habitué of the house by opening a door himself and striding though—only to discover he is in a kind of utility closet leading to a dark corridor from which he hears the voices of Madame de Restaud and Old Goriot—and the sound of a kiss. Then, having found his way to the drawing room, Rastignac from the window sees Goriot crossing the courtyard. The old man nearly collides with the carriage of a young man, who will turn out to be the Comte de Restaud and who greets Goriot with a pained expression of obligation and shame.

At last admitted to the Comtesse's presence, Rastignac finds her attention taken up by her official lover, Maxime de Trailles. But she does introduce Rastignac to her husband as "related to the Vicomtesse de Beauséant by way of the Marcillac family." As if touched by a magic wand, the Comte is now all attention, happy to discuss ancestors. But Rastignac remains preoccupied by the mystery of the Comtesse's relation to Old Goriot. "He wished to penetrate this mystery, hoping in this way to reign as sovereign over this so eminently Parisian a woman." (SC 66/P 3:100) He believes that such privileged knowledge will bring him power. So he mentions having just witnessed the departure of his boardinghouse neighbor, Père Goriot. At this, the Comte throws down the fire poker he is holding as though it had burned his hand and exclaims, "Monsieur, you could have at least said Monsieur Goriot!" The *père* attached to Goriot's name has a somewhat pejorative connotation—it's a term you apply to a peasant or a local character, not to someone deserving of respect, and a world of trouble lies in this exchange. Bringing up Goriot has had the opposite effect of the magic wand exercised by Eugène's relationship with Madame de Beauséant: it's as if he had barged into a private collection of figurines and knocked off some of the heads. As Eugène takes his leave, the Comtesse flatteringly invites him to call frequently. But the Comte instructs his valet to the contrary: never admit Monsieur de Rastignac again.

Those decapitated figurines evoked by Balzac are true to the violence that underlies this scene. Rastignac's allusion to Goriot in the Restauds' drawing room isn't the sort of social gaffe that we find in

Jane Austen. What Rastignac has done is to juxtapose two orders of reality that must be kept separate for "society" to function. The exploited labor and perverted familial networks represented by Goriot's relation to the Comte and Comtesse de Restaud must be kept beneath the surface. Just as Goriot must enter the Hôtel de Restaud via the backstairs—earning a kiss when he brings money—the polite and polished superstructure of society must never be seen in relation to the substructure of money-grubbing and exploitation that allows it to exist. The distinction of Anastasie de Restaud—like that of her sister Delphine de Nucingen, who is married to a rich Alsatian banker involved in highly dubious speculations—can only be maintained by hiding the sources of wealth.

The Comte de Restaud comes from a distinguished family that has sought to repair its lack of money by his marriage to the daughter of the merchant Goriot. Back in the dark days of scarcity during the French Revolution, Goriot made a fortune by cornering the grain market. Under the Restoration, with its claim to an unadulterated purity of its ruling class, such things are not to be mentioned. The question of money is plainly central to the life of Delphine; it is also the central, though secret, problem of Anastasie and her husband: Anastasie craves luxury for herself and for her lover Maxime de Trailles, who threatens to kill himself if she does not pay off his debts. When she pawns the Restaud family diamonds to do that, things will come to a head—both in *Père Goriot* and in Balzac's tale about the moneylender, *Gobseck*, where, as we will see, the reader is presented a different interpretation of the roles played by the Comte and the Comtesse. That is the sort of stereoscopic vision *The Human Comedy* gives us frequently, with the Restauds as with Rastignac's blunder in mentioning Goriot in the their drawing room.

It takes another social call to clue Rastignac in on what he has done. Summoning a hired carriage that he can ill afford, he goes to visit Madame de Beauséant at home, where another caller, the Duchesse Antoinette de Langeais (we will want to tell her story later) soon joins them. These two best friends exchange polished but venomous remarks on each other's lovers, both apparently on the verge of desertion. But they unite to give Eugène a lesson on the way of the world. The Duchesse fills in the backstory of Goriot, how he became rich, and how during Napoleon's empire his daughters seemed good matches for Restaud and Nucingen. Come the Restoration, however, Goriot was "a grease spot in his daughters' drawing rooms." Once they squeezed the money out of him he's discarded "like a lemon peel" in the gutter. The moral drawn by the Duchesse: "Society is a mudhole. Let's try to remain up on the heights." (SC 82/P 3:115)

Returning on foot to the Pension Vauquer, Eugène realizes that these great ladies have told him in polite language what Vautrin puts more crudely. If not birth then wealth alone will raise you above the mudhole. Eugène has pretty much given up studying law, but he is deep into learning about Paris and its social codes, just as Balzac devotes novels, essays, and sketches to the semiotics of the city and its inhabitants. How do you pin down the meanings of a world in constant transformation? In a century where all men dress in black, how do you know the distinctions among them? The women can be a clue, as Rastignac instinctively understands. But Rastignac the learner is provided with a master, who waits and watches in the Pension Vauquer. His mother and sisters scrimp and save to send him money, and he can summon a tailor whose suits provide a "hyphen between a young man's past and his future." (SC 102/P 3:130) Vautrin

19

draws the lesson. "Mama has bled herself," but that's not going to prove sufficient. "Do you know what you're going to need at the rate you're going? A million, and straightaway." (SC 108/P 3:136)

Vautrin Plots Eugène's Success

In Vautrin's analysis, there are only two paths in life: "stupid obedience, or else revolt." He vividly unfolds to Eugène the way of obedience: years of legal studies, painful attempts to make ends meet as a lawyer, pleading for the rich and sending "anyone with a spark of life to the guillotine," bare subsistence as a lower magistrate, then at age forty marriage to a miller's daughter with a small dowry. Only dirty tricks as a public prosecutor might secure some influence—and even so, his sisters will remain old maids since he will be unable to dower them; as for his own fierce desires for women, money, not a chance. "Here is the crossroads of life, young man: choose. But you have already chosen. You called on your cousin de Beauséant, and you caught the scent of luxury. You called on Madame de Restaud, Goriot's daughter, and you caught the scent of a Parisian woman. You came back here that day with a word written on your forehead that I could read: 'Succeed! Succeed at any price.'" To which Vautrin responds: "Bravo! That's the kind of fellow I like." (SC 111/P 3:139) To revolt is to take destiny into your own hands by a decisive act.

"Choose.... But you have already chosen." Vautrin's reading of the message written on Eugène's forehead summarizes the appetites that will drive the novel. Rastignac doesn't deny it. As Vautrin unfolds his future financial needs in a society where young men like "spiders in a teapot" are out to eat one another, Eugène responds "eagerly": "What do I have to do?" Vautrin has a plot for him—a revolt plot—and it turns on another boarder at the Pension Vauquer, Victorine Taillefer. She is the daughter of a banker who made his fortune by murdering his best friend (this is the subject of Balzac's novella *The Red Inn* [*L'Auberge rouge*]) and who, suspecting Victorine to be illegitimate, plans to leave it all to his son, Frédéric. "I don't like that sort of unfairness," Vautrin declares. "Like Don Quixote, I take the side of the weak against the strong." So his plan: Vautrin will set up a duel in which Frédéric Taillefer will be killed at the hand of a colonel who is Vautrin's friend and a master swordsman. "I will take on the role of Providence, I will make up God's mind for him." (SC 116/P 3:144) Vautrin further elaborates: "There are no such things as principles, there are only events; there are no laws, only circumstances." Rastignac reacts with horror, Vautrin retorts that if he doesn't take this path to success he is sure to do worse some day, whoring his youth and beauty for support from a woman. "Virtue, my dear student, is not divisible. It either is or it isn't." (SC 117/P 3:145)

Vautrin, the spirit of negation, has the eloquence of Lucifer or Mephistopheles. He is the only moral absolutist in the novel and the only character to see the world as it truly is. In sections of *Capital in the Twenty-First Century* entitled "Vautrin's Lesson" and "Rastignac's Dilemma," the economist Thomas Piketty demonstrates that the terms of Vautrin's choice are financially accurate, then as now.[2] Only an inheritance like Victorine's can satisfy Rastignac's demand for luxury and power. Salary alone won't do it. If Rastignac is to find an out from Vautrin's stark choice of obedience or revolt, he needs that kind of money. "The heart's a good guide," Eugène offers by way of a retort to Vautrin. (SC 119/P 3:147) We may react to Eugène's call upon "the heart" with the knowing smile of Vautrin:

the heart can indeed be used to open a path to fortune. And Vautrin will continue to tempt and to teach him, cornering him each time he returns to the pension from his latest foray into society.

Vautrin's presence in the novel raises the stakes for the reader as for Eugène. He voices the large issues that must be decided, permits no concealment of what's involved in the search for worldly success. This man, who will be revealed as a criminal mastermind and banker to a shadowy society of convicts, articulates the clearest moral message of the novel. He confirms in starker terms the lessons taught by Madame de Beauséant. As master of the urban world in its seamy underbelly, Vautrin has a pastoral and patriarchal dream: to become a planter in the American South, a slave owner, retired from the struggle. Rastignac, young, ambitious, and beautiful, can help him to realize that dream. "A man is all or nothing. He's less than nothing if he's like, say, Poiret. You can squash him like a bug; he's flat and he stinks. But when a man looks like you, he's a god." (SC 167/P 3:186) Vautrin's homoerotic attachment to Eugène never takes overt form—as it may in the case of the young hero of *Lost Illusions* (*Illusions perdues*), Lucien de Rubempré—but he does find vicarious fulfillment living in and through Eugène's success.

What can Eugène offer in opposition to such a vision of his future? He must quickly figure this out. Another call upon Madame de Beauséant leads to his escorting her to the Théâtre Italien: from their box he examines Delphine de Nucingen in hers. "She's charming," he tells his companion, who then proceeds to point out all that is lacking in Delphine's looks and manners for her to qualify as a true aristocrat. "The Goriot comes out in her every movement." (SC 126/P 3:153) It doesn't matter; Eugène declares himself stricken. The Vicomtesse questions his choice, and he replies: "Would my suit be listened to anywhere else?" He now understands that the social code does not allow him immediate access to the highest spheres, and that Delphine—the daughter of a Goriot, married off to an unappealing banker, about to be deserted by her lover, Henri de Marsay—constitutes just what he needs. The very first evening he spends alone with her she sends him to the gambling tables. Beginner's luck will allow him to win, and her to pay off a debt incurred by de Marsay. When he returns with 7,000 francs, he receives his first kiss as a reward.

Delphine is the perfect woman for Rastignac on his way up because she offers a nexus of "love" and money: the bank along with the heart. With Delphine, he can claim to be following his heart and at the same time advance socially and financially. He becomes the rich man we meet in later novels by making himself useful in her husband's speculations. Eventually, in later novels, the reader will learn (with something of a shock) that he marries her daughter, Augusta. As Comtesse de Rastignac, Augusta will be a dominant social figure in the 1840s—that is to say, during a new regime, that of the "bourgeois monarch" Louis-Philippe. So does society evolve, with yesterday's parvenus become tomorrow's social arbiters. Rastignac at the outset has the advantage of an inherited name in the provincial nobility, those known traditionally as *hobereaux*: of ancient lineage but not much else, reduced to eking out an existence on what is left of their land holdings. His alliance with Delphine and her husband aligns him with the dynamic forces of developing capitalist France, where the right investments—in an unregulated market—can bring enormous rewards.

Rastignac has in this manner found a good way around Vautrin's stark alternatives: stupid obedience or revolt, one that leads him as well to befriend the exploited father, Goriot, to whom he brings back news of his daughters from the upper world. Goriot conceives himself as the eternal father. "When I became a father, I understood God," he claims. Like God, like Vautrin with Rastignac, he lives through his creation, his daughters. Goriot and Vautrin offer two different models of paternity for Rastignac to choose between— models similar in their apparent altruism, yet utterly different in their proposed emotional satisfactions. Goriot, Lear-like, is the exploited father who will learn by the end of the book that patriarchy itself has been replaced by the cash nexus. Whereas Vautrin has espoused modernity entirely, and sees his chosen disciple as a way to use it.

Rastignac's returns from society to the Pension Vauquer always pose some form of a conundrum that he claims to have found in reading Rousseau, and puts to his friend the young doctor Horace Bianchon: If one could become rich by willing the death of one aged and unknown mandarin in China, should one do it? "Bah! I'm up to my thirty-third mandarin," Bianchon at first replies, but then the two young men solemnly decide that the mandarin must live. Yet Vautrin has not done with Eugène. This "fierce logician" points out that Rastignac can't be Delphine's lover and social escort while continuing to live at the Pension Vauquer, and comes back to the necessity of the murderous Victorine plot. "'What kind of a man are you,' cried Eugène. 'You were created to torment me.'" (SC 166/P 3:185) Vautrin in reply promises that once Frédéric Taillefer has been removed from the scene, Victorine's dowry will "wash you white as a wedding dress, even in your own eyes." (SC 178/P 3:196) He moves forward with his scheme, drugging Rastignac's wine at dinner so he can't run to warn Taillefer. The next morning, a messenger arrives at the pension to tell Victorine that her brother has died and her father has summoned her. Eugène's declaration that he will never marry Victorine is dismissed by Vautrin: "Young man, good comes to us while we are sleeping." (SC 196/P 3:212)

Then Vautrin falls unconscious to floor. "So there is a divine justice!" Rastignac exclaims. The words ring hollow. What has caused Vautrin's collapse is not justice, divine or otherwise, but a drug administered by the sinister Mlle Michonneau, who, along with Poiret, has been engaged by the police to find out if Vautrin is in fact Jacques Collin, an escaped prisoner long sought by the police. The drugged Vautrin is hauled to his room, where Mlle Michonneau pulls off his shirt and applies a sharp slap to his shoulder: "two fatal letters reappeared, white in the middle of the red spot." We may assume the fatal letters are TF, for *Travaux Forcés*, forced labor, to which Vautrin had been sentenced. His future attempts to efface the letters will be crucial to the plot of *A Harlot High and Low* (*Splendeurs et misères des courtisanes*). Here in *Père Goriot* their reappearance leads to his arrest. Gendarmes invade the pension. With his wig knocked off and his true identity revealed, Vautrin is seen by the lodgers in all his horror, as "a fallen archangel bent on eternal war." He declares himself a disciple of Jean-Jacques Rousseau who protests against the sham that the social contract has become. So revealed, he continues to exalt the criminal in revolt against society. "Are you better than I?" he demands of the assembled lodgers. "I have less infamy branded on my shoulder than you have in your hearts, flabby members of a gangrened society. The best among you couldn't resist me." (SC 203/P 3:219)

He is hauled off to prison, but not without reminding Eugène that the Victorine plot remains a possibility. "Our bargain still holds good, my angel," he says. Vautrin remains the master figure at the heart of the novel. But Rastignac has found an apparent way out of his dilemma. Old Goriot has rented and furnished an apartment for him, a place for his trysts with Delphine. She has summoned him to join her there, along with the present of an expensive time-piece. As he leaves the pension, he rereads her letter: "A love like that is my anchor to windward," he tells himself. Standing in the apartment, which has cost Goriot far more than he can afford, he exclaims: "I will be worthy of all this." (SC 216/S 3:231) Worthy, that is, of the charming luxury of his new bachelor's apartment. Balzac never allows us to be duped by Eugène's choices. If he manages to avoid the Victorine plot, his new arrangements result in a scheme that is only superficially less corrupt. And yet, the virginal Victorine is in fact far less corrupt than Delphine. In refusing Vautrin's bargain he is hardly embracing virtue.

Rastignac Chooses "Struggle"

With Vautrin gone from the novel, the final episodes will force Rastignac to discover his would-be mentor's world views on his own. The story plays out like this: Rastignac pressures Madame de Beauséant to furnish him with an invitation for Delphine to her grand ball, her farewell to society. Betrayed by her lover, she has decided to flee Paris for a solitary country retreat in Normandy (where we will catch up with her again in *The Abandoned Woman* [*La femme abandonnée*]). In true Faubourg Saint-Germain impertinent style, the invitation to Delphine does not include her husband, the Baron de Nucingen—and Eugène is "happy to procure her a pleasure for which he would doubtless receive the reward."

(SC 223/P 3:235) Such is the barter that will constitute his relation with Delphine.

When the evening of this great social event arrives, Goriot is on his deathbed. Delphine has no intention of missing the party, however. Eugène is appalled by such an "elegant parricide," as he calls it. He reflects bitterly but lucidly: "Infamous or sublime, he adored this woman for the voluptuous pleasures that he had brought her as dowry, and for those he had received in return; just as Delphine loved Rastignac as Tantalus would have loved an angel come to satisfy his hunger, or quench the thirst of his parched throat." (SC 253/P 3:263) The image is crude, picturing the relationship as one of brute need and satisfaction. He reflects that he has now witnessed "the three great attitudes toward society: Obedience, Struggle, and Revolt: the Family, High Society, and Vautrin." Vautrin offered only two, obedience or revolt. Rastignac, rejecting these absolutes, has added the intermediate term of "struggle," by which he means finding the way to negotiate between extremes, to compromise intelligently, to slip into good society.

The last part of *Père Goriot* plays out on a split screen, allowing us to see the deep contradictions undermining this society. On one screen we see Madame de Beauséant's farewell ball, on the other the sordid garret room where Goriot lies dying, destroyed by his daughters' desperate demands for cash and the revelation of their unhappy and perilous domestic situations. Delphine has discovered that her dowry is tied up in her husband's risky financial schemes. She has nothing to draw on for her own and her former lover's debts. The situation of her sister, Anastasie, is far more tragic. Her lover, the elegant but sinister Maxime de Trailles, the apparent father of two of her three children, has bankrupted her entirely, and she has pawned the Restaud family diamonds. Rastignac comes to fetch her to her father's deathbed, but she is not free: her husband is holding her hostage, demanding her signature on a document. (If the Comte appears a monster of cruelty here, *Gobseck* will shed a very different light on the story.) When she finally does appear at the pension, it is as a "grave and terrible apparition." (SC 280/P 3:285) But it is too late; her father has died.

In his protracted death agony, Goriot discovers all that is rotten in the social order. The betrayal of his absent daughters—and before that, their loss to marriage with husbands who exploit them—is the central theme of his ravings. "My two sons-in-law have killed my daughters. Yes, I no longer had daughters after they married. Fathers, tell the National Assembly to make a law on marriage!... No more marriages!" (SC 272/P 3:278) Marriage, which should assure social stability and continuity, has become a sordid financial bargain, as the novel amply illustrates. Its collapse represents a more general breakdown in the social order. "My daughters, my daughters. Anastasie, Delphine! I want to see them. Send the police to get them by force! Justice is on my side, everything is on my side, nature, the law. I protest. The nation will perish if fathers are trampled underfoot. That's clear. Society, the whole world depends on fatherhood. Everything collapses if children don't love their fathers." (SC 269/P 3:275) Here, and elsewhere in *The Human Comedy*, Balzac projects the drama of the father betrayed on a grand scale: the regicide of 1793 (when King Louis XVI died on the guillotine) was a national parricide that has left French society without clear principles of authority (the July Revolution would only make things worse), subject to what Balzac's fictional philosopher Louis Lambert will call "the law of disorganization." No longer an organic and hierarchical whole—

the nostalgic ideal of conservatives—it has become a struggle of individual egos with no unifying vision, like those spiders in a jar in Vautrin's exposition. Goriot's rants fall within the claim of conservatives across the ages that the family and its affects form the core social unit; if it has become so utterly denatured, society itself stands on the verge of collapse.

While Goriot lies dying, Rastignac is at once a participant and a disabused observer in the midst of Madame de Beauséant's spectacular ball. After an emotional moment with the Vicomtesse—who appears to him like a goddess from the *Iliad*—Rastignac makes the rounds of the ball with her. He sees the two sisters, Anastasie and Delphine, Anastasie "magnificent" in the diamonds that her husband has redeemed from the moneylender and wearing them, Rastignac suspects, for the last time. The spectacle only makes his sadness the greater. "Underneath the diamonds of the two sisters, he then saw once more the wretched pallet on which their father lay dying." (SC 257/P 3:266) Rastignac here achieves something like his creator's stereoscopic vision, which he unwittingly stumbled on when he first mentioned Goriot in the Restauds' drawing room. He seems to have attained a melodramatic articulation of the very structures of Parisian existence. To see through the diamonds to the deathbed: that is to have a truly penetrating vision needed to distinguish the truth from mere appearance. It may resemble the initial presentation of the Pension Vauquer and its inhabitants, where the narrator's insistent questions of appearances led to the postulation of hidden dramas. Here the hidden has been laid bare.

Early editions of *Père Goriot* included another scene at the ball, just before Rastignac's vision of the deathbed beneath the diamonds. Encountering a dancing couple of breathtaking beauty, he inquires of Madame de Beauséant who they are. She is Lady Brandon—"incontestably the most beautiful of all," and happily in love, even though her husband has sworn vengeance—and he is Colonel Franchessini, a "living Antinous," who three days earlier killed Frédéric Taillefer in a duel. Franchessini was provoked, says Madame de Beauséant; he killed the banker's son without meaning to. But for Rastignac the scene carries another meaning: "A cold sweat ran down his back. Vautrin appeared to him with his face of bronze. The hero of prison giving his hand to the hero of the ball changed the face of society for him."[3] Another moment of doubled vision, where the figure of Vautrin appears as if a ghost at the ball, linking this most beautiful dancer to the underworld. It is a vision that Rastignac alone is capable of—no one else at the ball has his knowledge of this link between the highest and the lowest. When Balzac in the last edition of *The Human Comedy* on which he made corrections (known as the "*Furne corrigé*") struck out this scene, it must have been from a judgment that it was too much, even for him. While Balzacian dramatizations can often be over the top, excessive, melodramatic, here the insertion of Vautrin's henchman, the killer of young Taillefer, into the grandest ball of the noble Faubourg possibly seemed too implausible and insistent. Rastignac's vision of Goriot dying beneath his daughter's diamonds can stand on its own.

Returning for the last time from the Faubourg Saint-Germain to the Pension Vauquer, Rastignac tells Bianchon that he knows he is in hell, but also knows he must stay there, to make his way in a society of "horror covered over with gold and jewels." (SC 258/P 3:268) Goriot's pauper's funeral—to pay for it Eugène pawns the watch Delphine has given him—is attended only by Eugène and the pension's servant Christophe, though on their way to Père-

Lachaise cemetery two carriages, emblazoned on their doors with the arms of the Comte de Restaud and the Baron de Nucingen, suddenly join the cortege—but they are empty. Rastignac sheds his "last tear of youth" over the grave. As dusk gathers he moves a few steps to the heights of the cemetery where his view can take in the city. He sees Paris lying serpentine along the banks of the Seine where lights are beginning to shine.

> His eyes fixed themselves almost avidly between the column of the Place Vendôme and the dome of the Invalides. There lived the fashionable world into which he had wished to penetrate. He threw at this murmurous hive a glance that seemed to suck out in advance all its honey, and spoke these grandiose words: "Now between the two of us!"
>
> And as first act of defiance to Society, he went to dine at Madame de Nucingen's.
>
> (SC 285/P 3:290)

This celebrated end to the novel shows us Rastignac in the midst of the contradictions he has cultivated to make his way in the world. His challenge to the city—"*A nous deux maintenant*" is the fencer's call to his opponent—is qualified by the preceding image of sucking the honey from a beehive, and by the realization of his "act of defiance": going to dine with his mistress. These suggest something other than defiance. Rastignac's resolution of his dilemmas, temptations, and moral choices lies in what he has named "struggle," the median term he has added to Vautrin's "obedience or revolt." Struggle it will be, but within society, not against it.

The Rastignac we encounter in other novels is a dominant figure,

socially and eventually politically. His arrangements with the Nuc-
ingens, serving the schemes of his mistress's husband (without always
understanding them), then marrying into the family by way of his
mistress's daughter, leave him affluent and powerful. When we see
him elsewhere in *The Human Comedy*, he appears to be amiable,
disabused, and cynical, and generally good company. Success has
not ruined him. It has merely confirmed those characteristics that
made him successful. A character in *The House of Nucingen* (*La
Maison Nucingen*) sums up Rastignac's moral career:

> he did not believe in any virtue, but rather in circumstances in which
> man is virtuous. This understanding was the matter of a moment:
> it was acquired at the height of Père-Lachaise cemetery, the day he
> buried a poor honest man, the father of his Delphine, who died the
> dupe of society, of the truest emotions, abandoned by his daughters
> and his sons-in-law. He resolved to fool everybody in this society,
> and to present himself in the clothing of virtue, probity, and good
> manners. Egotism armed this young noble from head to foot.[4]

We see that Vautrin's lessons have had their effect, capped at the
moment of Goriot's burial. And if there is a certain hollowness as well
as charm in the mature Rastignac, that may be the nature of success.

Learning to Read the City

We should not be taken in by Rastignac's final gesture of defiance
to Paris. Not to be taken in is something *Père Goriot* as a whole
teaches: it's about learning to see the world as it is, not as it claims
to be. Rastignac's position at the final moment of the novel, standing

at the highest point of Père-Lachaise, a hill of the dead, and looking down at Paris along the banks of the Seine, is crucial. It is a scene of reading: reading the city and its social meanings. The Paris on which Eugène focuses his "avid" glance lies framed between the column of the Place Vendôme, erected by Napoleon in celebration of his victories, sheathed in bronze taken from enemy cannon, and the dome of Les Invalides, home of former warriors. If Paris may itself be compared to a battlefield, in the post-Napoleonic, proto-capitalist Restoration the way you win in its struggles is not by arms—despite Vautrin's rigged duel—but by insinuation, charm, gathering information, possessing social secrets. These are Eugène's new skills, as they were his creator's. They want to make Paris legible.

How to read the manners, customs, speech, geography, and topography of Paris is a key Balzacian enterprise from the start of his work, as a journalist and a novelist. It was a time for "physiologies" and "physiognomies," classifications with a pseudoscientific, and often comic, purpose. Balzac produced sketches of the Bois de Boulogne, of the life of artists, of the shop signs of Paris; a *Treatise on Elegant Living* (*Traité de la vie élégante*), also a *New Theory of the Luncheon* (*Nouvelle théorie du déjeuner*), maybe a *Physiology of the Cigar* (*Physiologie du cigare*) and *A Study of Manners by Way of Gloves* (*Étude de moeurs par les gants*). (Since such occasional texts were generally signed with pseudonyms, if signed at all, the attribution of some of them to Balzac remains conjectural.[5]) The problem they all present is how to read signs when signs have been blurred. Postrevolutionary France has abolished the distinctive marks of identity of the ancien régime; the nineteenth century has brought a new social leveling and indifferentiation. How can you tell who people are, what milieu they belong to, what their past histories may be? The novella *Ferragus* (the first

33

of the three tales that make up *Story of the Thirteen* [*Histoire des Treize*]) begins with the narrator teasing out the moral attributes belonging to streets in Paris: those that are decent, honest, suspect, or homicidal. Balzac calls his *Treatise on Elegant Living* "the metaphysics of things"—metaphysics because things are always signs of something beyond their physical presence.[6] The unidentified Comtesse who is the principal character of the study of gloves (a very important accessory in Balzac's world) looks at gentlemen's gloves and deduces from them what each of the men has been up to that day. It's a kind of proto–Sherlock Holmes technique, for the detection of signs of the everyday, of the way people live now.

Balzac intended some of these studies to form part of his never-completed *Pathology of Social Life* (*Pathologie de la vie sociale*), a collection that includes, among other texts, the *Treatise on Elegant Living, Theory of Movement* (*Théorie de la démarche*), and *Treatise of Modern Stimulants* (*Traité des excitants modernes*). His title reminds us irresistibly of Sigmund Freud's *Psychopathology of Everyday Life*, and in fact the enterprise is not so far from Freud's effort to show how everyday actions, slips of the tongue, and other "parapraxes" speak of our unconscious desires. Balzac has no theory of the unconscious, but he is as concerned as Freud with how people reveal—or deceive—themselves.

Historians and sociologists have often turned to Balzac in order to understand France in the 1820s and after. As the historian Pierre Rosanvallon notes, in this moment on the threshold of the invention of "sociology"—soon to begin with the "social physics" of Auguste Comte—it is the novelists, and especially Balzac, who furnish the "principles of intelligibility" for the understanding of society.[7] Balzac's inquest into contemporary reality at times resembles such inquiries into social conditions as A. B. Parent-Duchatelet's *De la prostitution dans la ville de Paris*, a monumental study of the forms and causes of prostitution published in 1836, and Eugène Buret's inquiry into the condition of the working poor, *La Misère des classes laborieuses en France et en Angleterre*, from 1840. There was evidently at the time a felt need to seize social facts, decipher them, and find an analytic frame for explaining them.[8]

It was the era also of Kaspar Lavater, the inventor of physiognomy, and of Franz Joseph Gall, the phrenologist, and Balzac subscribed to these and other pseudosciences that promised a new legibility of the person and his milieu. At the outset of *Père Goriot*, as Erich Auerbach notes in *Mimesis*, milieu and person reciprocally explain each other:[9] Madame Vauquer "explains the pension, as the pension implies her." (SC 11/P 3:54) But implications and explanations are not always so straightforward. Other dwellers in the Pension Vauquer demand a greater effort of understanding. "These lodgers made one sense dramas past or ongoing." (SC 13–14/P 3:57) Mlle Michonneau makes you wonder: "What acid had stripped this creature of her feminine forms? She must once have been pretty and shapely. Was it vice, grief, cupidity? Had she loved too much, had she been a dealer in secondhand clothes, or simply a whore?" And then Monsieur Poiret: "What work could have knocked him up so? What passion had darkened his bulbous face, which even as a caricature would have been implausible? What had he been? Well perhaps an employee of the Ministry of Justice, in the office where the public executioners send their invoices, for black veils for parricides, sawdust for guillotine baskets, rope for the blades." And so on. The observer must have what Henry James referred to as the "penetrating imagination," seeking always to go behind appearances, to breech the façades of the real to get to the place of the true drama.[10] Recall Rastignac summoned from his early reveries of love and glory to observe Goriot through the keyhole, turning a silver tea set into an ingot, in order pay off Anastasie's debts. Before reaching his final vision from Père-Lachaise, Rastignac has gone through a long apprenticeship. One day, he shows up at Madame de Beauséant's seeking advice at the wrong time; she dismisses him "curtly, with an abrupt gesture." And then: "He perceived the iron hand under the velvet glove, the egotism and selfishness under the manners; the bare wood under the varnish." (SC 122/P 3:150) To see in this manner is to espouse Vautrin's vision, even though he rejects its criminal uses.

So exemplary are the life and career of Rastignac, the proverbial figure of ambition realized, that Balzac later encapsulates his character in the form of an entry in *Who's Who*:

> Elder son of the Baron and Baroness de Rastignac, born at Rastignac in the Charente Department in 1799, comes to Paris in 1819 to study law, lives at the Pension Vauquer, where he meets Jacques Collin, aka Vautrin, and forms a friendship with Horace Bianchon, the famous doctor. He becomes the lover of Mme Delphine de Nucingen, at the time she is abandoned by de Marsay, daughter of a Monsieur Goriot, former flour merchant whose funeral is paid for by Rastignac. He is one of the lions of society; he makes friends with all the young men of his time, with de Marsay, Beaudenord, d'Esgrignon, Lucien de Rubempré, Émile Blondet, du Tillet, Nathan, Paul de Manerville, Bixiou, etc. The story of his fortune is found in *The House of Nucingen*. . . .[11]

This bio (of which I quote only part) appears in Balzac's preface to a later novel, *A Daughter of Eve* (*Une Fille d'Ève*) in which Rastignac makes yet another cameo appearance—and it suggests how alive Balzac's characters were for him, how he could cite them in place of "real" people to define the dynamic roles in the society and the world he was in the process of creating. He notes, however, that such a chronology of Rastignac's life story comes only retrospectively: in *The Human Comedy*, as in life, we have to put a life story together from the scraps of knowledge that experience makes available. Nothing comes to us in a unified block: "everything," Balzac claims, "is a mosaic." Life precisely is not a *Who's Who*.

Other characters in *Père Goriot* will take their star turns in other novels. We encounter Madame de Beauséant often; *The Abandoned Woman* is all about her Norman retreat. Antoinette de Langeais will be the unhappy heroine of *The Duchesse de Langeais* (*La Duchesse de Langeais*). Dr. Horace Bianchon will reappear probably more than any other character, with the possible exception of the lawyer Derville. The usurer Gobseck is also ubiquitous and gives his name to a novella. As for Vautrin, the most powerful and also the most protean character of *The Human Comedy*, he too will return, reaching what is described as his "last incarnation" in *A Harlot High and Low*. He is the principle of unity and of dynamic force in the novels that make up the backbone of *The Human Comedy*: *Père Goriot*, *Lost Illusions*, and *A Harlot High and Low*. As the would-be mastermind of the destinies of Rastignac and Lucien de Rubempré, and some other young men such as the Corsican Théodore Calvi, Vautrin is as much a shaper of characters and a master of plots as Balzac himself. And just as these young men slip away from him, so Balzac's inventions acquire a free existence of their own.

Rastignac was still active and powerful in 1846; probably he outlived his creator, who died in 1850.

2. Jean-Esther van Gobseck
(1740?–1829)

The Lifeblood of Capitalist Exchange

MONEY IN *The Human Comedy* is crucial, the "lifeblood" of society, and at the very center of Balzac's fictional world stands the money-lender, the usurer called "the capitalist" who commands the supply of money running through society's veins. Gobseck is privy to the needs and intrigues and secrets of his clientele, and beyond: he banks on the value of erotic liaisons and the likelihood of future bankruptcies. His knowledge takes us into the machinations that enable modern society, fueled by credit rather than landed wealth, to function. The unmoved mover at the center of circulating capital, Gobseck's strange wisdom allows him to understand dramas enacted within the privacy of families. "Reach deep enough into the Parisian woman's heart, you find the moneylender even before the lover," Vautrin remarks on hearing of Anastasie de Restaud's visit to Gobseck early in *Père Goriot*, and in Anastasie's story the moneylender and the lover closely entwine: the debts she must liquidate, with her father's cash and then her husband's family diamonds, have been racked up by her lover Maxime de Trailles, a sinister though beautiful and elegant young man who is said to be a "ring" uniting high society and the underworld.[1] The story of the Restaud diamonds, and of the intense, murderous, and far-reaching struggle between the Comte and Comtesse de Restaud, appears in Balzac's first sketchy version of *Gobseck*, written before *Père Goriot*.[2] As finished, *Gobseck* and *Père Goriot* provide the same story told in split screen, to very different effect.

As the master of money, Jean-Esther van Gobseck is one of the characters who returns with the greatest frequency in *The Human Comedy*; only the doctor Bianchon and the lawyer Derville show up as often. Like the doctor and the lawyer, the moneylender is perpetually on call. There is a link between his functions and the lawyer's, and Balzac deputizes Derville to tell Gobseck's story. *Gobseck* begins at one o'clock in the morning after a soiree in the salon of the Vicomtesse de Grandlieu. The Vicomtesse accuses her seventeen-year-old daughter, Camille, of having paid too much attention to the young Comte Ernest de Restaud, the son of Anastasie and her husband. Ernest's mother's background is undistinguished, the Vicomtesse says. She has tarnished her reputation and eaten her way through millions. She behaved badly with her husband, and she doesn't deserve a son so loyal as Ernest. The Grandlieu family would never allow such a match. At this point, Derville steps forward, having overheard the Vicomtesse. Seating himself in a comfortable armchair, he announces that he has a story to tell; it will change their view of Ernest de Restaud.

An oral tale, then, emerging in the course of a social interaction, as many of Balzac's stories do: he seeks to re-create the traditional context of oral storytelling, including listeners' reactions to the story told. The tale told is to transmit information and to change minds.

It holds a moral; it has consequences. Camille reacts with joy: A story! Please begin. But before the tale comes to its end, her mother will bundle her off to bed: it has become much too risqué for a girl not yet permitted to read novels. The Vicomtesse and her brother the Comte de Born will, however, hear Derville out to the end.

The story of Gobseck is bound up with Derville's own story and the story of the Grandlieus. When Derville was an ambitious young lawyer, he and Gobseck lived in neighboring apartments, and Gobseck loaned him the money to set up a law practice. Later, he led him to his future wife. The Grandlieu family in turn owes much to Derville: it's he who by legal maneuver allowed them to repossess their Parisian town house, confiscated and sold off during the Revolution, with the return of the monarchy. Story is layered on story and other stories, in an interactive manner: Camille's future marital prospects depend on the story that Derville will tell, which is in part the story of his own beginnings and successes, but always and above all the story of the ubiquitous and indispensable Gobseck.

Yet this complex narrative layering arises also from the fact that in a deep sense, Gobseck himself has no story. He sits and waits, and stories come to him. Early in his life—he was only ten—his mother sent him to sea, and he came to know places and peoples. But now he is essentially immobile. In the new world of capitalist investment, the man with money merely sets it in motion, then waits for the return to accrue. Derville begins his story with a description of Gobseck. His face is impassive, like an old man by Rembrandt or Metsu (he is of Dutch Jewish origin); he speaks in a low voice; he never loses his temper. Is he prematurely aged, or old and well-preserved? He moves like a well-regulated clock. He economizes his strength. Derville even wonders which sex he belongs to, before deciding he is of "the neuter gender." (NY 231/P 2:967) He is like the antiques dealer we will meet in *The Fatal Skin*, who has reached the age of 102 by refusing to spend, by hoarding his pleasures within himself. As for Gobseck's own idea of himself, he tells Derville he is a "poet," not one who writes verse but that's not the only kind. His poetry comes from the observation of human emotion. "If you had lived as long as I have, you would know there is only one thing certain enough to bother about. That thing... is GOLD. Gold represents all human forces." (NY 233/P 2:969) If most believe happiness can be found in strong feelings, these exhaust us and use up life; better is to live in a well-ordered occupation, functioning like a mechanism. "Art or Knowledge, Passion or Calm": there lies the essential choice. And Gobseck goes further: "all human passions heightened by the play of your social interests come here to parade before me, while I live in calm.... In a word, I possess the world without fatigue, and the world doesn't have the slightest hold on me." (NY 233–34/P 2:970)

Here Gobseck tells a story, which Derville relays to his listeners. He spent his morning collecting two unpaid loans. First he went to the splendid Hôtel de Restaud. Anastasie is still sleeping, her maid tells him; he must come back at noon. When he returns, she hasn't the money to pay him, of course; but when her husband enters to ask what's going on, she quickly slips Gobseck a diamond as collateral. As he leaves Anastasie, he says to himself: "Pay for your luxury, pay for your name, pay for your happiness, pay for the monopoly you enjoy." (NY 238/P 2:973) And he intentionally tracks mud on the carpet of the stairway, to make her feel "the claw of necessity." His other visit is to the honest and hardworking seamstress Fanny Malvaut, who lives in a garret in the working-class district of the rue Montmartre. Fanny, in contrast, has her payment ready for him.

41

She, Gobseck tells Derville, would be the perfect wife. Derville took note. This sometime seamstress, now his wife, is, he tells the haughty Grandlieu, the very best of women.

"Can't you understand that underneath this pale mask of mine there are ecstatic pleasures?" Gobseck demands of Derville. Paris lies under the control of moneylenders—"silent and unknown kings"—who recognize that "Gold is the spiritualism of contemporary societies." They constitute a "Holy Inquisition" since they know what goes on in all social sectors, behind the closed doors of families. Celebrated beauties, men of power, merchants, artists all bow to the power of money and come to create scenes of exquisite drama in Gobseck's cold, bare apartment. "These sublime actors perform for me alone, without the power to deceive me. My gaze is like that of God, I see into hearts. Nothing is hidden from me." (NY 241/P 2:976) Like the novelist, the demiurgic usurer becomes, through his placement of money, the creator of dramatic lives. Balzac is fascinated by those who can witness the dramas they have themselves created.

Now we come to the story of the Restaud diamonds, the one we thought we knew from *Père Goriot*. Gobseck, having set Derville up in law practice (with a loan at fifteen percent interest), uses him as a go-between with Anastasie and the desperately indebted and unscrupulous de Trailles, her indifferent lover, who calls upon every emotional manipulation to force her to pawn her husband's family jewels. Gobseck reacts with visceral joy to handling the gorgeous diamonds. He holds them up to the light, brings them to his mouth as if to devour them. Color floods into his cheeks, his eyes sparkle, he swells with an infantile ecstasy. He's outdone his rivals Werbrust and Gigonnet: "Ego sum papa!" he cries out, and does a little dance. (NY 258/P 2:991) He possesses the real thing, as if to claim that

diamonds are realer wealth than money. But here Derville steps in
to warn Gobseck against his transaction with Anastasie. She is legally
subject to her husband, and so is not free to dispose of the diamonds.
And when the Comte soon arrives seeking to take them back, Gobseck accepts the compromise Derville negotiates: they will be
returned in exchange for the cash value of the loan made to Anastasie. This is when the Vicomtesse de Grandlieu sends Camille off
to bed. Derville has gone a bit too far. But what you read in the
newspapers is far worse, he protests. Do you think I let my daughter
read newspapers? the Vicomtesse rejoins. After her daughter has
gone, she urges him to go on. And he should feel free to name the
Restauds, whose names Derville has suppressed till now in deference
to Camille and her liking for Ernest.

And here is what happens. The Comte de Restaud still loves the
"demon" Anastasie—Gobseck himself is moved by her majestic
beauty—and yet her enthrallment to Maxime threatens to consume
his entire fortune. Why not, Gobseck suggests, put that wealth in
a trust to a third party. Advised by Derville that Gobseck, though
a "capitalist" whose god is money, is a man of absolute probity, the
Comte signs his wealth over to the moneylender, in a simulated sale
offset by a counter-deed that will upon his death restore the bulk
of the fortune to Ernest, the one legitimate child, while the other
children will receive a decent modicum. Derville is to hold the
counter-deed in safekeeping, and he grows anxious when the Comte
fails to return it to him. The Comte, he learns, is in fact ill. Derville
hurries to the rue du Helder to meet with him—only to be told by
Anastasie that the Comte will not see anyone. Derville fears that
Anastasie may be capable of anything. He demands to see her husband, but in vain. Anastasie for her part is desperate to find out what

the lawyer is after; she would even seduce him to know, but Derville is impervious. They part as mortal enemies.

Last Act in the Restaud Drama

Freud called dream "*ein anderes Schauplatz*," another stage, and that very much describes the relationship between *Père Goriot* and *Gobseck*. Anastasie, as we know from *Père Goriot*, must also put her signature on the fictive sale of the Comte's fortune: that is what delays her appearance at her father's deathbed. She shrewdly suspects the existence of the counter-deed, which she imagines will leave the Comte's entire fortune to Ernest. She wants to protect her other children by Maxime, fearing that they have been disinherited by the Comte. She sets up an absolute state of surveillance. She prevents anyone but Ernest from entering the Comte's bedchamber, and she grills Ernest about what his father tells him. She now knows Maxime has abandoned her. She begins to study the legal code in an effort to understand how she can get the family fortune back. Not only does she prevent Derville from visiting her husband; she also blocks the Comte's efforts to get a message to the lawyer. When he tries to use Ernest as an intermediary, she does her best to convince him that his father is not only ill but deranged in mind.

At this point, the Comte appears as from the dead.

"Ah, ah!" cried the Comte. He had flung open the door and stood almost naked on the threshold, already as dried and fleshless as a skeleton. His strangled cry had a terrible effect on the Comtesse; she sat frozen, as if struck dumb.

"You have flooded my life with bitterness, and now you mean to trouble my death, pervert my son's mind, make him a vicious person!" he cried in a rasping voice.

The Comtesse threw herself at the feet of this dying man whom the last emotions of life made almost hideous and poured out a torrent of tears.

"Mercy! Have mercy!" she cried.

"Had you any mercy for me?" he asked. "I let you devour your own fortune, now you want to devour mine and ruin my son!"

"All right, yes, be pitiless toward me, be ruthless," she said. "But the children! Sentence your wife to live in a convent, I'll obey; to expiate my sins toward you I'll do anything you command, but let the children live happy! Oh, the children! The children!"

"I have only one child," replied the Comte, stretching his fleshless arm toward Ernest.

"Oh, pardon! I repent, repent," cried the Comtesse, embracing her husband's feet, damp from her tears. Sobs choked her speech, muttered and incoherent words came from her burning throat.

"After what you were saying to Ernest, you dare talk about repentance!" said the dying man, who overturned the Comtesse with a thrust of his foot. "You turn me to ice," he added with an indifference that was frightening. "You were a bad daughter, you have been a bad wife, you will be a bad mother."

The wretched woman fainted. The dying man returned to his bed, lay down, and lost consciousness a few hours later.

(NY 274–75/P 2:1005–6)

Everything that has been seething under the surface comes to full articulation and acting out, as in a stage melodrama. This is among the most excruciatingly effective of Balzac's many melodramatic scenes, providing Freud's "other stage" of dream, producing a stark understanding of what has been repressed and unspoken, and what is at stake. Gobseck's transactions open to view the spectacle of what has come to pass in a marriage, and beyond that the unholy alliance of cash and love that perverts modern society.

The Comte dies at midnight. Derville and Gobseck force their way into the bedroom despite young Ernest's attempt to keep them out, claiming his mother is in prayer. They encounter a scene of wild disorder: "Her hair hanging loose in her despair, her eyes glittering, the Comtesse stood speechless in the midst of clothing, papers, and rags strewn everywhere." (NY 275/P 2:1006–7) Anastasie has forced open all the drawers of the Comte's secretary, overturned the furniture, broken into boxes, and evidently found the document she was looking for under the Comte's pillow. His corpse has been pushed aside, the pillow lies on the floor, marked with her footprint. An empty envelope addressed to Derville with the Comte's seal, broken, lies on the floor. The document itself she has cast into the fire; Derville finds only an unburnt corner. "Ah, Madame," he says to her, "you have ruined your children! Those papers were their titles to your husband's property." (NY 276/P 2:1007–8) The Comtesse staggers, speechless. Gobseck coolly announces that the house now belongs to him. Derville is left gasping for breath.

In the absence of the counter-deed, the estate indeed is Gobseck's, and he takes advantage of it, living like an unlikely member of the landed gentry. Anastasie is left to bring up her children in poverty, a heroically devoted mother. Ernest grows up charming and unspoiled. When Derville runs into Gobseck in the Tuileries, he suggests that the moneylender really should help Ernest. Help him? replies Gobseck. Never. "Hardship is our greatest teacher, hardship will teach him the value of money, of men and of women. Let him navigate the Paris seas. When he has become a good pilot, we will give him a ship." (NY 277/P 2:1008) Like Vautrin in *Père Goriot*, Gobseck is in his way a moralist. It's the disdained outsiders who have the capacity to analyze society and propose a vision of the moral life, even if it's not what they practice themselves.

A Miser's Death and Legacy

Derville is unhappy with Gobseck's appropriation of the Restaud fortune. But eventually he feels obliged to call upon him to urge him to support the union between Ernest and Camille de Grandlieu by providing the young man with the funds he needs. He finds Gobseck is bedridden. Death is near, and soon Gobseck summons Derville again, to charge him with finding his heir: he is aware that his grandniece Sarah, known in the world of high prostitution as "La Belle Hollandaise," has a daughter, known in the same milieu as "La Torpille," or "the Torpedo" (the stinging fish rather than the missile). "Look for her, Grotius!" (NY 280/P 2:1010) Gobseck is worth seven million francs, and the search for his great-grandniece Esther van Gobseck will take us into the murky intrigues of *A Harlot High and Low* (*Splendeurs et misères des courtisanes*).

When Derville pays his visit, Gobseck offers him, as his executor, all sorts of disparate items: pots of foie gras, sacks of coffee beans, a dinner set by the famous Odiot, tobacco. . . . It turns out that Gobseck has been named to a commission to settle claims for compensation against the new Haitian government (recognized by France in 1822), and has been receiving all sorts of emoluments and gifts—bribes—from landowners and merchants. Over the years he has acquired all the apartments on the first two floors of his building, and when he expires, stoic to the end, Derville undertakes an inventory. He finds a pile of gold under the ashes of the fireplace, gold that Gobseck had tried to burn since he was too ill to bank it. In adjoining rooms he finds what might be described as Gobseck's last remains, all the merchandise that he had hoarded in his final days.

In the room next to the one where Gobseck had died were rotted pâtés and masses of food of all sorts, even shellfish, fishes sprouting mold—the mix of stenches nearly choked me. Worms and insects crawled everywhere. These recently arrived presents were mixed pell-mell with boxes of every shape, cases of tea, bales of coffee. On the mantelpiece in a silver tureen were notices of arrivals in his name at Le Havre, for bales of cotton, vats of sugar, casks of rum, coffees, indigo dyes, tobaccos, a whole bazaar of products from the colonies! This room was piled high with furniture, silverware, lamps, and paintings, and vases and books, or beautiful engravings rolled up, without frames. . . . I saw jewel boxes marked with coats of arms or monograms, fine sets of linen, expensive arms, none labeled. Opening a book I thought out of its place I found thousand-franc notes between its pages. . . . In the course of my career in the law never have I seen such a spectacle of greed and eccentricity.

(NY 280–81/P 2:1011–12)

Returning to the bedroom, Derville discovers a pile of correspondence about sales he refused to close on. "Gobseck haggled over a few francs difference and meanwhile the goods spoiled." His powerful passion for ownership survives longer than his mercantile intelligence. Such is the fate of goods when their commercial circulation breaks down—a kind of depot of last resort, spelling the end to the exchanges on which modern economies depend. This master of the cash nexus who controlled the circulation of money at the last reverts to miser and hoarder, like a character from the ancien régime, in a Molière comedy for instance. There's a basic contradiction at the core of this character: he has entered the modern world of capitalism, but not quite. He remains tinged with attributes of traditional greed, unwilling to let go of the goods he has accumulated, as if they were more tangible, usable, even edible forms of wealth than money. Like his creature, Balzac is only on the threshold of a modern economy.

Derville is left with Gobseck's own question on his deathbed: "Who will all these riches go to?" Derville reluctantly honors Gobseck's dying request and searches in the brothels of Paris for the designated heir. But he is able to reassure the Vicomtesse de Grandlieu that the legal documents are in place for the young Comte Ernest de Restaud to come into a fortune that will allow him to marry Camille, while providing for his mother and siblings. The story that Derville undertook to persuade the Grandlieus has reached its happy ending: it's all right for Camille to love Ernest. The Grandlieu family needn't oppose a marriage between them; they will be a wealthy couple. But Derville's emphasis on money doesn't wholly convince the Vicomtesse. We will consider it, she tells the lawyer. "Monsieur Ernest must be very wealthy to have his mother accepted by a family such as ours. Think that my son will some day be Duc de Grandlieu, he will reunite the fortunes of the two branches of the family, and I want him to have a brother-in-law to his taste." (NY 282/P 2:1013) Here, the Comte de Born intervenes to note the Restaud family coat of arms, and its antiquity. True, says the Vicomtesse, and Camille could arrange never to see her mother-in-law. To which Born replies that Madame de Beauséant received Madame de Restaud. Yes, but only at her very large receptions—her "routs"—concludes the Vicomtesse.

So that the issue of Camille's marriage to Ernest remains at the very last suspended between aristocratic pride and greed. That is the balance point of Balzac's world, where the prestige and snobbery of the aristocracy remain intact, while the narcissism of small differences assures the dominance of the Faubourg Saint-Germain. But its power is in decline; it needs backing by the fortunes of the new mercantile and industrial classes. Gobseck isn't a pure product of the new commercial and financial world like the banker Nucingen, much less a representative of nascent industrialism. And yet his uses of his money clearly speak to the nineteenth century rather than the past. It is only with his death that he takes on the withered features of the traditional miser. During his active lifetime, his investments are very much part of the bloodstream of modern society, in which the landed gentry remain important but real power lies with capitalist accumulation that must often hide its naked ambitions in polite social trappings. The ambitious, like Rastignac, need the capitalists in order to become rich. The gentry need the capitalists to remain rich. The Grandlieu–Restaud marriage, supported by the wealth Gobseck has banked and multiplied, looks ideal in such a world.

We will learn elsewhere in *The Human Comedy* that the marriage does take place: Camille becomes Ernest's wife, and one of the pillars of high society. But the future of Gobseck's legacy to his great-grand-niece Esther, "the Torpedo," is far more troubled and troubling. That story takes us into new territory: not merely human need and greed but various regions of the criminal underworld only suggested in Vautrin's earlier appearance.

Gobseck, Esther, and the Fate of a Fortune

Esther may be the most beautiful young woman of the whole *Human Comedy*. In her beauty and her sexual experience, she transgresses class boundaries. As the journalist Étienne Lousteau describes her early in *A Harlot High and Low*:

> At the age of eighteen, this girl has already known the greatest opulence, the most abject poverty, men at every social level. She holds a kind of magic wand with which she unleashes the brutal appetites so violently repressed in men who still have passions while working at politics or science, literature or art. There is no other woman in Paris who can say as she does to the Animal: "Out with you!" And the Animal comes out of its cage and wallows in excess...."[3]

Lousteau seems to allude to Homer's goddess Circe, who turns Odysseus's men into swine. Esther has a kind of protean ability to change herself as well. When she meets Lucien de Rubempré, she falls madly in love. She renounces prostitution and tries to live a secret life with him. But at the Bal de l'Opéra in 1824, she is recognized, despite her disguise, by Jean-Jacques Bixiou, one of the journalist pals she once hung out with. In despair at her unmasking she tries to commit suicide—lighting a charcoal brazier in a room without ventilation. She is saved at the last moment by Vautrin, in the guise of the Spanish priest Carlos Herrera, who now is masterminding Lucien's existence. Herrera sends Esther off to a convent to have a religious education that ends with her baptism, after which she is restored to Lucien, but only as a well-kept secret mistress. She is allowed out for exercise only at night. And one moonlit night when she is walking in the Bois de Vincennes she is glimpsed by the Baron de Nucingen, who is struck as by lightning. He must have her. Her Jewish ancestry appears to be partly responsible, activating Nucingen's repressed origins.

Esther will become ever more deeply a part of Herrera/Vautrin/Collin's schemes to further the career of his beloved Lucien: he hopes to convert her beauty into money. Esther will serve in Collin's scheme to extort from Nucingen the money Lucien needs to get a secure foothold in society. She exercises a social function fully opposed to Gobseck's accumulation of wealth: her role is to spend, "to repair the misfortunes created by Greed and Cupidity." (P 211/P 6:617) The prostitute is the old equalizer, squandering the wealth of the capitalists. Esther exposes the hypocritical arrangements of the social order that she both transgresses and is cabined by. But the moment must come when she is obliged to pay what she calls the "debts of dishonor": give herself to Nucingen, though she warns him that this will be the one and only time. When that moment arrives, she dresses as if for a wedding, spends one night with the besotted Nucingen, then swallows poison. Her suicide comes on the eve of the day when Derville would at last have tracked her down as Gobseck's legatee, and set her and Lucien free from want.

Gobseck's fortune arrives too late to save Esther, and too late also to save Lucien, who descends into a downward spiral following her death. Where does it go? Lucien commits suicide not knowing he is now the legatee, and the fortune disperses through Lucien's family: to Eve and David Séchard and their children, to an honest provincial family that really doesn't need it. Gobseck's legacy never quite arrives at the right time or place. And in fact by the time it reaches the Séchards, the July Revolution of 1830, already looming at the end of *A Harlot High and Low*, has broken out, as perhaps the true legacy of the financial legerdemain of Gobseck, Nucingen, and others. Though this revolution will solve very little. It will mainly consolidate the regime of the "capitalists." The large-scale banking practiced by Nucingen will eclipse the artisanal moneylending of Gobseck.

The presence and necessity of Gobseck stand at the core of *The Human Comedy*: stories that turn around the moneylender, from the Faubourg Saint-Germain to the world of prostitution, exemplify the power of money to set everything in motion. Social consequences, such as Ernest de Restaud's marriage to Camille de Grandlieu and Derville's to Fanny Malvaut, originate in the unmoving and unmoved figure of the usurer. He incarnates the needs of an older world of the decaying and needy aristocracy as well as the more voracious demands of the new mercantile and industrial bourgeoisie, where his fortune will end up, bypassing the prostitute sacrificed to Lucien's ambitions and Nucingen's geriatric ardor. Gobseck is a structural necessity of Balzac's world. It wouldn't be imaginable without him.

Yet one should not leave Gobseck without noting that this seemingly wholly unscrupulous moneylender also claims a certain moral stature. He appreciates the honest, hardworking seamstress Fanny Malvaut. He provides Ernest the hard knocks to make him a better person. He has nothing but contempt for the likes of Maxime de Tailles. That the old miser recalls the Dutch masters makes him a representative of tradition as well as the financier of the modern. Our ambivalent attitudes toward saving and spending, toward the whole issue of money, where it comes from and where it goes, cling to Gobseck. He embodies the physicality, the indispensability, the abstractness and concreteness and necessity of money that runs through modern life. He is horrifying and amoral, yet the partisan of sound values. He is finally a kind of figure of destiny in the dawning age of capitalism: this is what it all comes back to.

3. Antoinette de Langeais
(1795–1823)

Desire and Its Discontents

A NOBLEWOMAN WHO DESIRES TO DESIRE but is blocked by
what her social caste permits, a soldier who has only an elementary
education in the ways of love, and a milieu where class and politics
force desire to assume devious guises: such is the stuff of a drama of
desire at an impasse from which it appears only violence can bring
release. Balzac's novella *The Duchesse de Langeais* (*La Duchesse de
Langeais*) takes us to the wilder shores of love, posing stark questions
about eros and understanding, and in particular a woman's experience of them. It will begin in medias res, with the soldier's search
for his lost love object, and then will go back to the origin of an
extreme and exacerbated eros. It asks whether there can be any social
solution to the absolute demands of desire.

The most recent film adaptation of the novella opens with a
breathtaking long tracking shot across water to a brilliant mass of
ocher-colored buildings on an island of the Mediterranean.[1] We
then enter a church where the organ is playing, eventually to find
the title character under a nun's habit. Here the story begins, but

readers of *Père Goriot* will realize they met Antoinette de Langeais when Rastignac calls on Madame de Beauséant, and the noble ladies and self-declared best friends spar with each other about their fickle lovers. Their barbed conversation reflects the extremity of the situations in which they find themselves: both are on the verge of abandonment and at a moment of crisis while explaining to Rastignac how to get on in society. The Vicomtesse de Beauséant, as we know, has decided to leave Paris for a life of expiation and repentance in Normandy after throwing a final grand ball. At the ball, the Duchesse de Langeais tells her friend that she is about to make a last attempt with General de Montriveau—if that fails, she too will disappear from Parisian society.

The story of Antoinette de Langeais doesn't proceed in linear fashion. In one of Balzac's most effective dramatic unfoldings, we begin late in the story, as the Marquis and General de Montriveau comes to the rocky Mediterranean island in order to search for the lost Duchesse. He suspects she may be hidden under the severe habit of a Carmelite nun. After this opening we return in time to Montriveau's courtship of the Duchesse and hers of him, and the accumulated misunderstandings that define their nonetheless passionate relationship, then in the final part turn to the outcome. *The Duchesse de Langeais* follows a logic of passion and discovery rather than chronology. It is a story about the claims of eros, in turn bound up with a story of knowing. It recounts an eroticized quest for knowledge that may be best captured by the term James Strachey coined to translate Freud's word *Wisstrieb*: "epistemophilia," a compound of sexual and intellectual drives to know.[2]

Montriveau, who comes to the island simply as "a French general" participating in the Franco-Spanish War of 1823, seeks "to satisfy a secret curiosity"; he has, we learn, searched every other convent in Spain in his desperate quest to find the Duchesse. From outside the convent walls, he listens to the chants of the nuns, intent on detecting the voice of his lost love.[3] At the mass celebrating the restoration of King Ferdinand VII at the war's conclusion, Montriveau senses a French hand on the keyboard of the organ during the Te Deum since it appears to feature motifs from French songs, including a melody that the Duchesse would play for him in her boudoir. The next day at vespers, he again finds a trace of France in the playing of the Magnificat. The organ, the narrator tells us, this most magnificent of instruments, is the only one powerful enough to transmit human prayers to God, to "translate" them, to overcome the distance between men and God: the word Balzac uses is *truchement*, meaning originally a go-between. And in fact Montriveau hears an erotic charge in the artistry of the nun at the keyboard as she "seized upon the music to express the overflow of passion that still consumed her. Was this an offering of her love to God, or rather the triumph of love over God?" (NY 292/P 5:914) It is the Duchesse, Montriveau convinces himself.

Montriveau in this manner attempts to make out the presence of the Duchesse deep within the convent through the traces of her spirit in the nun's music, in her touch upon the organ keyboard. How can he use that knowledge to gain love, how can he align love with knowledge? He manages to arrange a meeting with the nun in the convent parlor, where she speaks from behind the barrier of a grille. Antoinette, he calls her, but she maintains that she is now Sister Theresa, dead to any other identity. The mother superior intervenes to ask if she already knows the man to whom she is speaking; the nun replies he is one of her brothers, and Montriveau admires this "Jesuitism," which reveals that she still loves him. Her husband the Duc has died, he tells her; she blushes but reminds him that she is now bound by other duties and oaths. She speaks of divine love; Montriveau insists that he must possess her. He accuses her of never having loved him. "You don't wish to leave this tomb; you love my soul, you say? Well then! You will lose it forever, that soul: I will kill myself." Without replying to him, the nun turns to the mother superior. "My mother" she says in Spanish, "I lied to you...this man is my lover!" (NY 300/P 5:923) The curtain behind the grille falls, doors violently slam shut. The general leaves the church, convinced that Antoinette still exists and loves him still. He makes up his mind to abduct her from the convent, to ravish her from God himself.

Here ends part one, to take us back to the beginning of the story. Part two, entitled "Love in a Fashionable Paris Parish," begins, in contrast to the intense opening, with a long political excursus on the role of the Faubourg Saint-Germain aristocracy during the Restoration of the monarchy following the fall of Napoleon. Antoinette will be characterized as the very epitome of that caste at that moment. The narrator reflects on the place of aristocracy in a well-ordered, harmonious society, expressing a good deal of nostalgia for the supposedly organic society of the ancien régime, as in Talleyrand's remark that those who hadn't lived before the Revolution never knew "*la douceur de vivre.*" But Balzac criticizes the Faubourg Saint-Germain aristocracy of the Restoration for failing to recognize its obligations toward the rest of the nation. A true ruling class needed to control a monopoly of the creative forces of the nation, in industry, commerce, statesmanship, and the arts. If it lacked these forces within its own ranks, it should have gone to recruit them from other classes, as, the narrator claims, the English Tories did:

"if genius wasn't within it, to go search for it in the cold attic where it might be dying, and to assimilate it." The Faubourg Saint-Germain instead assumed that intellectual superiority came with its social superiority, and failed to recruit the young talent of France, such as the underemployed young writers of *Lost Illusions*, or Balzac himself. (NY 308/P 5:931) Like greedy parvenus, the gerontocratic leaders of the Faubourg Saint-Germain grasped all the wealth and kept all the honors and powers for themselves. If they had opened their ranks to the bourgeoisie, they would have deprived the opposition of its leaders, but no: at this moment of intellectual and artistic creativity they "all hated art and learning." They became obsessed with etiquette and the markers of class distinction rather than the true foundations of power—and thus the Restoration collapsed, in a mere three days of revolution, in July 1830. "This was a cold, petty era, one without poetry. Perhaps it takes a long time for a restoration to become a monarchy." (NY 316/P 5:939)

Balzac always comes back to what is essentially the intellectual failure of the Restoration, its incapacity to analyze what was going on in a nation that had emerged from revolution and the Napoleonic adventure with a need for order and stability but also with new dynamics of ambition and the conquest of power, and a new belief in the potential of the individual to change his own status and even that of the nation. The example of Napoleon was on the mind of all young men, even those who adhered to the monarchy. The story of the Duchesse and General de Montriveau will on the level of a private passion illustrate a failure similar to that in the public sphere.

Like the Faubourg, Antoinette is "superior and weak, grand and petty." (NY 312/P 5:934) She is described as "a woman artificially educated but in reality ignorant, full of lofty sentiments but lacking the thinking to coordinate them; squandering the richest treasures of her soul in obedience to convention ... speaking much of religion without loving it, yet ready to accept it as an end." Born Antoinette de Navarreins in 1795, she was married in 1813, at the age of eighteen, to the Duc de Langeais. With the coming of the Restoration in 1815, the couple entered society and public life—while living separate lives. Essentially incompatible, "they had secretly hurt one another's feelings, secretly wounded each other, and separated forever." (NY 315/P 5:937) The Duc commands a military unit far from Paris and visits the court only when on leave; the Duchesse serves as a companion to a royal princess. The beautiful Antoinette lives in a kind of "fever of vanity," adored in society, listening to stories of scandal that enable her to "discuss theories of the love that she did not know." Surrounded by a court of male and female admirers, she is "coquettish, lovable, seductive up to the end of the party, the ball, the soiree; then, the curtain come down, she found herself alone, cold, uncaring." (NY 317/P 5:939) In this state of erotic latency, she is described as a "miser satisfied to know his caprices could be satisfied: perhaps she didn't even go so far as desire."

Armand de Montriveau's situation is quite different. He is a well-educated and intelligent artillery officer who comes from a noble family but served Napoleon and was wounded at Waterloo, then undertook an exploration into Upper Egypt, undergoing a period of captivity and a brave desert crossing. And yet he knows nothing of love. "Having lived always on the battlefield, he knew about women only what the hurried traveler, moving from inn to inn, can know of a country." (NY 327/P 5:950) Despite his age he is "as new in love as the adolescent who has just read *Faublas*," a mildly erotic eighteenth-century novel of a young man's initiation.

Even before meeting Montriveau, Antoinette is taken with the image of the brave soldier traversing the burning sands of the African desert. She wants him to be her conquest and no one else's. And yet she does not want to surrender herself to him. The situation quickly becomes impossible. Their social small talk "is like the body of a letter; there should have been a postscript in which the main idea was stated." (NY 326/P 5:948) But the postscript never is delivered. Instead, we have a protracted, fetishistic game of offering and withholding. Montriveau is "a virgin at heart" who swears, in the manner of Arabs among whom he has lived, that he will possess the Duchesse. But the Duchesse surrounds herself with "fortifications" that he will have to overcome. She offers herself to him piecemeal, first her feet (NY 330/P 5:953), then her hand to kiss (NY 333/P 5:956)—after which her hands become "insatiable" for kisses. Next, her forehead and her blond curls. Courtship becomes "the work of a Penelope," with the Duchesse forever undoing the progress Montriveau thinks he has made. (NY 336/P 5:959) Like the fetishist, she contents herself with substitutes for sex, with way stations toward the intercourse that Montriveau ardently desires. Finally, Montriveau demands to know why she has asked for his life, and when he's made himself hers totally, accepted the gift? She replies that her marriage to her husband allows her to dispose of her heart but not of her "person": that is to say her body. The two come to resemble "those Indian fakirs who are rewarded for their chastity by the temptations it gives them." (NY 341/P 5:965) Montriveau falls at her knees in her boudoir: "He kissed the hem of the Duchesse's dress, her feet, her knees; but for the honor of the Faubourg Saint-Germain, it is necessary to respect the mysteries of its boudoirs, where one wanted everything from love except that which would prove love." (NY 355/P 5:978)

What exactly goes on is left to the reader's imagination. It implies a kind of oral progress on Montriveau's side, but one fetishistically limited, again, to parts, never arriving at his goal.

This "preface to what society calls a lapse" appears ready to go on without end, until Montriveau runs into his friend the Marquis de Ronquerolles, an experienced man of pleasure, who asks him if the Duchesse is his. When Montriveau "naively" lays out the situation, Ronquerolles tells him that the women of the Faubourg Saint-Germain have "compromised with nature," permitting themselves everything but a "positive sin." (NY 359/P 5:981) His counsel: "Strike. When you have struck, strike again. Keep on striking, as if you were giving her the lash." (NY 360/P 5:982) Montriveau at once rushes to the Hôtel de Langeais, entering unannounced. The Duchesse is in her peignoir preparing for bed. He endeavors to embrace her. Disaster: she rings for her maid, who arrives to escort him out. "Be good enough to return when I will be ready to see you," the Duchesse tells him. (NY 363/P 5:985)

The picture of sexually charged and frustrated love in *The Duchesse de Langeais* thus far makes it a remarkably impassioned story that seems ever on the brink of catastrophe. But strange and unexpected developments are in the wings. Montriveau belongs to a secret society known as the Thirteen, Les Treize. (*The Duchesse de Langeais* itself stands with two other novellas, *Ferragus* and *The Girl with the Golden Eyes*, in a trilogy called *Story of the Thirteen*.) Other members include Ronquerolles and Delphine de Nucingen's sometime lover, Henri de Marsay. The Thirteen are bound together by a secret pact by which all must come to the aid of each in a time of need, and such is their collective audacity and ingenuity that, as he puts it to Antoinette, Montriveau can summon "a power more absolute than that of the czar of all the Russias." Now, rebuffed by the Duchesse, he activates the Thirteen. The following week, they abduct Antoinette during a ball given by the Comtesse de Sérizy: when she enters what she thinks is her carriage she finds herself in another that takes her to an unknown town house where several men grab her and bind her. She faints. When she comes to herself, she finds she is tied up—with silk rope—lying on a sofa, while next to her Montriveau smokes a cigar.

Montriveau here makes an uncharacteristically long speech, explaining in detail his case against her for having "played" with his love, which came to her "pure and candid." (NY 371/P 5:993) She has given him an understanding of what love and happiness might mean, only to snatch them away, robbing him of "his future of good fortune"—"a frightening crime." Antoinette objects: "The gift of my heart was not enough for you, you insisted brutally on having my person...." (NY 374/P 5:996) And she makes her own long speech, accusing him of having come to her without respect, as to a fallen woman. But now she sees it was all for love, and subdued to his power, Antoinette falls at his knees: "I love you! I am yours!... For you! For you, my one and only master!" (NY 375/P 5:997) Bondage seems to elicit consent. But now Montriveau claims he doesn't believe her. "Antoinette can no longer save the Duchesse de Langeais. I don't believe in either one."

A bright flame from the fireplace in the next room lights up three masked figures, and Armand describes the punishment he has devised. His confederates are heating an iron brand, shaped in the form of the Cross of Lorraine, with which he will brand her full on the forehead with a mark that can never be hidden. "You will finally have on your forehead the mark of infamy applied to the shoulders of your brothers the convicts." (Shades of Vautrin, exposed as the convict Collin in *Père Goriot*.) Montriveau has become judge, jury, and executioner for Antoinette's crime against love, in a scene that offers an S/M variant on the traditional Court of Love, and anticipates *The Story of O*.

Montriveau has feared that Antoinette will resist. But on the contrary:

> "Resistance," she cried, striking her hands with joy, "no, no I would wish the whole world here as witness. Ah! My Armand, mark, mark quickly your creature as a poor little thing belonging to you....When you will have singled out in this way a soul in bondage who will wear your red mark, well then you can nevermore abandon her, you will be mine forever. By isolating me upon the earth, you will be responsible for my happiness if you are not a coward, and I know you to be noble and great! But the woman in love always brands herself. Come, gentlemen, come brand the Duchesse de Langeais. She is forever Monsieur de Montriveau's. Come quickly, all of you, my forehead burns hotter than your iron."
>
> (NY 376/P 5:998)

What are we to make of this unexpected and instantaneous conversion of the Duchesse to erotic love? Is it simply one more move in the fetishist's games she has played before, that his proposed violent act should break the impasse and bring repressed passion into the open? Antoinette convinces us that it is more, that the game really ends here. For the first time in her life, she feels something close to erotic fulfillment. To us today, the scenario appears hopelessly masculinist and misogynist: we might feel more comfortable if it didn't so completely succeed. But the text claims that what emerges with Montriveau's threat of branding is "the true woman" —"*la femme vraie*" indeed is the subtitle of part three of the novella, which contains this scene. The brand will assure Antoinette herself of what the games of love in the Faubourg Saint-Germain have always lacked: a promise of eternal fidelity. Recall the political failures of the Restoration. Montriveau has managed to shake the status quo, to create something newly romantic and strange. Balzac has brought together the political, the erotic, and the quest for knowledge in one scene that is both excessive and convincing.

An Erotic Impasse

And yet Balzac doesn't stop here. The lover who proposed the red-hot brand turns out no longer to believe in so obvious (so phallic?) a solution. Armand, repressing a tear, tells Antoinette that he will spare her, even as he bids her farewell. "I no longer feel the faith," he tells her. They must henceforth be strangers to each other. "Look," Antoinette responds, "I am young, and you have just made me younger still. Yes, I am your child, you have just created me. Oh! Don't banish me from my Eden!" (NY 377/P 5:999) Her logic here is curious and interesting: Armand's godlike threatened act of violence re-creates Antoinette as a yet-unfallen Eve, pleading to stay in her Garden of Eden. Her sexual relationship with him would not be sin but rather the eternal love of two social outcasts, "branded" by their love, thus bound only to each other. This seems to be an outlandish ideal in Balzac's erotic imagination, of lovers exiled and so forever united, but an ideal never possible of realization. The love idylls in Balzac all are doomed.

Antoinette tries to explain to Armand what he doesn't understand: the joy created by her sacrifice of all her social and moral characteristics. While a queen to others, to him she will be a simple seamstress, in order to please him. Montriveau will have none of it. He leads her blindfolded from the room and the house, though he can feel the heart palpitations of this woman "so suddenly invaded by a true love." (NY 378/P 5:1001) The word "invaded" suggests a breech in those "fortifications" with which Antoinette surrounded herself. Montriveau, however, simply returns Antoinette to the ball at Madame de Sérizy's from which he abducted her. He is not convinced or converted. He doesn't get what has happened—there is a crucial failure of erotic and amorous intelligence on his part.

And now begins a new contest between Montriveau and the Duchesse. She has made known her love for him, and is convinced that he will come to realize that their union is inevitable and necessary. For him, however, the old game continues. The Duchesse is not to be believed, she must be spurned. Antoinette cannot believe she has uttered the words "I love you" in vain. She must either be loved or else abdicate her place in the world. "Feeling then the solitude of her voluptuous bed where lust had not yet placed its warm feet, she rolled about restlessly, repeating to herself: 'I want to be loved!'... the true woman glimpsed happiness, and her imagination, avenger of time lost by nature, pleasured itself in stoking the inextinguishable fires of pleasure." (NY 381/P 5:1003) Her desire is as inflamed as was Montriveau's, but again it lacks its other. We will see that Antoinette's experience is repeated by Henriette de Mortsauf in *The Lily of the Valley* (*Le Lys dans la vallée*), but Henriette admits only retrospectively to a rigorously repressed passion. Now

Antoinette puts her intensely physical desire at the center of her life. She wants to act according to its demands.

But it is frustrated passion, and daily she grows paler and thinner. Her "striving toward pleasures always hoped for, always betrayed" undermines her social self. "She was paying for the arrears of her life of deceptions." (NY 386/P 5:1008) The Duchesse writes daily to ask Montriveau to visit—but he does not come. Finally she sends her carriage, empty, with its attendants, to stand before Montriveau's front door, from eight in the morning till three in the afternoon, where it is seen (as she intends it to be) by passersby and especially those aristocrats on their way to meetings at the nearby Chamber of Peers, who draw the conclusion that she is within, having become Montriveau's mistress. What she earlier forbade—any public sign of love—now stands reversed. She wants to create a public scandal: she is marking herself with the brand that Montriveau refused to place on her forehead. Everyone thinks her in Montriveau's arms; meanwhile "she lay throbbing deep within her boudoir." (NY 387/P 5:1010) In a largely comic episode, the members of her family meet to find an appropriate resolution to such shocking behavior. The old Princesse de Blamont-Chauvry advises Antoinette that she is no longer living in the Renaissance, when great ladies could behave with disdain for social consequences. There are ways, this figure from the ancien régime explains, to love and live in disguise. Antoinette finds inspiration in these suggestions. In disguise, she slips into Montriveau's house. In his bedchamber she finds all her pleading letters—unopened.

She resorts to one last, drastic expedient. She asks her eighty-year-old uncle, the Vidame de Pamiers, to take a final letter to Montriveau, and to insist that he read it in the Vidame's presence. The letter states that if he does not come to her within three hours—by eight o'clock in the evening—he will never see her again. She is not threatening suicide, but she will disappear, never to be found.

Along with Armand, we read the letter. "If you love me, put an end to a cruel game," she says. "You are killing me"—the game is no longer hers but his. "After having given myself entirely to you in thought, to whom else can I give myself?...to God." (NY 403–4/P 5:1025–26) Her letter is touching. But here the machinery of melodrama kicks in. Montriveau is in a meeting with friends. He tries to bring it to an end in order to meet the deadline—but his clock is slow. Meanwhile, the Duchesse waits outside his door, and at a quarter past the hour, she loses faith. When Montriveau steps out to go to the Hôtel de Langeais, Antoinette is already fleeing through the streets of Paris. She reaches the Boulevard d'Enfer and bursts into tears. After casting a final glance at the reddened, smoky city, she gets in a cab and leaves Paris, never to return. As in a stage melodrama, deadlines are absolute: a quarter of an hour brings the disaster that separates Antoinette and Montriveau—forever.

How to Do Sex?

"God Makes the Endings" is the title of the fourth and final part of the novella. Montriveau, having enlisted the Thirteen to help him abduct Antoinette from the convent, returns to the island in a brig flying the flag of the United States as a disguise. He and his confederates decide they need to attack the island convent from its most inaccessible side. In a light skiff, they approach the island through perilous reefs, bringing cables and baskets with which to construct a rigging like a spiderweb, and after eleven days, the "thirteen human demons" prepare to scale a sheer cliff, "as difficult for men to climb as would be the polished round belly of a porcelain vase for a mouse." (NY 411/P 5:1033) "Belly" (*ventre*) is strange for a cliff, but the following sentences confirm this sexualized topography: "This granite face was fortunately cleft. The opening, whose two sides had the inflexibility of the straight line, allowed them to attach every two feet stout wooden wedges into which these bold workmen drove in iron crampons." Here I am translating very literally, to show how the original suggests a kind of violation, not only of the island and of the convent but of Sister Theresa herself. The repressed charge of sexuality in the tale emerges into the open and onto the landscape.

They reach the wall of the convent, and Montriveau stops to listen to the muffled music within, seeking "airborne promises of happiness." By "a strange aberration of the heart," he loves the nun aged twenty-nine, made older still by grief and prayer, more than the insouciant young woman he remembers from her Parisian boudoir. "Montriveau was destined to love those faces where love reawakens in the midst of lines of pain and the ruins of melancholy. Doesn't a lover then call forth, with the voice of his own powerful desire, a new being, young, throbbing, who breaks for him alone the envelope he finds beautiful and the world judges destroyed?" (NY 413/P 5:1034) In snatching the Duchesse from the convent, the demands of desire seek to restore a prior state and make good a seduction never completed.

The next evening, the members of the Thirteen infiltrate the convent, with one of them, Henri de Marsay—whose feminine looks are mentioned often in *The Human Comedy*—dressed as a nun. It's he who leads Montriveau to the nuns' cells, and finally to that dedicated to Saint Theresa. Ronquerolles comes to whisper that all the nuns are at church, at a mass for the dead. Montriveau enters the cell—to find the Duchesse dead, lying on a wooden plank, lit by two candles. What is to be done? They will take her away. The nuns now are coming in a procession to the cell but with the "magic swiftness that an extreme desire gives to our movements," the body is taken from the cell, out through a window, down the sheer cliff, into the boat. By the next morning, the brig is at sea. Montriveau remains alone in the cabin with the body of the woman now designated by her maiden name, "Antoinette de Navarreins."

In a final dialogue, Ronquerolles tells Montriveau:

> "...that was a woman, now it is nothing. Let's attach a cannon ball to each of her feet, throw her overboard, and don't think about her any more than as we think of a book read during our childhood."
>
> "Yes," said Montriveau, "for it's now only a poem."

The Duchesse as a book read during childhood and as poem gives a kind of wistful romantic coloring to this elegiac moment. But then Ronquerolles cuts in to say: "Now you are being reasonable. From now on, have your passions; but as for love, you need to know where to invest it wisely. It's only a woman's final love that can satisfy a man's first love." (NY 415/P 5:1037)

What is the worldly-wise, cynical Ronquerolles getting at? All along he's been wary of his friend's naiveté and lack of experience in love. Passion is fine, but love is an investment, he seems to say. Choose it wisely. But the final aphorism? It corresponds to a traditional view that young men should be initiated into love by older women. But its application to this story is hard to fathom: it's certainly true that Antoinette is Montriveau's first love—he is a "virgin" so far as true love as opposed to casual sex is concerned—but it's hard to see Antoinette's love for him as her last, since she has never loved before. Though the novella has made it her first and last. This may be the wisdom Ronquerolles intends: you made a mistake in choosing a woman who, for all her social and coquettish skills, was not experienced in love, and therefore could not understand the absoluteness of what you were offering her.

It comes back to that problem of desire and knowledge with which the story begins, as Montriveau tries to make out the presence of the Duchesse within the convent through her voice in the choir and her touch upon the organ keyboard. Once you have found her, what can you do with that knowledge? The Duchesse excels at managing Montriveau's desire with a striptease, a game that resembles the fetishist's avoidance of the traditional goal of genital sex by investing eros in substitute objects. There appears to be a fear of reaching the object. It is almost as if they both need to be taught how sex works. They are caught in an impasse that they can't break out of. This heightens the erotic and emotional stakes but never gives them the release, the way through to mutual satisfaction that they both come to want. So that their love must end with a tragic denouement.

In Balzac's novella, a story not only of love but of politics as well, states of submission and domination are strikingly reversible. Balzac has much to say about romantic love, but he treats it generally with a certain deflationary skepticism.[4] What interests him is what lies beyond the romantic on one hand and the purely calculating seduction on the other: something wilder, something that assaults and sometimes destroys the everyday self. Another tale from *Story of the Thirteen, The Girl with the Golden Eyes,* about the fashionable young fop Henri de Marsay (the disguised nun of *The Duchesse of Langeais*—and, as it happens, a future political leader) and his erotic adventure with the mysterious Paquita Valdès, leads to her death, and his confrontation with her lover, the Marquise de San-Réal, who turns out to be his half sister. Sex with Paquita offered "infinity," perhaps because it was quasi-incestuous. It is lovemaking with yourself as other. Proust said of *The Girl with the Golden Eyes* that "here under the apparent and exterior action of the drama circulate the mysterious laws of flesh and emotion."[5]

Even more extreme is Balzac's story *A Passion in the Desert* (*Une Passion dans le desert*), about a French soldier who gets lost in the desert during Napoleon's Egyptian campaign and spends the night in a cave that is part of a small oasis with palm trees, to discover in the morning that he shares it with a panther. The panther is female—though its powerful tail is phallic—and both alluring and dangerous. Soldier and panther forge an amorous friendship but their playful caresses come to a bad end when he overreacts to her biting his thigh—though just a little bite—and stabs her in the throat. Panther as woman is a way for Balzac to talk about female sexuality in ways censored in a more public language. As in Vautrin's relationship with Rastignac and Lucien de Rubempré, Balzac finds a figural language to speak of loves that dare not speak their name. A full gamut of possible sexual pleasures lies close to the surface. Proust was right to admire Balzac's audacity in opening up kinds of sexuality not represented in "mainstream" (non-pornographic) novels. Exploration of sexuality in *The Duchesse de Langeais* points us toward a world of unconventional sexual relations and fantasies that Balzac doesn't so much describe directly as allude to, touch upon, make evident. It is there when you pay attention.

Eros, Feminism, Androgyny

Gustave Flaubert was severely criticized, at the trial of his *Madame Bovary* for outrage to public morality, for showing Emma Bovary as embellished by adultery: "Never had Madame Bovary been so beautiful as at this moment. . . .": adultery provides a kind of fertilizer to her beauty, bringing it to its full flower.[6] Balzac precedes him here, in glowing portraits of women who are sexually fulfilled. A notable example can be found in *A Woman of Thirty* (*La Femme de trente ans*), where Hélène d'Aiglemont has eloped with a pirate, and found happiness:

> The tropical sun had embellished her fair face with tan, a marvelous coloring that gave her a poetic expression; one felt there an air of grandeur, of majestic command. . . . Her long and full hair, falling in large curls on her noble neck, added another degree of power to the pride of this face. Hélène gave full evidence of her awareness of her own power. A triumphant satisfaction welled up in her pink nostrils, her tranquil happiness was signed in all the maturation of her beauty. There was in her an indescribable mix of the sweetness of the virgin and that special kind of pride of the well-loved woman. Slave and sovereign, she liked to obey because she could command.[7]

That is what sex can do for you. Note again the slight S/M implication: "slave and sovereign." Both sex and politics seem to demand domination and submission—but they can change places.

The leading contemporary critic Charles Augustin Sainte-Beuve accused Balzac of building his reputation on women in an unhealthy way: conquering them like the plague. Sainte-Beuve's jealousy of Balzac's success is evident, and he never could bring himself to do justice to *The Human Comedy*. But he is largely correct that Balzac's appeal was first to women, unsurprising in that the history of the novel is largely built on the genre's allure for women, who were the ones with the leisure for reading, and whose restricted lives thirsted for imaginary satisfactions. From Samuel Richardson onward, the inner experience of women has also been a prime subject of the novel, whether written by men or by women. (Ian Watt in *The Rise of the Novel* notes the role "tradesmen's wives" with time on their hands had in the success of Richardson's novels.[8]) Balzac's young male protagonists—Rastignac, Lucien, and others—make their way in large part through their appeal to women. His female characters claimed enormous attention during his lifetime, and still today can appear extraordinary creations. He won early recognition with his *Physiology of Marriage* (*Physiologie du mariage*), a somewhat cynical account of the institution that nonetheless indicated to many women that he understood the conditions of their existence, and then in *A Woman of Thirty* he gave definitive form to the figure of the married woman, at the height of her beauty and sexual desire, trapped by the conventions of marriage, by loutish husbands and the double standard that permits men sex outside marital constraints but severely punishes the adulterous woman. And again in *The Lily of the Valley*, though the perspective is that of the young would-be lover Félix de Vandenesse, Balzac creates a rich inner portrait of Henriette de Mortsauf, badly married, persecuted by her husband, greatly tempted by Félix's devotion but enlisted with virtue to the end—and then at the very end, on her deathbed, crying out in an anguish of regret that she never knew sexual love of the kind that Félix offered. Letters from women readers to the novelist make clear that he evoked something real in their lives, some self-recognition in his fictions. They found he spoke to their inner experience in ways that elicited a response.[9]

There is a case to be made for a feminist Balzac, who espoused with imaginative sympathy woman's condition. It's not that he militates for the improvement of woman's lot—that is not part of his conservative politics—but that he understands that women, even so privileged a woman as Antoinette de Langeais, have a bad deal in life. They are brought up in an enforced ignorance by parents and in convents, then married off young to older husbands who have no interest in tenderness or sexual nurture. The pleasures of whoring are widely available to men, and the salons of the upper echelons of harlotry a place of free and witty conversation as well as pleasure. Nothing comparable is open to women. The aristocrats, such as Antoinette or Claire de Beauséant or Anthénaïs d'Espard, find pleasure in their salons and sometimes in discreet love affairs—but these always seem to end badly. Middle-class and provincial women, like Dinah de la Baudraye in *The Local Muse* (*La Muse du département*), can try to escape their condition in espousing the arts and letters. But on balance there are not so many happy women in Balzac's work—or their happiness is of limited duration. They find a typical response in a letter to the novelist from one Louise Abber: "Worn out from a painful life, I need to unburden myself of my sufferings" ("*Fatiguée d'une vie douloureuse, j'ai besoin d'épancher mes souffrances*").

It might be more accurate to see a certain androgyny in Balzac's attitudes, sympathies, and creative imagination. Not only does he appear able to move with ease between male and female perspectives in any given situation, he seems at home in imagining somewhat androgynous beings who appeal both to women and to men. Lucien de Rubempré is the outstanding example, but we will find others, in *The Fatal Skin* (*La Peau de chagrin*), for instance. The love of half siblings for the same woman in *The Girl with the Golden Eyes* makes a similar point, as does *Sarrasine*, where the painter-protagonist falls in love with a "woman" singer who is in fact a castrato, whom he at the moment of this revelation accuses of being "nothing," a person without sexual identity, thus someone who creates a certain panic of gender identity in general.[10] Androgyny was a subject of some interest in Balzac's time. The Girodet painting of Endymion for which the castrato Zambinella served, in Balzac's fiction, as a far-off model offers a visual androgyny. And perhaps androgyny is a metaphor for the artist who creates life from his sole self and body.

If Antoinette is a prisoner of Faubourg Saint-Germain conventions, which eventually she is willing to shatter, her status as a duchess gives her a potential for freedom that isn't vouchsafed to bourgeois women. Balzac is of course fascinated by the aristocracy, and especially the noblewoman who seems to have the capacity to define her own life. One of the most memorable examples comes in *A Murky Business* (*Une ténébreuse affaire*), where the beautiful, chaste, passionate, brilliant Laurence de Cinq-Cygne (the family takes its name from five virgins, "swans" who defended their château against enemy assailants), at the time when Napoleon is consolidating power, lives with the freedom of the Amazon, riding miles every day to maintain contact with her four cousins—who become implicated in a plot to overthrow Bonaparte and restore the monarchy—and loves at once her twin cousins, Paul-Marie and Marie-Paul Simeuse, to the point where she refuses to distinguish between them, loving a kind of doubled person who alone would seem capable of satisfying her enormous demands on life and love. She travels all the way to the battlefield of Jena to demand grace for them from Napoleon himself. Sadly, both will be killed on the battlefield, and she will have to accept the diminished eros provided by the least beautiful of her other cousins, Adrien de Hauteserre. The kind of freedom from constraint Laurence represents cannot survive in the modern world. But it is exhilarating and arousing while it lasts.

Antoinette, to return to her in conclusion, appears to represent a glimpsed possibility of erotic happiness when she undergoes her "conversion" with Montriveau's proposed act of violence, which she sees, perhaps correctly, as an act of love: a needed violence to overcome a resistance that she cannot herself bring an end to—since it is part of her nature and nurture as a Faubourg Saint-Germain aristocrat—but desires in some manner, at some level of consciousness, to go beyond. In asking to be branded, she looks forward to a life of erotic belonging to Montriveau, which may resemble slavery but to her implies an absolute commitment on the part of her lover that is rare in the world of *The Human Comedy*. When she implores Armand not to banish her from the Eden she has discovered in her re-creation as a woman, she asks for an opportunity to enter the world of sexual satisfaction that she and her life experience have denied her. That Montriveau doesn't understand—only comes to grasp, perhaps only partially, when it is too late—is Antoinette's tragedy. If Balzac pulls out all the melodramatic stops in his presentation of the story (think of that organ of the first part of the tale, the "translator" between man and God that Antoinette so expressively plays) to give us a tale that may appear over the top, the situation he discovers and lays bare seems deeply true.

4. Raphaël de Valentin
(1804–1831)

Life Lived as Parable

BALZAC CALLED *The Fatal Skin* (*La Peau de chagrin*), the book with which he emerged as a major novelist, a "philosophical tale." Raphaël de Valentin finds his life caught up in a primordial struggle between love and death. As he discovers the potential of magically fulfilling every wish, he at the same time becomes subject to the inexorable consequences. Balzac, very much like Freud in his most speculative essay, *Beyond the Pleasure Principle*, discovers that the pleasure principle is inextricably bound up with its opposite, the death drive.

We first meet Raphaël as an unnamed young man, entering a gambling den in the Palais-Royal by day, when the true bloody dramas of desperation take place, ready to play his last piece of money. Only a few spectators are present at this hour, and they look "for a drama in the fate of this single gold piece, perhaps the final scene of a noble life."[1] When the young man loses, he rushes from the gambling house, down toward the Seine. No, it's too early to throw himself into the river, he decides: better to let darkness cover his suicide. Now he wanders aimlessly in the streets near the Palais-Royal, casting a piercing glance at an elegant young woman, as his farewell to love. She doesn't notice him. Soon he drifts into an antiques shop. Told that the truly precious objects are to be found on the second floor of the shop, he climbs the stairs to encounter "the dry bones of twenty worlds." (S 19/P 10:69) The showrooms are piled with stuff, providing a kind of unedited inventory of world civilization. "All the countries on earth seemed to have brought some debris of their sciences, some sample of their arts. It was a sort of philosophical dunghill. . . ." (S 20/P 10:69) To the young man on the verge of death, the confusion of this dunghill, the weird juxtapositions of things within it, sacred and profane, becomes overwhelming. "The ear seemed to hear stifled cries, the mind to grasp unresolved dramas, the eye to perceive half-hidden flickers of light." The youth leaves the real world behind him, his spirit lost in the joys and sorrows of others. Climbing to the third floor, he finds himself "suffocating under the debris of fifty vanished centuries." (S 25/P 10:74)

He falls into a meditation on the panorama of human life, and on the earth before life, only to be interrupted by the arrival of the owner of the shop, a small, unworldly old man who seems to live alone in a sphere without joy or pain. He offers to show his visitor a painting of Christ, by Raphael, and then when he learns of the young man's intention to commit suicide, he proposes something else, a shagreen, or wild ass's skin, engraved with a message in Arabic that proclaims that whoever possesses the skin will possess everything—but his life will belong to the talisman.

> If thou possess me, thou shalt possess all things
> But thy life shall belong to me. So hath God
> Willed it. Express a desire and thy desire

Shall be fulfilled. But let thy wishes
Be measured by thy life. Here it lies.
With every wish I shall diminish
Just as thy days shall be
Decreased. Thou dost
Desire me? Then
Take and God
will hear. So
be it.

(S 35–6/P 10:84)[2]

This is the stuff of *The Arabian Nights*, which always fascinated Balzac. Moving beyond the world and its cluttered things, he turns to address the occult forces that move the world.

The old antiques dealer—he is 102, an age he has attained by rigorous self-restraint, including sexual abstinence—evokes those forces. It's he who unfolds the laws of life:

Man depletes himself by two instinctive acts that dry up the sources of his existence. Two words express all the forms taken by these two causes of death: DESIRE and POWER. Between these two poles of human action, there is another principle seized upon by the wise, to which I owe my happiness and my longevity. Desire sets us afire and Power destroys us; but KNOWLEDGE leaves our fragile organism in a state of perpetual calm.

(S 37/P 10:85)

The antiques dealer in his own way resembles Gobseck: he lives as observer rather than participant, avoiding all desire while finding vicarious pleasures in the mind. "My sole ambition has been to see. To see is to know, is it not? Oh, to know, young man, isn't it to have pleasure intuitively?... I have an imaginary harem where I possess all the women I haven't had." (S 38/P 10:86) He has soared above the world, making himself something close to a god. "How could one prefer all the disasters of our baffled desires to the sublime faculty of summoning the universe to appear within oneself... to lean over the edge of this world in order to interrogate other spheres, and to listen to God!"

Raphaël will promptly ignore the antiques dealer's advice, like other young Balzacian heroes who typically dismiss such wisdom. An existence removed from the world might seem similar to the writer's ideal life, but that never was Balzac's choice. He lived amidst the demands of desire, attempting to devour everything in his path. Renunciation was only a necessity, one forced upon you by poverty, thwarted desire, and the need to spend long nights writing. Raphaël's reaction simply dismisses the antiques dealer's disquisition on wisdom. "All right, then, yes, I want to live with excess," he says, taking hold of the magic skin. So, like many young men in folktales, he makes a wish that is scarcely pondered, even foolish. "I wish for a royally splendid dinner.... Let this night be graced by women of flaming ardor! I want a delirious and roaring debauchery to sweep us away on his chariot with four horses, beyond the bounds of this world, to deliver us to unknown shores." (S 39/P 10:87) The antiques dealer laughs and tells Raphaël that his suicide now is merely postponed. In return, Raphaël wishes that the old man would fall in love with a dancer—and runs off.

The magic skin may be fantasy, but the way the wishes it grants come true is the stuff of realism: such are the rules of Balzac's fiction.

Rushing out of the shop, Raphaël runs headlong into three young men, who turn out to be friends, strolling toward the Pont des Arts. In the wake of the July Revolution—which brought the reign of the Citizen King, Louis Philippe, and the emergent power of the financial and industrial bourgeoisie—these young men have decided to start a newspaper. "Journalism, you see, is the religion of modern societies," says one of them, "and that's progress." Why progress? asks another. "Because its popes don't have to believe, and the people don't either...." (S 45/P 10:93) (Premonitions of *Lost Illusions*.) A rich banker named Taillefer, reputed to have made his fortune by killing his best friend (see the novella *The Red Inn* [*L'Auberge rouge*]), is throwing a banquet to launch the paper. Taillefer is the father of the Victorine of *Père Goriot*, whose millions Vautrin dangled before Rastignac.

So it is entirely within the realm of the probable that Raphaël finds himself at a banquet, which will develop into an orgy. A number of characters assembled there—the notary Desroches, the caricaturist Bixiou, the vaudeville writer de Cursy, Raphaël's good friend Émile—will figure elsewhere in *The Human Comedy*. Late in the evening a group of women join the party, and Raphaël and Émile have a conversation with two of them, Euphrasie and Aquilina, who have chosen a flaming life of orgy, however brief, over a long life of virtue and restraint. Don't you ever worry about the future, Émile asks Aquilina, and she responds: "Why would I worry about something that doesn't exist yet?" (S 68/P 10:114) And then: "Besides, don't we live more in one day than a good bourgeoise lady in ten years, and that says everything." (S 70/P 10:116) Raphaël presses the claims of virtue, and Euphrasie exclaims: "Virtue! We leave that to the ugly and hunchbacks. What would they be without it, poor things?" Yet when Raphaël envies their life of wild abandon, Aquilina's response is sobering: "'Happy!' said Aquilina with a smile of pity, or terror, in giving the two friends a horrible look. 'Oh! You don't know what it's like to be condemned to pleasure with death in your heart.'" (S 71/P 10:117) In her linking of pleasure and death, Aquilina cuts closer to the truth than her listeners realize.

Now pandemonium erupts at the banquet. Drunk, Raphaël confesses to Émile that before all this he was about to throw himself in the Seine. What for? Émile wants to know, which provokes Raphaël's lament: "Oh, if only you knew what my life has been." Émile responds that this is a trite thing to say, but he agrees to listen to Raphaël's life story, at least if he makes it brief. "'Please, spare me the preface,' said Émile, half laughing and half piteously, taking Raphaël's hand." (S 75/P 10:120) In the more usual narrative contract, story is produced in response to a request; here it's the opposite. Raphaël needs to tell more than Émile wishes to hear.

Here the first part of the novel, "The Talisman," ends and the second, "The Woman Without a Heart," begins. Raphaël will give a first-person narrative of his life from its start to its near end in his aborted suicide. The young man, who is at first unnamed, simply a poor unfortunate who has reached the end of the line (he becomes Raphaël only upon meeting his friends), offers us his own version of his identity and life story. Until the age of twenty-one, he tells Émile, he lived bent under a despotism as cold as a monastic order. The despot was his father, who denied him comfort, distraction, and money, despite the family's aristocratic origins. But one evening, when he was nineteen, at a ball hosted by the Duc de Navarreins, a relative, his father asked him to take care of his purse: and Raphaël, defying paternal interdiction, gambles. He gambles and wins, and can restore the purse undiminished. As a result, he receives for the first time his father's praise and a promise of future emancipation, with a stipend, in preparation for becoming a great statesman. But then comes the Restoration, forcing his father give up lands he had acquired in the aftermath of the Revolution, and Raphaël is obliged to play the part of lawyer and litigant. Now he becomes his own despot, internalizing his father's prohibition of pleasure in what would later be a classic Freudian scenario of the formation of the superego. He sells off his inheritance to pay his father's debts. When his father dies, Raphaël is left alone in the world with a total fortune of 1,112 francs. For all his ardent nature, women can only be a dream.

What to do? He decides to embrace a big idea rather than a mistress: to compose a treatise on the will. He can live on 365 francs per annum for three years, moving into a garret in a dingy building once occupied by a young Jean-Jacques Rousseau, in a forgotten corner of the Left Bank, up in the cheapest mansard room. He works night and day on his opus in this "aerial sepulcher," looking out over the rooftops of Paris. His intense desires for love and for women are sublimated into his work. He gives lessons to his landlady's daughter, Pauline, and she in turn brings him meals and does his housework. Pauline is like a sister; there must be no question of desire. But then in December 1829 he meets Rastignac, well-established in the world and a friend to young men of good birth like Raphaël, who introduces him to what he calls the "political system" of dissipation. Rastignac points out that Raphaël's treatise will need backing if it's to be published and read; he will take him to the salon of the influential Comtesse Fœdora, a half-Russian beauty, though Raphaël will have to squander his savings on the necessary gloves and cabs. That evening he explains to her his great work on the will, which, like his creator, he conceives as a kind of fluid force, something like magnetism or electricity, that can be brought to bear on others, and Fœdora is impressed. "Fœdora or death!" he exclaims as he walks back through the dark streets to his bare room. (S 112/P 10:152)

But the beautiful, intelligent, coquettish Fœdora, a rich young widow who should be in need of a lover, seems to be impervious to love, for reasons that no one can explain. One evening, returning from the theater, she tells Raphaël that she has had many offers of love and of marriage, but that she has no intention of giving up her freedom. He is by turns passionate and sarcastic in response; nothing moves her. He leaves in despair. Worse yet, his hat—that necessary accessory and emblem of respectability—is dissolving from going back and forth in the rain. It is "wounded, dejected, finished, truly a rag, a worthy representative of its master." (S 121/P 10:160) The good Pauline, in contrast, offers her love, a love simple and true, but what is that next to the Comtesse's social prestige?

Rastignac again steps in to help, finding him work as a ghost-writer for a volume of pseudo-historical memoirs. This allows Raphaël to renew his wardrobe. But his pursuit of Fœdora remains hopeless. She is indifferent to his passionate appeals, and unmoved even by the sublime music of Rossini and Cimarosa. She is, as Rastignac admits, an enigma to male desire. Why is she immune to desire? Is she hiding some bodily defect? In order to find out, Raphaël comes up with a thoroughly infantile project, something like one of Freud's scenarios of the male child curious to understand sexual difference. He resolves to spend a night hidden in Fœdora's bedroom. During a large reception, he sneaks off and slips behind the bedroom curtains. Past midnight, Fœdora arrives, humming an aria from Cimarosa, "Pria che spunti," and then bursts into song—no one has ever heard her sing—in a voice that becomes rich and sensuous. Stopping before her mirror, she contemplates her tired face, and rings for her maid Justine. The name made famous by the Marquis de Sade is not insignificant: Raphaël has suspicions of a lesbian love between the mistress and this tall, well-built young brunette. Instead, Justine comes in and tells her she should marry, an idea Fœdora, as always, rejects. She is, Raphaël decides, an "atheist in love." (S 151/P 10:183)

Now comes the crux of the scene. Justine unlaces her:

> I contemplated her with curiosity at the moment when the final veil was lifted. She had a virgin's bosom that dazzled me: through her shift, by the candlelight, her white and pink body shone like a silver statue that gleams under its transparent wrapping. No, no imperfection could have made her fear the furtive eyes of love. Alas! A beautiful body will always triumph over the most martial resolutions.
>
> (S 150/P 10:184)

Virtually naked, slightly veiled by the gauzy shift, Fœdora presents a body that is all too perfect: virginal, like a silver statue. Physically and emotionally, she is apart. There seems to be no way into her for the prying, spying lover. The final sentence above may suggest that the lover is rendered impotent in catching sight of her body, as in, once again, Freud's scenario of the male child discovering the female genitals and feeling the cut of castration. The airbrushing out of the genitals is all the more to the point. Epistemophilia, as in *The Duchesse de Langeais*—the need to see and to know, like the child puzzled by sexual difference—deprives Raphaël of the power of seduction. Spying is something like castration, an inability to complete any contemplated act of seduction. When Fœdora, after crying out "Oh God!," finally falls asleep, Raphaël thinks about slipping in next to her, anticipating Marcel's attempted possession of the sleeping Albertine in Proust's novel.

He resists this temptation. He decides instead that he must tell her his life story, as he is telling it now to Émile, in order to try to reach her. He requests an evening alone with her and speaks till nearly midnight, but though she is touched by his tale of poverty and study, that is all. His declarations of love leave her unmoved. Intending to renounce her forever, Raphaël returns to his garret. He finishes the fictional memoirs and receives final payment. Suicide beckons, but then Rastignac reappears to talk him out of it. Stupefy yourself with pleasure, he advises, plunge into a profound dissolution. Gamble! But Raphaël, still subject to the paternal interdiction, can't do that himself. He gives his money to Rastignac, who goes off and returns with a small fortune, 27,000 francs. With his share, Raphaël rents and furnishes an apartment in the rue Taitbout (where Goriot and Delphine set up a bachelor's apartment for Rastignac; where Jacques Collin will lodge Esther) and embraces the life of a high liver: a viveur. He encounters "Debauchery, in all the majesty of its horror." (S 164/P 10:227)

Debauchery, he tells Émile, demands a strong soul; it is an art, like poetry. It creates a more dramatic life within life—Balzac's own ambition as writer, you might say. "War, Power, the Arts are corruptions placed as far from human reach, and as deep, as debauchery, and all are of a difficult access." (S 165/P 10:196) A version of the romantic quest to go beyond finitude. "All excesses are brothers.... The thought of the infinite maybe exists in these precipices...." These artificial paradises, as Baudelaire would call them, offer "a perpetual embrace of all life, or better, a duel with an unknown power, with a monster." (S 166/P 10:197) The result of the duel is "to create yourself a second time, as if in revolt against God!" Raphaël soon runs through his money; *viveurs* always do. He sells his only piece of real estate, an island in the Loire River where his mother's tomb stands. (We have heard little about his mother; she died when he was still a boy.) Selling off the site of her tomb makes him feel a chill like that in a cave. It is a bad omen. After paying his debts, he is left with 2,000 francs. He cannot bring himself to go back to his studious life in his garret, the life of vision and renunciation and wisdom represented by the antiques dealer. He has become "a galley slave of pleasure." (S 172/P 10:202) At the last, he finds himself reduced to a single twenty-franc piece. Now we have circled back to the opening of the novel. He recalls Rastignac's success at the gambling table, and despite his lifelong fear of gambling.... But just as he is about to tell Émile of his loss of his last coin and his decision to kill himself, he suddenly recalls the talisman in his pocket. He becomes exalted like a madman.

"To the devil with death," he cries out, brandishing the skin. "I want to live now! I am rich." He remembers to have wished for 200,000 francs of income, and he believes he will have them. His exclamations awaken Émile, who picks up with "Fœdora or death!" So you were asleep? says Raphaël. No, mumbles Émile, "Fœdora or death, I'm with you." (S 173/P 10:203) For some fifty pages, for the last hour or so, Raphaël has been talking to no one. His life history has fallen on ears made deaf by drink and sleep. Only the impassive Fœdora, and Rastignac perhaps, and we readers know his story. Raphaël, who as a ghostwriter composes fake memoirs, cannot impose his own personal narrative on an inattentive world.

Now the magic skin is the center of his attention. It is, he explains to Émile, an "antiphrasis": it grows smaller with every wish, whereas desire ought to expand and extend. (The analogy of magic skin and penis becomes evident and will be alluded to a number of times.) With a flash of lucidity, Raphaël decides to measure the skin: he spreads it on a napkin and with a pen traces its outline. Then, like Émile, he falls asleep.

Orgies in Balzac must be followed by mornings after, when daylight enters the devastated apartment to show up spilt wine, wrinkled clothes, fatigued faces. Around noon, the orgiasts struggle to wake. But now the *notaire* Cardot enters, looking for Raphaël, demanding to know his mother's maiden name: O'Flaharty. It turns out that he is the sole and unique heir of Major O'Flaharty, deceased in August 1828 at Calcutta, leaving a fortune of six million. Raphaël at once seizes the magic skin and places it over the outline he traced during the night, to see how it has shrunk. The skin moves easily within the margins of the inked perimeter. A frightful pallor spreads over his face, making it into a livid mask. "He saw DEATH." (S 179/P 10:209) He can doubt no longer. He now knows that his life belongs to the skin. He comes to the instant realization: "The world belonged to him, he had the power to do everything and he no longer wished for anything." (S 180/P 10:209) Like a traveler in the desert with only a modicum of water, he will have to measure out desire with care. But now others are all over the rich young man with their demands: Euphrasie wants a pearl necklace, Aquilina horses and carriage, others wish for cashmeres, the payment of debts, the death of a rich uncle, or a cure for gout. Raphaël glowers at them: "I almost want to wish death on all of you."

Beyond desire lies the death drive. Émile accuses him of becoming

89

an egotist and, what's more, of believing in the talisman. Raphaël remains silent and drinks himself into a stupor to forget, for a moment, his fatal power.

A Life Beyond Desire?

Here ends the second part of the novel. The third and final part, "The Agony," returns us to third-person narration following the first-person narration of Raphaël's life to Émile. Raphaël, now the Marquis de Valentin, lives in a quiet, even gloomy town house on the rue de Varenne, in the aristocratic Faubourg Saint-Germain. His servant, Jonathas, commands a staff that must serve as the buffer between their master and the outside world. Raphaël has arranged his life in such a way that he never has to express a desire. Doors open by themselves; Jonathas is never to ask him what he wants—any verbal formulation of wishing, liking, has been entirely forbidden. "The better to combat the cruel power whose challenge he had accepted, he had made himself chaste in the manner of Origen, by castrating his imagination." (S 189–90/P 10:217) In this denial of the quest for pleasure, Raphaël ironically takes up the stance of the antiques dealer, but bereft of his mental orgies. In his drawing room hangs the fatal skin, outlined in red so that any shrinkage will be immediately visible. Raphaël receives a visit from his former professor, Pourriquet, who has lost his post following the July Revolution and seeks to have it restored. Raphaël can do nothing, he says, before politely wishing that Pourriquet succeed—which instantly produces a white margin between the skin and its outline. Raphaël, furious, accuses Pourriquet of costing him ten years of life, and he chastises Jonathas for admitting the old professor. Raphaël goes to the theater, and whom should he meet but the antiques dealer: hair dyed and face made up, and accompanied by the beautiful and venal Euphrasie. When Raphaël asks him about his ascetic philosophy, he replies that he had it all wrong: "There's the whole of life in an hour of love." (S 197/P 10:224)

The theater is full of beautiful women, including Fœdora, and to guard against temptation Raphaël has had an ingenious opera glass made for himself: it is designed to distort, destroy, and make hideous the harmony of the most beautiful features. This opera glass gives us an emblem of the relation of the Balzacian self to the world: if you don't desire anything, the world is without appeal, it loses its beauty. You lack for everything, yet nothing now triggers the need to devour, to incorporate, to make the beautiful object one's own. If the self's relation to the external world no longer is subtended by desire, it loses all meaning. Raphaël's life is a kind of vegetation, a life without movement or meaning.

A woman takes a seat in the loge next to his. The theater buzzes with admiration, but Raphaël refuses to look at her, until at last that proves impossible. There is Pauline, now richly and tastefully dressed, who at once tells him to meet her in his old room in the Hôtel Saint-Quentin the next day at noon. Back home, he boldly declares: "I want to be loved by Pauline." (S 201/P 10:227) The skin does not budge; no doubt this wish had been fulfilled long since. Perhaps love has freed him from its maleficent power? The next day, Pauline awaits him in his garret, playing his old piano. Her long-lost father, it turns out, has returned with a fortune. She is now a rich Comtesse. They profess their love for each other as in an operatic duet, and we are given to understand that they make love then and there. Pauline has no use for social conventions.

"Let death come when it may," says Pauline in ecstasy. "I have lived." (S 206/P 10:231)

Money, as so often in Balzac, comes when it can no longer do any good. If Raphaël hadn't deserted the Hôtel Saint-Quentin for Fœdora, and a life of gambling and dissipation, if he had just stayed put, the diabolical skin would never have been his, and all his desires would have been realized. He and Pauline plan to marry in a fortnight. But back by his own fireside, he notices that the skin has shrunk a bit. For the male lover, that's the price of desire fulfilled. Enraged, he grabs the skin from its place on the wall, runs out in his garden, and throws it into the well. To hell with all this nonsense, he decides. Life must be lived without a thought for the wretched talisman.

One morning, while Pauline and Raphaël, now inseparable, are breakfasting in his hothouse room, the gardener comes to show them a curious discovery he has made: in drawing water from the well he has brought up the skin, now shrunk to a six-inch square. Raphaël's voice goes hollow, his face pale. The novel takes a satiric turn, as Raphaël consults various scientists to see if the world of modern progress can counter the force of this ancient talisman. The zoologist Lavrille tells him all about the habits and habitat of the wild ass, but the skin won't stop shrinking. The physicist Planchette delivers a disquisition on movement, a subject that Balzac never ceased to think about, but when he and his colleague put the skin under a kind of hydraulic press, the machine explodes and the skin shows no damage. Other attempts to beat and smash the skin are equally unsuccessful. The chemist Japhet applies various acids and other substances on it, to no avail.

Raphaël now is obsessed with death, he tells Pauline. She reacts: "What matter the number of days, if in one night, one hour, we have exhausted a whole life of peace and happiness!" (S 229/P 10:253) She has signed on to the credo of romantic love, extending back (at least) to Saint-Preux, the hero of Rousseau's epistolary novel *Julie, or the New Heloise* (*Julie, ou la nouvelle Héloïse*), who after his first night of passion with Julie writes: "*Oh! mourons, ma douce amie!*"—"Let us die, my sweet friend." And so on to Wagner's Tristan and Isolde, and to Villiers de l'Isle-Adam's Axël and Sara: when Sara proposes to Axël a night of love followed by a double suicide, Axël replies that the night of love is superfluous, they must die at once. "Live?" he says. "Our servants will do that for us."[3] Raphaël accepts Pauline's view: "Give me your mouth to kiss, and let us die." And she replies, laughing: "Let us die, then."

But Balzac's novel doesn't ratify romantic self-immolation. The next morning, when they wake up after a night of passionate love-making (Pauline is one of Balzac's most uninhibited heroines), she tells him there is something disquieting in his breathing when asleep. And now he begins to cough, "with one of those deep and resonant coughs that seem to come from a coffin." (S 232/P 10:256) He emerges from the fit of coughing pale, trembling, exhausted. Doctors are summoned, but like the scientists they are at odds and can't come up with any useful diagnosis—which allows Balzac to satirize different schools of medicine, from the idealist to the empirical. Horace Bianchon alone among them shows empathy with the patient. Raphaël is advised to seek a cure of mountain air, and travels to Aix-les-Bains, in Savoie. His indifference and egotism and his racking cough offend and alienate the other denizens of this proto–Magic Mountain. One of the young men provokes him to a duel. Raphaël warns him that he possesses a terrible power that will not let him lose the duel, and when the young man insists, he toys with

93

his power, showing no concern as his opponent fires—wide of the mark. "Shooting without taking aim, Raphaël hit his adversary in the heart; and without paying attention to the young man's collapse to the ground, he pulled out the magic skin to see how much a human life cost him. The talisman was now no bigger than a small oak leaf." (S 255/P 10:276) The interplay of eros and the death drive that has been dramatized throughout the story of the skin now takes the form of sadism, the aggressive and destructive drive turned outward toward others.

Raphaël leaves for the spa of Mont-Dore in the Auvergne, reflecting sadly that the possession of power doesn't guarantee its good use. In fact, "Raphaël could have done everything, and he had done nothing." (S 255/P 10:276) In the volcanic mountains of Auvergne, he seeks to do even less. Arriving at a small mountain farm where the patriarch has reached the age of 102, like the antiques dealer, he resolves to settle there, "to become one of the oysters clinging to the rock" (the same image is used to describe Gobseck). Balzac writes: "He was overcome by a profound egotism in which the universe sank away. To his eyes, there was no more universe, the universe passed into him completely. For the sick, the world begins with the head and ends with the foot of their bed. This landscape was Raphaël's bed." (S 261/P 10:281) He falls into reveries on the material world. "He attempted to associate himself to the innermost movement of this nature, and to identify himself wholly with its passive obedience, in order to fall under the despotic and conservative law that controls instinctual existences. He wanted no longer to be burdened with himself." He aspires to what Geoffrey Hartman dubbed "Romantic anti-self-consciousness": those instants when poets and thinkers seek to disburden themselves momentarily of the trials of self-consciousness.[4] Yet still Raphaël's condition grows worse.

Back in Paris, he orders Bianchon to give him a dosage of opium that will allow him to sleep most of the time. "Sleeping is still living," he says. (S 269/P 10:288) But now Pauline, dressed all in white, makes her way into his bedroom. When he awakes from his opium-laden sleep, he tells her to leave him. He pulls out the magic skin, as fragile and small as a periwinkle petal, to show how little is left. "If you look at me like that," he says, "I am going to die." Pauline takes the talisman—this appears to be the first time in the novel it is in her hands—and examines it under the lamp.

> Seeing her so beautiful from terror and love, he was no longer master of his thoughts: the memory of scenes of caresses and delirious joys of passion triumphed in his soul so long asleep, and awoke like the flames of a dormant fire.
>
> "Pauline, come! Pauline!"
>
> A terrible cry came from the throat of the young woman, her eyes dilated, her eyebrows arched upwards from the force of an unspeakable anguish, she read in Raphaël's eyes one of those furious desires, once her great glory; but as this desire grew greater, the magic skin, in contracting, tickled the palm of her hand.
>
> (S 272–73/P 10:291–92)

Balzac is here at his most explicit in his depiction of desire and the consequences of its satisfaction. Terrified, Pauline runs from the room. Raphaël pursues and finds her lying on a sofa, half naked. She has tried to stab herself, now she is trying to strangle herself with her shawl. If I die, he will live, she cries.

> Her hair was falling disheveled over her bare shoulders, her clothes were all in disorder, and in this struggle with death, her eyes filled with tears, her face afire, her body twisted from a horrible despair, she displayed to Raphaël, drunk with love, a thousand charms that increased his delirium. He threw himself upon her with the quickness of a bird of prey, tore apart her shawl, and tried to take her in his arms.
>
> (S 273/P 10:292)

Sadism and masochism, love and death are terminally entangled as, struggling to find the words to express "the desire that was devouring all his strength," Raphaël gasps and dies, biting Pauline on the breast.

The Stakes of Life

The wild and effective melodrama at the end of *The Fatal Skin*—does Raphaël at the last return in punishment to the absent mother's breast?—gives us pause for reflection on Balzac's "realism." We tend to think of him as firmly committed to the real—to fighting it out within the things and the constraints of real life—and we may find it odd that this first great novel of his *Human Comedy* should have at its core a magical object. There are various ways to think about this. It is clear, for instance, that Balzac has in mind his beloved *Arabian Nights* and the capacity to produce magical occurrences within banal everyday life. Even when there are no magical objects around, Balzac is performing similar feats: making the everyday world give rise to a heightened, hyperbolic, parabolic drama. You might say that Raphaël's talisman is no more than a convenient shorthand for representing the large forces that animate all of Balzac's novels. In reading *The Fatal Skin*, it is easy to take it as a largely realist novel where Raphaël's successive choices are the product of normal human will, though given a symbolic representation in the talisman. And yet it is not quite that. The talisman lays bare and makes palpable what is hidden behind the curtain in most of Balzac's novels: the life-and-death stakes of the drama played out every day in society. On the threshold of Balzac's vast project, Raphaël's story already goes to its heart.

When Balzac conceived a classification of his novels for the large framework of *The Human Comedy*, he assigned *The Fatal Skin* to the category of Philosophical Studies. There were to be three basic categories: Studies of Manners (*Études de moeurs*), Philosophical Studies (*Études philosophiques*), and Analytic Studies (*Études analytiques*). The philosophical category was supposed to show the reasons that explain social effects, that is, the large forces moving social life, what you see when you strip off the surface, peer behind the curtain. The analytic studies were then to give the causal principles behind the effects and the reasons, but these studies remain fragmentary.

Balzac wrote to the Comte de Montalembert shortly after publication of the novel: "It is the blueprint [*formule*] of human life . . . everything in it is myth and figure."[5] Myth and figure, yet embedded in human life. The novel has a curious figural epigraph, a wiggly line that resembles a snake. The source is provided: Laurence Sterne's *Tristram Shandy*, chapter 322 (which should in fact read chapter 312). The reference is to the moment Corporal Trim brandishes his cane in the air to represent the free, unfettered life of the bachelor. Balzac's printers didn't quite understand, and from edition to edition the squiggle became a snake, and Balzac never bothered to correct it, perhaps because the French *serpent* represented well enough what he had in mind: the serpentine, wandering, undulating line of human life.[6] The very figurality of the figure that introduces the novel somehow literalizes itself as a snake, somewhat in the manner that the magic skin, which can realize desire but shrinks while doing so, can (if one wishes) be literalized as the penis.

When the novel was reprinted in its second edition, as part of the group then labeled the *Romans et contes philosophiques* (Novels and Philosophical Tales), it came with a preface by Balzac's friend, the critic Philarète Chasles—inspired and possibly dictated by Balzac himself—which ended by foregrounding the issue of individual identity dramatized in the novel. Writes Chasles: "It is this individual personality that ravages the heart and devours the entrails of the society in which we live. The more it increases, the more individuals become isolated: no more ties, no more communal life. Individualism reigns: it is its triumph and its fury that *The Fatal Skin* has reproduced. In this book there is the whole of an epoch."[7]

We hear in Chasles's words the voice of the political conservative who believes that the decline of an organically hierarchical society headed by monarch and church has issued in a disordered competition of individual egos. Though *The Fatal Skin* is less obviously concerned with social life than a novel like *Père Goriot*, it contains as least as much social theory. It suggests that we are to read Raphaël's hyperbolic life of desire, fulfillment, and death as a parable of modernity as seen through the eyes of a traditionalist. Desire is out of hand, and it leads directly to egotism—recall Raphaël's response to his companions in orgy after learning what the talisman can do: he would like to wish death on all of them. As Émile tells him, he is becoming "furiously egotist." To understand the interplay of desire and death can be, as in Pauline's case, the willing sacrifice of life to the ecstasy of desire. Yet it is far more likely to result in Raphaël's egotism, his attempt to preserve life no matter what. And Raphaël, who commands desire, who can do anything and everything, ends up doing nothing. Whereas the antiques dealer, who has renounced desire in order to live in knowledge, ends up in pursuit of a prostitute who mocks him. If desire, power, and knowledge figure all of human existence, no one seems to have the key to their usage.

Choosing Raphaël de Valentin as one of Balzac's biographies may seem a bit perverse since his life is so short. Yet his life is of course parabolic. On the very first page of the novel, when the as yet unidentified Raphaël enters the gambling house, a pale old cloakroom attendant behind a counter asks for his hat. "When you enter a gambling house, the law starts by stripping you of your hat." (S 7/P 10:57) It's not clear why it should be "the law" that your hat be taken, but the narrator continues with a query: "Is this a scriptural and providential parable? Isn't it rather a way of striking an infernal pact with you by exacting a sort of security? Would it be to oblige you to keep a respectful manner with those who are going to take your money? Is it the police lurking in all the sewers of society who insist on knowing the name of your hatter, or your own if you have inscribed it on the headband?" You must go to the gaming tables without your hat, suggesting that you no longer belong to yourself but to the wheel of fortune. Hats may be considered emblems of social identity—recall that Raphaël's will become a disgraceful, deformed mess from too much walking in the rain during his courtship of Fœdora—and the young man, nameless throughout the early pages of the novel, must go unprotected to the gambling tables, and the encounter with desire unleashed and fate subjected to chance. There is an ill-fated heroism in this entry into the gambling den.

But perhaps what is most important here is not the precise meaning of the hat, or the demand to surrender it, but rather the narrator's need to interrogate the gesture, to see it as a possible parable, of indeterminate meaning—to read meanings from it. This we have seen before in Balzac, for instance in his presentation of the lodgers in the Pension Vauquer, where details of appearance raise questions about their meaning, about the past lives of the lodgers, about this milieu. And the presence of the magic talisman in *The Fatal Skin* makes this novel as a whole something close to a parable, a presentation of the large forces of existence—Desire, Power, Knowledge—in dynamic interaction. It offers a dramatic summary of the forces that shape life unto death.

The Fatal Skin is more focused on a single individual and more figural—"philosophical" in Balzac's terms—than many of Balzac's novels. It is openly concerned with human beings as desiring agents and the problem of desire. It displays characters trying to realize desire or divest themselves of desire (the two female love objects are on the one hand without desire and on the other endlessly desirous), and the book suggests that we must continually struggle, in our own lives in the world, to do both those things: realize and restrain desire. But Raphaël cannot do either in a manner that would make him whole. That's the curse of the skin. He is a case study in the pure dynamics of desire, which left to its own devices is always as fettered as it is unfettered and takes all sorts of weird forms, scopophilia, sadism, masochism, of which those opera glasses are such a beautiful emblem.

Raphaël's first-person story to Émile loses its listener midway, his account to Fœdora gets him nowhere. Yet for the reader, his auto-biographical moment, in the midsection of the novel, "The Woman Without a Heart," is impressively exemplary as it puts into visible play those large forces that preside over human life. But it is the story of a life out of control, subject to what we sometimes call destiny— like the toast proposed by one of the orgiasts "to unknown gods." Whereas the first and third sections, told by an impersonal narrator, may in their control of Raphaël's wild tale represent something like the reality principle. Yet one sympathetic to the unconscionable demands of desire.

If *The Fatal Skin* offered a clear parable, a moral message about life, it would no doubt be intolerable. It remains a completely read-able and exhilarating novel because its claim to parable is so inde-terminate. It is subject to the reader's interpretation, in a kind of duck-rabbit rebus that lets the reader choose between the novel of a young man's reality and the parabolic understanding of life. Nor does that choice have to be made once and for all. In reading the novel, I think we can alternately see it as Raphaël's life story and as "myth and figure." We can assign various kinds of reality to the ele-ment of magic, or see the magic as simply figural. Figure and ground can reverse, frequently. Holding them both in some kind of suspen-sion may offer the best reading. It seems to me significant that in his first fully achieved fiction Balzac began what would prove an unre-mitting commitment to the biographical account of fictional per-sons with the case of Raphaël, at once the story of a life, from childhood to death, and a kind of meta-narrative of Life itself, its forces and choices. It's as if *The Fatal Skin* were a kind of introduction—consciously so? I can't tell—to the many lives to come.

At the very end of his life—just before he asked his physician Max Schur to fulfill a long-held promise to inject him with a lethal dose of morphine when the pain of his cancer had become unbearable—Sigmund Freud finished what was to be his final reading. "Freud did not read at random," Schur tells us, "but carefully selected books from his library."[8] His final choice fell on Balzac's *La Peau de chagrin*. When he finished the book—the day before he called for the fatal injection—he remarked to Schur: "This was the proper book for me to read; it deals with shrinking and starvation." Not only with shrinking and starvation but with all that precedes the final outcome of human desire: wanting, having, possessing, devouring. *The Fatal Skin* seems so perfect a final reading for Freud that Schur's anecdote appears almost contrived. In fact, Balzac's novel captures the essence of Freud's late thought, from *Beyond the Pleasure Principle* onward, given its final expression in one of his last essays, *Analysis Terminable and Interminable*, where he claims a precursor in the pre-Socratic philosopher Empedocles of Agrigentum. Empedocles sees the world as the struggle of *eros* and *neixos*, love and destruction.[9] For Balzac as for Freud, to choose love, desire, is also inevitably to choose destruction, death. The organism seeks to return to primal quiescence.

The emblem of the magic skin figures the overall logic of desire and its fulfillment. Desire sets us afire and power destroys us, as the old antiques dealer tells Raphaël early in the novel: desire turned into power, realized in the world, inevitably leads to death. Any attempt to arrest this logic leads to sadism, for instance—that is, the internal destructive force turned outward toward other human beings, as in war—or to the life of "wisdom" that, however admirable it may be judged, seems always to give a result that is sterile, barren. To refuse life in desire is to condemn yourself to that analogue of Origen's castration described in Raphaël when, after learning the power of the skin, he tries to castrate his imagination, turn the world ugly—as through his special opera glass. A world that denies desire is ugly, lifeless. As all of Balzac's young protagonists instinctively understand, it is desire that makes life worth living. But as Raphaël is given a special dispensation to understand, the choice to live the gratifying life of desire is at the same time the choice of death. There is no way out of that stark conjuncture.

5. Lucien Chardon de Rubempré

(1798–1830)

A Poet Seeks His Fortune in Paris

LOST ILLUSIONS (*ILLUSIONS PERDUES*) may be the most prescient novel of its time, one that lays out the future of the novel itself. Set in the 1820s, the story of Lucien de Rubempré, the novel's complex hero, is all about the relation of literature to life and to the growing business—industry—of publishing in early nineteenth-century France. The newspaper was becoming a fact of life, and literature was more and more dependent on it for publicity and reviews, and then, with the creation of the serial novel running daily in the paper, for publication. The whole story is present here, from Lucien's betrayal of poetry for journalism, to his discovery that words are only worth what they fetch in the marketplace. Writing can have talismanic power—if you know how to use it. And not just literature but love, or "love," is caught up this overheated early capitalist economy that can bring quick riches, or bankruptcy and moral ruin. Papermaking, printing, copyright, censorship, and the commodification of literature, everything that was transforming French life, politics, and thought come together in this most far-reaching of Balzac's works.

What to call Lucien is an issue from early in the novel. Lucien Chardon, he is baptized, son of the late pharmacist Chardon in the provincial city of Angoulême. But his mother descends from a once proud aristocratic family, the de Rubempré, which, as is often the case in *The Human Comedy*, lost property and fortune in the Revolution. Lucien will be driven to trade the humble Chardon (which, a satiric sonnet written by a detractor will note, means "thistle") for the noble de Rubempré. The Bourbon Restoration saw many French families simply help themselves to a noble name—as Balzac did. Contemporaries might make fun of your name change, but you were one among many so it scarcely mattered in the end. Lucien is more demanding: in order to enter the aristocratic circles where he would like to shine, and to marry, he needs a genuine title, awarded by royal decree.

We first meet Lucien as an aspiring poet in Angoulême; he lives with his mother and sister, Eve, on the paltry annual income of 800 francs. Angoulême is divided into a lower town, l'Houmeau, and an upper town, Beaulieu, a division that means a class distinction. Lucien has been taken up by a grand lady of the upper town because he appeals to her literary aspirations, and in person as well. "The poet himself was poetry," we learn, and throughout his life both women and men will find Lucien's slightly feminine male beauty irresistible.[1] Madame de Bargeton—née Marie-Louise Anaïs de Nègrepelisse, related to the cream of the aristocracy—has a void in her heart that her old, vacant husband can't fill. When a member of Louise's circle catches Lucien at her knees, a duel ensues: M. de Bargeton, defending his wife's honor, wounds the accuser. Louise proposes that she and Lucien escape to Paris, which she tells him is the natural sphere of the aspiring poet. Members of Lucien's family put together a loan that they can ill afford, and Lucien will miss the wedding of his sister and his best friend, David Séchard. But the lure of Paris cannot be resisted.

Louise arrives in the city by coach, Lucien on foot, covered with all the dust of the highway. Now inevitably betrayal ensues. Paris is the culprit: it offers the contrast of true elegance and feminine beauty—against which Louise appears frumpy—and wealthy, well-turned-out masculinity, by which even Lucien can judge himself as deficient. As he walks in the Tuileries Garden, he discovers the existence of "necessary superfluities" that give a man distinction: cuff links, cravats, lorgnons, canes, grooms. (ML 169/P 5:270) What he needs is a fortune. But alas, even after managing to spend the last of his savings on dressing himself, he looks like a provincial mannequin in the opera box of Louise's cousin the Marquise d'Espard. The Marquise is shocked. Learning that he is not even a real "de Rubmepré," she picks up her skirts and hustles out of the box with Louise. How fortunate that Louise has not become Lucien's lover. A break is necessary. Lucien, now penniless, is abandoned in Paris.

Louise writes a note, unsigned, to say that she and the Marquise won't be meeting Lucien as planned—the Marquise is "indisposed"—and one of the great early scenes of the novel follows. Lucien, wondering at this reversal in his fortunes, wanders to the Champs-Élysées: high society is out in force, "three or four thousand carriages" are gathered there. In one, Lucien spies the Marquise and Louise, now fashionably dressed, and no signs of indisposition. Elegant gentlemen on horseback surround them. Lucien attempts to greet them; they pretend not to see him. The dandy Henri de Marsay is in attendance on the two great ladies. He inspects Lucien through his lorgnon, and then lets it fall like "the blade of the guillotine." Enraged, Lucien imagines himself in the role of the Jacobin public prosecutor, commanding the guillotine. But what he really needs, he quickly realizes, is different: money, "at any price!" With money will come possession: "I'll have my Marquises d'Espard! I'll roll down the Avenue in a carriage myself!" (ML 188/P 5:287) Like Rastignac, like Raphaël and many another young Balzac hero, he wants to devour the world.

But the sonnets (*Les Marguerites—The Daisies—*they're called) and the historical novel (*L'Archer de Charles IX*) he's brought with him from Angoulême are not going to get him what he wants: no publisher will touch an unknown author. In the cheap restaurant Flicoteaux, where students dine because the wretched meal is accompanied by unlimited free bread, he makes a new friend, Étienne Lousteau, once an aspiring poet himself, now on the make as a journalist. They take a walk in the Luxembourg Gardens at twilight, and Lucien bids farewell to poetry. Lousteau takes him to the theater—Paris abounded in theaters and new productions—where a play in which two young actresses display their legs will provide an opportunity for Lucien to write his first drama review. He dashes it off and reads it at an after-theater party. It is a success; he enters the guild of journalists; already people envy him. His rise is rapid. He is soon named as theater critic for a new journal that Lousteau will edit.

Commerce and Language

At the party, conversation turns to the role of journalism. A German diplomat who is present recounts an anecdote: after the defeat of Napoleon, the Germans considered burning Paris; General Blücher, commanding a view of the city from the heights of Montmartre, dismissed the idea: "Don't you dare. France will only be destroyed by *that*"—meaning the intelligentsia gathered in the great city. (ML 318/P 5:403) And, the German diplomat suggests, that is what is happening with the newspaper; it marks the destruction of authority. Bringing information to the masses of the people will sow revolt. The journalist Claude Vignon agrees: newspapers are an evil, though one the government would be better off making use of to its own ends, instead of fighting it. Yes, says Émile Blondet, another journalist, newspapers are "poison shops," and Vignon piles on:

> The newspaper, instead of being a sacred mission, has become an arm for the political parties; and from that it became a commercial enterprise; and like all commercial enterprises it knows neither faith nor law. Every newspaper, as Blondet puts it, is a shop where one sells to the public words in whatever color it likes . . . all newspapers will in due course be cowardly, hypocritical, shameless, mendacious, murderous; they will kill ideas, systems, men, and will thrive from doing so.
>
> (ML 320/P 5:404)

Well launched on his tirade, Vignon goes on to say:

> We all know, such as we are, that newspapers will go farther than kings in ingratitude, farther than the dirtiest business dealings in speculations and calculations, that they will devour our brains every morning to sell their intellectual narcotics; but we will all write for them, like workers in a quicksilver mine who know that they will die from their labor.
>
> (ML 322–23/P 5:406)

Lousteau then describes his new publication: "The newspaper holds to be true whatever is probable. We start from that." (ML 357/P 5:437)

Journalists attacking journalism: their ferocity reflects Balzac's own obsessions and a crucial moment in the history of the press, of printing, and of politics in France and indeed the Western world in general. To Balzac, newspapers incarnated the very anti-principle of the kind of political and social authority he wanted to believe in, and claimed to think necessary for his country. France in the 1820s saw an extraordinary burgeoning of newspapers, which were becoming a daily reality and a political force of a sort never seen before. It was largely the effort of the Restoration monarchy to muzzle the press that brought it down in the revolution of July 1830. Journalists and printers were in the vanguard of the July Revolution. Someone during the party remarks that journalistic excess is sure to lead to new repression. The novelist Raoul Nathan replies, in what sounds like a belated response to General Blücher: "Bah! What can legislation do against French intellect?" (ML 320/P 5:403)

Balzac was himself both a journalist and a novelist, two roles that for many of his contemporaries were virtually indistinguishable. Most of his fiction appeared in part or entirely in the periodical press before publication in book form. He was the first French novelist to publish a *roman-feuilleton*—a serial novel running daily in a newspaper: in 1836, shortly before undertaking the composition of what would become *Lost Illusions*, his novel *The Old Maid* (*La Vieille Fille*) ran in *La Presse*, a right-leaning newspaper owned by Émile de Girardin.[2] He would publish as well in its liberal rival, *Le Siècle*. And in 1835 he bought his own periodical, *La Chronique de Paris*, which early the following year made its debut with a stellar group of writers, but soon succumbed to bankruptcy. Earlier yet,

Balzac had attempted to master the means and modes of literary production by purchasing and presiding over a printshop and a type foundry. That enterprise also went bankrupt; nonetheless, in creating it Balzac displayed a prescient understanding of the means of production of literature.

Lost Illusions gives Lucien an alternative to journalism: the austere devotion to art represented by the novelist Daniel d'Arthez and his faithful group of young talent gathered in the cenacle of the rue des Quatre-Vents: they live in a kind of "decent misery" and stake their lives on future success in their vocations. The book makes much of the noble life of d'Arthez and his friends, and he will be instrumental in the posthumous success of Lucien's novel. And yet the reader doubts that this option has any reality for Lucien. He is predestined to enter the quicksilver mine. He will become one of its doomed workers.

No one knew better than Balzac what it meant to try to live by one's pen—and living by the pen is the profound subject of *Lost Illusions*. Before the Revolution, a poet or a novelist generally depended on some other source of income: inherited wealth, or a pensioned position in the bureaucracy, or else aristocratic or royal patronage. The professional writer who lived from the proceeds of his published work did not yet exist. And even in the postrevolutionary moment of Balzac, such a life was fraught with difficulty, in part because the concept of copyright, of what we now call "intellectual property," remained undefined and unsettled. Balzac railed against pirated editions of his work published in Belgium or by unlicensed provincial publishers in France. It was in fact Balzac who, in an open letter of 1834, first called for the creation of an association in defense of the writer's rights. This would take form as the Société des Gens de Lettres, founded by Balzac along with Victor Hugo, George Sand, and Alexandre Dumas, which still exists today as a guild for the protection of copyright and what the French call the "moral right" of a creator over his creation.

Lucien for better or for worse is launched as a journalist, and professional success is followed by personal success. An actress in the play he reviews, the delicious Coralie, is smitten with his beauty. They quickly end up in bed. She proves a divine mistress, with unfortunate consequences. When her official lover and keeper, the merchant Camusot, is angered to discover Lucien's boots at the door of the apartment that Camusot has of course paid for, she breaks with him. She will devote herself exclusively to Lucien's happiness. They live the high life of the young, accumulating debt, while Lucien discovers that journalism offers not only freedom but servitude. Lousteau wants revenge on the publisher Dauriat, and Lucien is ordered to trash a novel by Raoul Nathan that Dauriat has published. But Lucien admires Nathan above all living writers. How can he criticize his book?

> "Hah! My dear boy, learn your trade," Lousteau replied with a laugh. "Even if it's a masterpiece, under your pen it must become a stupid piece of trash, a dangerous and unhealthy work."
> "But how?"
> "You'll change its beauties into flaws."
> "I'm incapable of such a tour de force."
> "My dear, a journalist is an acrobat...."
>
> (ML 363/P 5:442)

And Lousteau goes on to explain how to destroy the book with, as it were, a kind of good faith, by using it to illustrate a certain tendency in modern literature that breaks with classical ideals.

With this instruction, Lucien rises to the occasion, producing another masterpiece of journalism, while Nathan is reduced to despair and Dauriat shows up to offer 3,000 francs for *Les Marguerites*, which he has not read. Lucien basks in the power of the journalistic word. But then a new order comes down from on high: Lousteau and his pals, Hector Merlin, Émile Blondet, and Félicien Vernou, want him to write a new article in *praise* of Nathan's book; it's necessary to preserve good relations with an author who will be useful to the future of his periodical. But Lucien now can't think of anything good to say about the book.

> "You actually believed what you wrote?" Hector asked Lucien.
> "Yes."
> "My boy," said Blondet, "I thought you smarter than that!"
>
> (ML 380/P 5:457)

Blondet then goes on to offer a new lesson to Lucien: everything is bilateral in the domain of thought. "Ideas are binary. Janus is the god of criticism and the symbol of genius." Vernou piles on: "You believed in what you wrote?... But we are salesmen of sentences, and we live off that commerce." Blondet then explains that after rehabilitating Nathan's novel, anonymously, Lucien will write a third article (the only one to be signed with his name) in which he reconciles the two earlier critiques as part of a debate provoked by all important works of literature.

Lucien, ever the quick study, goes to work with a sense of energy:

"taken by the paradox," he produces the two articles. Coralie draws the parallel to her profession: "Don't I go on this evening dressed an Andalusian, tomorrow as a gypsy, and another day cross-dressed as a man? Do like me, give them disguises for their money, and let's live happily." (ML 385/P 5:461) Coralie's response to Lucien's "paradox" recalls Diderot's famous *Paradox of the Actor*, which says that the stage performance of emotions is all the more effective the less one believes in what one is representing. This is no less true of the journalistic word, a linguistic sign that has exchange value but not representative value—what matters is what you can get for it. Similarly, new money is not tied to the possession of land, the true and traditional measure of a person's worth, but obtained through exchange, speculation, debt, inflation. In the bourgeois and capitalist century, the reign of bankers such as the ubiquitous Baron de Nucingen has replaced that of the ancien régime aristocracy, and journalism is an indispensable part of the new order. The equivalence of words and money will play out over the whole of *The Human Comedy*: what you can do with both of those means of exchange takes the place of their source and their orderly use. *Pecunia non olet*: money does not smell, as a proverb has it. But that's only if you accept its exchange value without poking too much into its origins.

How to Live Beyond Your Means

Lucien lives high off the "paradox" he discovers in writing articles against, for, and in-between on Nathan's novel. He discovers that the journalist has something like the "fantastic power granted to the desires of those who possess talismans in Arabian tales." (ML 386/ P 5:462) Allusions to *The Arabian Nights* in Balzac always signal the opening up, above and beyond the normal bounds of human desire, of superhuman possibilities of power and possession. Lucien, for instance, now has the power to take advantage of his old flame Louise de Bargeton, now the inseparable friend of the haughty Marquise d'Espard, and newly eager to have this successful young man for a lover. Lucien is a success but he doesn't know how to use success. He lives in luxury and spends money as freely as the luxury-loving Coralie. Taking Louise as his mistress would give him a real foothold in the best social circles. It would be the smart thing to do. But though Lucien flirts with her, Coralie leaves him so sexually satiated that he lacks the willpower to complete the seduction of Louise. He "had, like an ogre, tasted fresh flesh." (ML 414/P 5:487) He is enchanted by the voluptuous Coralie.

Lucien has fallen into the group Balzac calls *viveurs*: one of those underemployed young people who lives with a fine carelessness, getting by on the value of their wit. Balzac views this new social grouping through a political lens: "No other fact marks so clearly how the Restoration condemned its young to become Spartan helots." The narrator continues:

> Young people, who didn't know what to do with their energies, threw them not only into journalism, into conspiracies, into literature and art, they dissipated them in the strangest excesses, so great was the sap and the luxuriant powers of young France. Those who were ready to work wanted power and pleasure; the artistic wanted rewards for their talent; the idle wanted to stimulate their passions. In all cases, youth wanted a position, and the political regime denied them any chance at one.
>
> (ML 418–19/P 5:490)

We find a version of this diatribe in *The Duchesse de Langeais*, and it recurs often in Balzac's work. For all his devotion to legitimate monarchy, he judges the Restoration a failure because it left the young with nothing to do. The Restoration was largely administered by aristocrats from the ancien régime who had fled abroad during the Revolution in order to save their lives, only to return from exile to a country that had changed enormously. Rather than recognize and adapt to the changes, old King Louis XVIII and his even older successor, Charles X, and their aged ministers sought to restore life just as it had been before the Revolution, with all its privileges and pleasures, making another revolution inevitable. That inevitability looms over *Lost Illusions*.

Lucien and his ilk have some excuse for their idleness, then: more productive careers are closed to them. Journalism doesn't in the end count as a career—it's a parasitic enterprise, an anti-career—and if the newspapers are largely in the political opposition that's because their readership is found in the restive youth. As the acid Claude Vignon puts it: "I will never cease to be astonished to see a government abandoning the dissemination of ideas to such a pack of scoundrels as ourselves." (ML 404/P 5:478) The fourth estate was busy showing that opposition was both more intellectually lively and more amusing than submission to governmental policies.

And yet Lucien is not content with the talismanic powers of journalism. Madame d'Espard and her circle persuade him to pursue royal legitimation of the name de Rubempré; that will give him true status and power. This renewed ambition invites the attention of his enemies, and they are legion, stung by his satiric articles and jealous of his success. They plot to convince him that he can never make it in good society as a star of the opposition newspapers. They press him to seek a title; after all, what can mere Lucien Chardon expect in the way of a marriage? Whereas the handsome Marquis Lucien de Rubempré would see a bevy of rich heiresses ready to welcome him. He needs two things: to move from the opposition to the royalist press, and to obtain the royal decree. Lucien, now hugely in debt, joins the staff of the royalist paper *Le Reveil*, ignoring the warnings of d'Arthez, a royalist himself, that he will be seen as a turncoat. Lucien naively believes he can trust the editors of *Le Reveil*, all dedicated to monarchy and religion. But he is still under contract to Lousteau's liberal journal, and his old friend forces him to write a piece that satirizes the very Garde de Sceaux, and the King, from whom Lucien expects benefits. It's published anonymously, but his enemies leak the identity of the author. As a result, when he shows up at the ministry of the Garde des Sceaux to receive the royal decree changing his name, he is told that the King has ripped it up. He is ordered to leave the premises at once.

The whole business of royal authorization of name change has in fact been nothing but a charade mounted by Lucien's enemies to undercut his once powerful position in journalism. Lucien's mistake is to believe too much in the power of the word: if you say it's so—if you declare yourself a royalist, if you get your name changed—it is so. Falling as it were for his own lies, he is manipulated by the language he as a journalist was an expert in manipulating. As Lousteau will later explain, it's fine to turn your coat out of necessity, but in that case you need to alert your pals to what you are doing, and why. Better to make these moves cynically than in the mystified belief that they are sincere.

After his dismissal from the ministry, Lucien, stupefied, wanders through the city, and comes upon one of the *cabinets de lecture*, the reading rooms that were beginning to be very popular in Paris, for newspapers originally and then for novels. In the window is the announcement of a new novel, the novel he brought with him to Paris but now bearing a "bizarre title," and the author's name: Lucien Chardon de Rubempré. (ML 473/P 5:538) His name—yet not quite. His novel is out! And yet he knew nothing about it. The newspapers have been silent, and that, far more than a bad review, is the ultimate defeat. Silence condemns you to nonexistence. This novel, the product of Lucien's youthful enthusiasm, reworked by d'Arthez into what posterity will recognize as a masterpiece, stands as a potent symbol of the alienation of intellectual production: the process that Georg Lukács labels the "capitalization of spirit."[3]

Now all of Lucien's hopes and schemes come crashing down at once, in a total collapse of the speculative economy that he has built around him. Besotted with Coralie, *"heureux tous les jours,"* an expression that means he's having sex all the time, he squanders his substance (as we know from *The Fatal Skin*, male potency for Balzac is a zero-sum game). Lucien misses the chance to make the smart move of taking Louise de Bargeton as his mistress. "Coralie has been that boy's undoing," says one of his enemies. (ML 456/P 5:524) Burdened by debt, Lucien had sold his novel to a new publishing house, Fendant and Cavalier (a kind of Dickensian name: you might translate it as Slashing and Nonchalant), operating entirely on credit, leveraging a tiny capital by way of loans, which compensated him in *lettres de change* payable over twelve months. Attempting to negotiate them, Lucien discovers that the firm's credit is so flimsy he'll lose fifty percent of their face value. Just enough is left for Lucien and Lousteau to gamble it away.

In the meanwhile, *Le Reveil* demands that Lucien launch an

attack on his friend d'Arthez, who now is seen as a threat by the ultra-royalists because his pal Léon Giraud's journal has become a powerful support for the moderates who oppose Charles X's absolutist tendencies. Lucien must carry out this assignment or the royalist press will trash Coralie, already a butt of attacks by the liberal press because of Lucien's desertion. When Lucien, tears in his eyes, explains the cruel dilemma to d'Arthez, his friend understands and even agrees to edit the venomous review. But d'Arthez's friends are not in the loop. As Lucien stands in front of the *cabinet de lecture* contemplating his disfigured novel, another member of d'Arthez's circle, Michel Chrestien, arrives to spit in his face. The duel that follows will leave Lucien wounded and bedridden, while Coralie goes onstage every evening to support him, even begs money from her ex, Camusot, and then collapses from the strain. She dies, and Lucien writes drinking songs to pay for the burial. But he also forges his sister's husband's name on *lettres de change* to raise cash. His disgrace complete, he decides to return once more to his native Angoulême. He will go on foot, but even that requires daily bread. He hasn't any money left, so Coralie's maid Bérénice goes out to sell herself. She returns with 20 francs for Lucien, the "final stigma" of his Parisian existence. (ML 488/P 5:551)

Presses, Paper, Plots

Balzac crashes Lucien's speculative economy down to zero. Lucien is the test case of what journalism can do to the once idealistic poet. Journalism, it turns out, is just so much hot air, hot type rather, that has an extraordinary importance at the moment but leaves nothing behind. It is the very opposite of the true poetic word that endures—

what Lucien originally aspired to but betrayed. The inflation of the word in journalism comes to be represented by the debt it passed on from Lucien's Paris adventure to his provincial brother-in-law David Séchard. And this allows Balzac to turn his attention back to Angoulême in the third part of *Lost Illusions*, "The Sufferings of the Inventor," published some four years after the Parisian episode. David owns the printshop full of outdated equipment he bought from his father, but what really interests him is his quest to find a cheaper material for making paper. This would be a key to the transformations of literature at the behest of journalism dramatized in part two of the novel. So long as paper was expensive—in fact, the most expensive part of the printing process—publication was restricted. The more copies of whatever you published, the more it cost, since you would need more paper. When paper costs were reduced, the opposite would become true: the more you published a given text, the cheaper the per copy cost became.[4] Paper was largely made from cotton fabric, which was costly even when recycled (the ragpickers of Paris were legion at the time). Chewing on a wild reed that becomes a kind of paste in his mouth, David chances on the discovery he needs.

David works in secret to realize his invention—but becomes a victim of a plot hatched by the rival printers in Angoulême, the Cointet Brothers, compounded by the burden of the *lettres de change* Lucien has forged in his name. The Cointet Brothers learn of his progress toward creating cheap paper, and they want to know the secret of his invention. He has to go into hiding to escape his creditors and protect his invention. The intricate machinery of Balzacian plotting is cranked up in the machinations to find his hiding place and force him to give up his secret, and a cast of professional intriguers comes onstage, from the resentful and vengeful lawyer Petit-Claude to David's father, old Séchard, hell-bent on the castration of his son. Balzac is able also to turn seemingly uninteresting financial transactions into a plot. One story is that of the *compte de retour*, which the narrator calls a "*conte plein de fictions terribles*," punning on *compte*, the account, and *conte*, or story, and in the telling the *compte de retour*—a "commission for change of place," in Kathleen Raine's translation—becomes a *compte fantastique*, a fantastic account and tale. (ML 535/P 5:591) The original sum "borrowed" by Lucien from David increases extraordinarily as the demand for its repayment circulates from Paris back to Angoulême, with every intermediate step adding a substantial fee. Balzac's sheer exuberant inventiveness is part and parcel of what Henry James called his love of his created characters, his love of their "acting themselves out."[5]

While David struggles, Lucien is trying to get back into the social game after his Paris disgrace. He tries to reawaken the affections of Louise de Bargeton, attending a soiree she has organized in dandyish garments that he has borrowed and begged from his former Parisian colleagues. His vanity is incurable and will lead to David's downfall as the wily lawyer Petit-Claude leads him on until he unwittingly lures David out of hiding. David is forced to make a deal with the Cointet Brothers in which he relinquishes his formula for making paper. Another lost illusion. He indeed gives up his profession as a printer to retire to the country for the rest of his life. Industrial progress goes forward, having brushed him aside, one of the many victims of the forward march of the nineteenth century.

When it's a matter of the publishing industry, Balzac was a close observer of that march. The making of cheap paper would go forward using a variety of vegetable substances, then mainly settle on

wood pulp, and simultaneously inventors made it possible to produce paper in the long rolls needed for the presses that printed
newspapers—newsprint. Balzac had seen printing presses themselves
transformed, from the cast-iron mechanical Stanhope press at the
start of the century, to the steam press, to the press with rollers
(hence the roll of newsprint), and in *Lost Illusions* he makes the
material substance of his book the stuff of its story. It is there from
the very beginning, in what is one of the strangest opening paragraphs in the history of the novel, seemingly unrelated to character
or story, focused only on printing and its situation now and in the
future:

> At the moment this story begins, the Stanhope press and inking
> rollers weren't yet functioning in small provincial print shops.
> Despite its skill in paper making that kept Angoulême in touch with
> Parisian printing, the provincial city was still using the wooden
> presses that gave us the expression "to make the press groan," no
> longer applicable today. . . . The devouring mechanical presses have
> today made us so thoroughly forget these old techniques to which
> we owe, whatever their imperfections, the beautiful books of such
> as Elzevir, Plantin, Alde, and Didot, that it is necessary to mention
> the old tools to which Jérôme-Nicholas Séchard brought a super-
> stitious affection, because they play a role in this small yet great story.
>
> (ML 3/P 5:123–24)

What's most interesting here is the play of tenses: the industrial
machines that "weren't yet functioning" at the time the story opens,
around 1820; the "devouring mechanical presses" that aren't yet in
action. Yet they will be, and already are in Paris, where they will

devour Lucien, and eventually David himself, and will change literature, which, Balzac claims in the preface to part three of the novel—written six years after the first paragraph—has been devoured by the newspaper. The dynamic of historical change reflected in that not yet/only later reflects the very production of novels, their transformation into what the powerful critic Sainte-Beuve would a couple of years later label "industrial literature."[6]

The Capitalization of Spirit

"On Industrial Literature," published in 1839, is not so much a probative analysis of the situation of publishing as it is a snobbish diatribe against it. Sainte-Beuve's main target is the *roman-feuilleton*, the serial novel that ran at the foot (the *rez-de-chaussée* or "ground floor") of the front page of daily newspapers. The essay attacks the democratization of letters while anticipating a version of Andy Warhol's prediction that in modern times everyone will be famous for fifteen minutes. In Sainte-Beuve's analysis, the government relaxed restrictions on the press in the late 1820s (it would clamp down again on the eve of the July Revolution) even as it raised the cost of obtaining a permit needed to publish. Newspapers compensated by the creation of the *annonce*, the *réclame*, and the *entrefilet*: advertising of various kinds, which book publishers snapped up. To pay for these ads, publishers jacked up the price of their books; to make those books seem like a good value to their buyers, they pushed novelists to provide matter for two volumes rather than one. When a newspaper depends on book advertising, can you trust its book critics to be objective? Sainte-Beuve asks. Especially when you write for the less expensive "forty franc newspapers," which had cut subscription prices dramatically, more or less in half, and so were that much more dependent on advertising and growing circulations, which in turn led to the invention of the *roman-feuilleton*. Writing, Sainte-Beuve claims, becomes filling up columns, full of needless adjectives and empty dialogue (for which Alexandre Dumas was particularly notorious), and a general lowering of stylistic standards.

This, Sainte-Beuve should know, is precisely the situation dramatized by Balzac in *Lost Illusions*. But since he was never able to appreciate Balzac—in fact they detested each other—he simply sees *Lost Illusions* as part of the problem rather than a reckoning with it. It's really both: a telling analysis of the commercial and industrial transformation of the novel that is at the same time caught up in the processes it describes. Writing the novel, Balzac is what anthropologists would later dub a "participant observer," seeking principles for understanding his own lived experience. At this moment before the invention of sociology, it is, as the historian Pierre Rosanvallon noted, the novelists who are seeking to formulate the "principles of intelligibility" of the social world, and we've seen in *Père Goriot* that Balzac (and after him, Rastignac) learns the "semiotics" of modern urban life.[7] To be sure, Balzac often professes to reject the modern world he is so very much a part of, condemning it for an incoherence born of a lack of true and visible authority. Lucien himself in his farewell letter to his sister, Eve, tells of a family that he describes as *"malade de son père"*—suffering illness from its father—and he appears to extend that diagnosis to France as a whole. (ML 645/P 5:685) France suffers from a lack of paternal authority that dates, symbolically and really, from the execution of Louis XVI by the guillotine on January 21, 1793. Ever since, the country has been wandering, lost, without guidance. But that serves as much as anything to make clear that the novel, and the novel alone, permits a true understanding of the way we live now.

In *Lost Illusions*, Balzac colludes with the system he condemns, and colluding and condemning provide an unequaled picture of the dynamics and contradictions of early capitalism. In the age of the Baron de Nucingen, literature, as much as canals or railways, presented an opportunity for speculation. Edmond Werdet, who was Balzac's publisher until the novelist's mania for rewriting his work in proofs bankrupted him, wrote about this time, describing an extraordinary efflorescence of novels in the 1820s. By 1830, he says, all of France seemed to have become a vast *cabinet de lecture*, where "everyone impatiently waited his turn to devour the freshly delivered work."[8] Writers lived in a boom-and-bust economy, from which Balzac tried to protect himself. At one point, he sold the whole of his work to a new, proto-industrial publishing enterprise that promised him a steady income, but the plan could not work with so chaotic a writer as Balzac. The very idea of *The Human Comedy*—ninety-some novels and tales together representing the whole of French society—also represents a commercial speculation that enabled Balzac to reprint already published material, to group and regroup work in new categories, and to offer ever "more complete" versions of the whole oeuvre. Balzac's 1842 "Author's Introduction" to the great work, the "Avant-Propos," is in part a publicity stunt, a prospectus for an encyclopedia that one can buy volume by volume, though in this case it will never be complete.

The historian Hippolyte Taine, in one of the earliest serious studies of Balzac, characterized him as "a businessman chronically in debt" ("*un homme d'affaires endetté*"), and it is true that he was always struggling to keep his creditors and the publishers to whom he had promised material at bay.[9] He would sign a contract and receive an advance, and spend the advance in the course of fulfilling another writing obligation—or by furnishing an apartment or buying clothes or his famous cane with the jewel-encrusted head—and then be under the gun to meet another deadline. He was not a reliable contributor. But as he pointed out in his public letter to fellow French writers in 1834, writers had little to rely on themselves. The French Revolution had essentially abolished copyright, making intellectual production the property of the nation. So that, Balzac protests, where the law fully respects the rights of the propertied, even the house of the "sweaty proletarian," "it confiscates the work of the thinking poet."[10] Balzac was soon embroiled in a lawsuit with François Buloz, the editor of the *Revue de Paris* (as well as the *Revue des Deux-Mondes*), who had betrayed the novelist by selling the uncorrected proofs of his novel *The Lily of the Valley* at the very time it was in the midst of serial publication in France, allowing it to be published without Balzac's final, all-important corrections. Balzac would eventually win the lawsuit, and by 1838, he joined with other writers to found the Société des Gens de Lettres. If Balzac and his associates sought to shore up the writer's position as a professional, Sainte-Beuve makes clear his dislike of this new organization, which lacked restrictions on membership, reached its decisions by majority vote—and, to him, looked all too much like a labor union.

As we approach the end of part three, *Lost Illusions* appears to be winding down. David and Lucien have both been "devoured" by the printing press, but if the former is left materially well-off, though shorn of ambition, Lucien feels no course is open to him but suicide. He writes Eve and David a farewell letter, describing himself as being like the number zero, without value unless attached to another integer; he bemoans his failure to attach his fortunes to a strong woman such as Louise de Bargeton. This reversal of the common-places of male and female roles is given a more sinister cast in Eve's remark that in a poet there lies concealed "a pretty woman of the worst sort," which reiterates the large issue of prostitution that runs through the novel. (ML 607/P 5:653) Poets turned journalists are whores.

Lucien gets ready to drown himself in the Charente River. And now something truly astonishing happens. Lucien's plan is inter-rupted by the appearance of a Spanish priest, Carlos Herrera. When he discovers that Lucien is on the verge of self-destruction, he pro-duces a sack of gold with which Lucien can pay off David's debt (it is of course too late for that). And the priest takes Lucien's arm, to propose another future, one in which Lucien will become his crea-ture. Slowly, doubting at first but then with more and more convic-tion, the reader comes to realize the priest can only be Vautrin, who must somehow have escaped from the prison we saw him con-demned to in *Père Goriot*. He appears as "a hunter who finds his quarry long and vainly searched for," in a scene that greatly impressed Marcel Proust, who reworked it in the meeting of his Marcel with the Baron de Charlus in *In Search of Lost Time*. (ML 649/P 5:690) There is a deep store of emotion here, only obliquely expressed.

"I am starting again, a terrible existence," Lucien writes to David and Eve. "Instead of killing myself, I have sold my life." (ML 690/P 5:724) Herrera/Vautrin/Collin also imagines a new life, one he will experience vicariously through Lucien:

I wish to love my creature, mold him, shape him to my use, in order to love him as a father loves his child. I will ride in your tilbury, my boy, I will take pleasure in your successes with women, I will say: "This handsome young man, it's me! This Marquis de Rubempré, I created him and placed him in aristocratic society; his greatness is my work, he speaks or falls silent with my voice, he consults me in everything."

(ML 670/P 5:708)

It's a scene of magical double reanimation, which also brings the novel back to life and indeed engenders an entire sequel, *A Harlot High and Low* (*Splendeurs et misères des courtisanes*), the first part of which had already been published as *La Torpille*. The sequel will unfold the story of Lucien as Herrera's protégé, in a relationship that mimes *The Arabian Nights*: "I fished you out, I brought you back to life. And you belong to me, like created to creator, as the afrits in fairy tales belong to genii, or the Icoglan to the Sultan, or the body to the soul!"

The image of the *Thousand and One Nights* seems never far from the surface, ready to burst through when the right magical words are spoken. It's not only that Collin's presence promises a new exercise of nearly demonic power on the world, and hence the possibilities of extraordinary happenings in Lucien's existence. The book itself springs back to life. Like the storytelling of Scheherazade that must be renewed every night if she is to save her life, Balzac's inventions pick up and restart even as the end imposes itself. It's as if it's impossible for him not to be in storytelling mode.

The end of *Lost Illusions* puts a new twist on exploration of the life of the modern writer, who is both Prometheus and prostitute. He always has a new story at hand—indeed he must, because he always has a new contract to honor, a new column to fill. The contrast between Balzac and Sainte-Beuve is significant: the latter snobbishly deplores the industrialization of the novel, the former deplores it and dramatizes how it works and what it means, yet also situates himself and his work squarely within its functioning. There is a moment, in part two of the novel, when Lousteau is explaining to Lucien the mechanisms of journalism and how the journalist can bring famous writers to beg for his favors, that provokes the dissent of the yet untested idealist: "I'd rather die." To which Lousteau responds: "Rather live." (ML 292/P 5:379) The narrative responds in an analogous manner: just when there seems every reason for it to give up, to die like its central figure, it rebounds. Better to throw yourself into the struggle of journalism than to give up, whatever d'Arthez and his friends may say and the narrator overtly declare. That's where the action is. That's where stories are to be found.

Agents of Unrest

Here it is worth noting that the third part of this novel full of denunciations of the debasing influence of journalism is given a preface that strangely gives an out-and-out defense of journalism, provoked by a set of three speeches by a representative in the National Assembly, the Baron Chapuys-Montlaville, who denounced the immoral influence of the *roman-feuilleton*, which, he claimed, was driving out serious political news in favor of distracting fantasy.[11] His proposed legislation was repressive in a curious way: he would abolish the tax stamp on those newspapers that agreed not to publish serial novels, preferring serious political news, while maintaining it on those that continued to offer up fictional poison. He singled out for attack the newspaper *Le Messager*, which had been entertaining its readers with Balzac's *The Provincial Muse* (*La Muse du département*). Chapuys-Montlaville argues that the illusory life of novels is dangerous because it makes people discontent with their lot in life; it teaches them contempt for the social status of their fathers, makes them embarrassed of their origins, and gives them false notions of social mobility. The novel in the newspaper leads to *déclassement*, the attempt to change one's social condition and class. Popular novels are agents of social unrest.

Chapuys-Montlaville goes on to lament the very kind of situation presented in *Lost Illusions*, as well as in other Balzac novels: ambitious, inconsiderate young people who, without reflection and without vocation, leave their honest, unpretentious lives in the provinces to hazard their fortunes in Paris, where they too often encounter misery and shame. The serial novel is the cause of social unrest, subversive of established class definitions and relations. His speeches will lead, in June 1843, to a debate in the assembly on whether Eugène Sue's *The Mysteries of Paris* (*Les Mystères de Paris*), which ran for over a year in 1842 and 1843 in the staid *Journal des Debats*, constituted wholesome fare for its readers.

Balzac knew himself to be directly implicated in Chapuys-Montlaville's attacks. He, like his spokesman Claude Vignon, was a laborer in the quicksilver mine. There was no way out because the newspaper had become the principal organ of intellectual expression in France. He concludes his preface by noting of Chapuys-Montlaville: "He, like his four hundred colleagues, is the direct product of the *Social Contract* and *Émile*, which were burned by the executioner in response to an order from the Parlement de Paris [France's high court]." (P 5:121) Balzac's allusion here to Rousseau's books, banned and burned by the authorities in Paris and Geneva in 1762, argues that the elected National Assembly, like the constitutional monarchy of which it is part, derives from those writings that stand behind the French Revolution. Despite his avowed rejection of the parliamentary regime and his longing for what he conceives as the organically ordered sociality of the ancien régime, Balzac understands that he lives in a world in which certain ideas have made history irreversible. Chapuys-Montlaville's laments on *déclassement* offer a dangerous anachronism rather than a solution to the problem of modernity. The repressive measures contemplated by the legislature are irrelevant in the newly constituted public sphere that emerged in postrevolutionary France. The prostituted pen of journalism is for better or worse the new power in France.

Like the journalist, Lucien himself is an ambiguous, somewhat protean figure, utterly charming but unreliable, ready to prostitute his talents while still believing in his purity of intention—until the moment he collapses and sees himself as nothing, a zero. When we encounter Lucien's new life as the creature of Collin/Vautrin/Herrera in *A Harlot High and Low*, we may be prompted to ask: Is this person still Lucien? Yes of course, but now so thoroughly dominated by his protector that he appears drained of personal willpower. He lives on the main floor of his building, while Collin inhabits the top floor, directing all activities, dictating the terms of Lucien's commerce with Esther, then imposing her sale to Nucingen in order to obtain the million francs needed for the marriage to Clotilde de Grandlieu. I think rather than telling Lucien's further biography here, it will be best to fill it in as part of Collin's.

6. Jacques Collin
(1779?–after 1845)

The Occult Power of *The Human Comedy*

AT THE HEART of Balzac's portrait of contemporary society stands a superman, an outlaw who exercises his occult influence in all social spheres, a creator and manipulator of the lives of others, a man beyond good and evil yet also a moral absolutist. Largely hidden from view, he makes things happen. What is it about him that so attracts the novelist—or is he himself the very representation of the novelist, the creative author of reality? Appearing first as Vautrin, in *Père Goriot*'s Pension Vauquer, as the would-be mastermind of Rastignac's career, then as the Spanish priest Carlos Herrera who rescues Lucien from suicide, he is a formidable figure who exudes a dynamic, even demonic energy that drives *The Human Comedy*. His power appears to be erotic in origin, even though the beautiful young men he adopts never yield to his sexual desires. Instead, he finally invests his drives in the political sphere. Whenever he appears, he masterminds breathtaking reversals of fortune.

It is in *A Harlot High and Low* (*Splendeurs et misères des courtisanes*), the sequel to *Lost Illusions*, that we come to know his full identity, even as he takes on strange new roles. Balzac called Collin the "backbone" of *The Human Comedy*, the colossal figure who links *Père Goriot* to *Lost Illusions* to *A Harlot High and Low*, who links also the two most notable young men, Eugène de Rastignac and Lucien de Rubempré, who links as well good society, even in its higher reaches, with the criminal underworld and prison. He appears always in disguise. He is always in a state of infraction of the laws. We learn in *Harlot* that he was educated in a college run by the religious order of the Oratorians, then sent to prison the first time in 1812, to five years of hard labor for the crime of fraud, later extended to seven years for attempted escape. In fact, the crime probably was not his but was committed by a very beautiful young Italian man (no doubt that Colonel Franchessini he calls upon to provoke young Taillefer into a fatal duel). We may surmise that his long criminal career starts from his taking this bum rap. As a convict he became the chief banker to his fellow prisoners. After his rearrest in the Pension Vauquer, sentenced to life at the prison of Rochefort, he escapes again almost at once, in 1820—disguised as a gendarme.

Collin appears to have developed Rousseau's insight, in his *Discourse on the Origin of Inequality*, that law comes into being along with property, to protect the haves from the have-nots. His antisocial behavior, Collin claims, responds to the perversions of the social contract. Crime is a social stance, a protest against a world in which, as he puts it in one of his tirades to Rastignac, the police exist to protect the rich crooks and to repress the poor. Like many a romantic outlaw, Collin has his Robin Hood side. Yet his cynicism is thorough, and the rewards he seeks are for himself and for his favored young men.

Harlot completes Lucien's story, but it is Collin's book. The novel opens at the Bal de l'Opéra, with all the women in disguise, though the men need not be. An unmasked beautiful young man, Lucien, is present, followed everywhere by a muscular masked man, described as a kind of "wild boar" (which is what a *vautrin* originally was). Some members of the milling crowd recognize Lucien. "I thought him fallen too low to ever be able to rise again," says Sixte du Châtelet, a notable from Angoulême who now is married to Louise de Bargeton.[1] He addresses Lucien as "Monsieur Chardon," and Lucien impertinently replies that he now is Lucien de Rubempré, having at last received the long-sought royal decree. We detect backing of a sort he did not have before. Rastignac is also at the ball, and the masked man whispers in his ear that it's now his duty to treat Lucien as lovingly as a brother. "Silence and loyalty," he commands him, and Rastignac is seized with panic. "It could only be *him* who could be in the know... and who would dare." To which the masked man replies: "Act as if it were *him*." (P 22/P 6:434) By the end of the evening, the man unmasks himself, briefly and privately, to Rastignac, who is astonished by his complete change of appearance—except for those unforgettable eyes. Rastignac's friends find him at three in the morning, leaning against the pillar where Collin left him. They take him to breakfast, after which he returns home, completely drunk and silent.

Such is the Collin effect, and it will continue to be felt throughout the baroque episodes of *Harlot*. The plot of the novel is complex and breathtaking, not least because it was composed over a period of years and serialized in various periodicals, including, by the end, the daily newspaper, as Balzac competed with Eugène Sue, whose *Mysteries of Paris* had been all the rage in France in 1842 and 1843. The opening scene at the Bal de l'Opéra provides a dazzling triple revival, offering not only the newly successful Lucien and the sinister mastermind Collin but also the masked Esther, who appears so much a lady that Rastignac maintains she must be the Comtesse de Sérizy, only to be recognized by the journalist Bixiou as des Lupeaulx's former "rat," that is, a young actress in training and potential prostitute. She has been redeemed by her love for Lucien, renounced the life of prostitution, made application to the police to be struck from the register of prostitutes (far more difficult, she points out, than being put on the list), and fears above all else being returned to her identity as a whore. Following her exposure at the ball, she attempts suicide, lighting a charcoal brazier in her frugal room.

Collin—wearing a cassock, still in the guise of Carlos Herrera—saves her from death. And then he takes over her life, as he has Lucien's. If she is to see Lucien again, Collin dictates, she must be purified: confined in a convent in order to be educated in the Christian virtues. When she is ready for baptism, she will be allowed to see Lucien again, all in all a strange and somewhat sadistic idea, especially when we remember that he soon will be scheming to advance Lucien's fortunes by selling Esther to the Baron de Nucingen—yet Sue's novel also included a sensational attempt to "redeem" a prostitute, and this was indeed a matter of public debate.[2] Collin claims to have obtained the document that strikes her from the rolls of prostitution, which he will give her once the process of rehabilitation is complete.

When we next see Lucien, Collin has made the momentous step of revealing his true identity to his protégé, binding him to secrecy and loyalty. Lucien has been living a life of spoiled boredom since his return to Paris, behaving with the utmost diplomacy, keeping his distance from his former journalist friends, cultivating the salons and the boudoirs of Diane de Maufrigneuse and Léontine de Sérizy (who is close to the Archbishop of Paris) and preparing his suit for the hand of one of four daughters the Duc de Grandlieu has to marry off. Collin has a political career in mind for him, but Lucien can't stop pining for the lost Esther. When Collin restores her, "purified," he stipulates that she must remain concealed from all the world, so as not to stand in the way of Lucien's social career. She is placed in an apartment, guarded by two maids devoted to Collin and a colossus of a coachman, where Lucien visits her only late at night, arriving in a cab that enters the courtyard with its blinds down. Lucien and Collin themselves inhabit a building on the Quai Malaquais, with Lucien in the official apartment on the main floor and Collin hidden upstairs on the fifth floor. Lucien and Esther's passion for each other is so fulfilling that he can be perfectly self-controlled in society, impervious to provocation or insult.

Lucien must have someone strong backing him, as the dandy de Marsay remarks. But his life is not his own. Collin, living upstairs in the same building as his protégé, keeping him under surveillance, reduces Lucien to a puppet in the plot hatched by Collin that will destroy the love idyll. That plot takes off from Nucingen's "celestial" moonlit vision of the half-Jewish Esther in the Bois de Vincennes. He must find her again and must love her. That opens up possibilities for Collin, who has been waiting four years to discover a way to raise the million francs that Lucien needs in order to marry Clotilde de Grandlieu—well-born and witty, but resembling "an asparagus" and unmarried at age twenty-seven—and obtain the title of marquis. Such is the price tag of the ancestral Rubempré lands, which are needed to make Lucien irreproachably respectable. His and Collin's current situation, funded by an inheritance that Collin, as Herrera, stole from a dying man for whom he performed the last rites, has raised a certain suspicion: Where does their money come from? Nucingen's fortune and his overwhelming passion can solve the problem.

Lucien, whose first impulses are usually good though unsustained, is horrified by Collin's proposal to sell Esther, but his protector soon persuades him there is no other choice. Even Esther succumbs to the inevitable. "*Incedo per ignes*," Collin tells Lucien: I walk through flames. (P 94/P 6:505) First he must hide Esther— Nucingen has hired spies combing Paris in search of her—then he must stoke Nucingen's desire, until he is prepared to spend anything, without reserve. Collin packs Esther off to the country, thoughtfully providing a substitute mistress, a young Englishwoman, for Lucien. There is no indication Lucien refuses the gift.

Nucingen vs. Collin in Dubious Battle

The second part of *Harlot*, subtitled "How Much Love Costs Old Men," follows the shadowy and sordid battle between Collin's and Nucingen's agents in almost too great detail. A range of characters from the fringes of society (some from Balzac's earlier novel, *A Murky Business* [*Une ténébreuse affaire*]), Contenson, Corentin, Peyrade, shady types capable of multiple disguises, enter the story as Collin tantalizes and leads on his prey, Nucingen. He plans to make up the million francs in several installments. He has Esther's maid promise the banker a night with her mistress for 30,000 francs, only to produce instead Lucien's blue-eyed, blond Englishwoman, not at all what Nucingen wants. Esther is said to be hiding from the law because she is deeply in debt. Another rendezvous, arranged for 100,000 francs, brings Esther and Nucingen together, but she postpones sex with him, and in the morning a gang of thugs, backed up by gendarmes, comes to arrest Esther for the feigned debt of 300,000 francs. Nucingen is obliged to come up with the sum (plus expenses) to keep Esther out of prison. Collin's inventive schemes continue. Nucingen is persuaded to purchase Esther a town house and to furnish it sumptuously, with the promise that as soon as she moves there, she will be his.

When Collin divines Esther's suicidal intentions, he rebukes her for her fainthearted love of Lucien, unlike his own: "I crowned him king, my Lucien! You could rivet me for the rest of my days back to my old chain, I think I could be peaceful still in saying to myself: 'He is at the ball, he is at court.' My soul and my thought would triumph while my carcass was in the hands of the cops! You're only a miserable female, you love like a female!" (P 207/P 6:613) Esther, stung by these words, sends Nucingen another letter in which she signs herself: "Your pleasure machine." She emerges as an exceptional figure even among Balzac's remarkable cast of prostitutes. As the moment of her sacrifice approaches, she lives with a kind of double consciousness, holding in herself the ideal of her pure love for Lucien at the same moment she expresses contempt for "the infamous and odious role played by the body in the presence of the soul." At once "spectator and actor, judge and accused," she realizes the myth found in Arabian tales of the sublime being hidden in a degraded envelope. (P 239/P 6:643) She lives with full, ironic awareness of who she wants to be and what she is forced to be.

Meanwhile, Nucingen's and Collin's agents circle round each other, disguised variously as mulattoes, English nabobs, justices of the peace, this last one of Collin's own impersonations. (There is a love of disguise for its own sake on Balzac's part: he delights in detailing the costumes and manners adopted by his characters to simulate other kinds of characters, as if his own acts of creation were proliferating.) Contenson succeeds in penetrating Collin's Carlos Herrera identity, and realizes that Nucingen is being bilked of money so that Lucien can buy the Rubempré lands. Indeed, things have advanced so far that Lucien has signed a purchase agreement with 500,000 francs extorted from Nucingen but ostensibly supplied by his sister and brother-in-law. In comes Corentin, disguised as an elderly bureau chief from the Ministry of Finance, who tries to black-mail Lucien by threatening to reveal the Esther business. Collin listens from the adjoining room, plotting his next move. But Lucien discovers that Corentin has already struck by sending an anonymous letter to the Duc de Grandlieu, telling all. Arriving at the Hôtel de Grandlieu, Lucien is turned away, while the Duc, seeking to inves-tigate the murky business, is advised by a friend to hire a spy employed at the Ministry of Foreign Affairs, who happens to be: Corentin. And so the plots thicken, while Lucien's social position is ever more menaced.

Collin's vengeance on Nucingen's agent Peyrade produces the grimmest episode of the novel, maybe of all Balzac's novels: his sixteen-year-old daughter, Lydie, is kidnapped, raped, and placed in a brothel, and goes mad. Peyrade himself dies as a result, or perhaps he is poisoned. It's hard to describe the effect of this episode in the novel. All the dirty tricks on both sides so far have been plenty harsh, but also amusing, a kind of stagey violence that is largely enjoyable. The rape of Lydie makes us sit up and realize we have descended into depths of human viciousness: that we are in fact dealing with persons, including Collin, of an utter immorality and disregard for human life. We are now in what Balzac calls the "third underground," a reference to the lowest level of a theater, where props are stored, and where the machinery that moves traps and curtains operates. It is at this level, we are given to believe, that we find the persons and the motives that, themselves out of sight, drive social existence. Balzac's constant fascination with the behind and beneath, those operative forces that have to be dug out from behind the surfaces, here takes the form of the machination hidden deep underground. But of course all the more effective for that. There is a direct link between the door of the Hôtel de Grandlieu shut in Lucien's face and the willed destruction of Lydie.

Nucingen, on the verge of bedding Esther, provides her an income from treasury bonds that she promptly sells to realize the capital of 750,000 francs, which she puts under her pillow in a packet addressed to Lucien. Then, following her one night of sex with Nucingen, she kills herself with a potent poison provided by the courtesan Suzanne du Val-Noble—before she can learn that Derville is looking for her as the sole legatee of Gobseck's seven million francs. Now everything comes apart. The supposedly faithful servants of Collin find the money under the pillow, succumb to temptation, and decamp with the fortune. Collin, learning of Esther's death, quickly has a forger make up a fake will in which Esther leaves all her possessions to Lucien. After placing this under her pillow, Collin exits via the skylight. But Contenson has concealed himself behind a chimney on the roof; he attempts to apprehend Collin—who sends him flying down into the gutter, dead.

Lucien meanwhile has set out toward Fontainebleau, in a plan to intercept Clotilde de Grandlieu, sent by her parents to Italy to be out of Lucien's way, traveling with the young Duchesse de Lenoncourt-Chaulieu. Clotilde has just assured him of her eternal love when the gendarmes arrive on horseback to arrest Lucien for complicity in theft and murder—accused of participating in killing and robbing Esther. The ironies accumulate: Esther kills herself before learning of Gobseck's immense legacy, which would have spared her from being sold to Nucingen; Carlos Herrera, along with Lucien, is accused of the one crime he didn't commit.

The Illegible Criminal

We plunge in part three of *Harlot*, "Where the Paths of Crime Lead," into the world of criminal justice, and into the medieval palace that was the central house of detention in Paris, which Balzac had visited for documentation. Two *paniers à salade*, "salad baskets," paddy wagons, bring Lucien and Collin separately to the Conciergerie, where Lucien immediately falls into despair, weeping for hours in his cell. Collin in contrast is scheming even before he reaches the prison. His faithful aunt Jacqueline, playing the role of a servant called Asie, creates a traffic jam to halt the paddy wagon and, in a private language concocted from Italian and Provençal, informs Collin of Lucien's arrest. Collin slips her a note (he is equipped with a minuscule piece of paper stashed under his wig) instructing her to put "Lucien's women" to work to save him. Collin is the first of the two suspects called before the examining magistrate, the *juge d'instruction*, Camusot de Marville, who was appointed to his important post in Paris largely thanks to the influence of the Duchesse de Maufrigneuse, whom he helped when her young admirer, Victurnien d'Esgrignon, was accused of fraud (the subject of *The Collection of Antiquities* [*Le*

Cabinet des antiques]). Then again, Camusot enjoys the protection of the Marquise d'Espard, of whom Lucien has made an enemy, and Camusot's ambitious wife, Amélie, has been summoned and relays to her husband the message from the Marquise promising a promotion if Lucien is convicted. But the Duchesse de Maufrigneuse also intervenes, summoning Amélie to her house to demand Lucien's release that day and dangling the promise of the presidency of his own court for her husband. She warns that the King himself, who is about to issue the royal decrees of July 1830 that sparked a revolution in response, counts on the devotion of his magistrates.

So Camusot is caught between competing powerful aristocratic women, and his conflict will only grow worse as he walks to the Palais de Justice to begin his interrogations of the suspects and is met by the Comte de Granville, the attorney general, who assures him that Lucien is certainly innocent, that he knew nothing of Esther's will and thus had no interest in her death, and that the theft of the cash under her pillow must have been the work of servants. But once in his office, Camusot is visited by Bibi-Lupin, the chief of the Sûreté Nationale, something like the FBI, who was in charge of the arrest of Collin in *Père Goriot* and suspects the true identity of the Spanish priest. The police, it seems, have deep in their archives a "universal ledger" on all suspicious individuals, and this suggests that the Reverend Carlos Herrera is almost certainly Jacques Collin, known as "Cheat-Death." (P 330/P 6:726) If this is confirmed, Lucien de Rubempré must be considered his confederate. What, given these competing interests, will Camusot do?

Herrera/Collin now is summoned before Camusot for the "vital, interesting, curious, dramatic and terrible struggle of a criminal interrogation," where "eyes, tone of voice, a quiver of the facial muscles" can be fatal, like those signs noted "by savages mutually seeking to find and to kill one another." (P 352/P 6:746) The crucial evidence should be *la marque*, the decisive brand on the suspect's shoulder that we know from *Père Goriot*. Collin must take off his shirt, and he tells the judge that there are scars on his back: he was shot by partisans because of his devotion to the Spanish "royal cause." Camusot questions him on "the cause of his affection for Monsieur Lucien de Rubempré," and Collin hesitates before "confessing" that Lucien is his son, then managing to faint. (P 315/P 6:748) A brilliant stroke on Collin's part that both covers their actual relationship and promotes the ideal of a relationship he might wish to have.

Now Collin's wig is removed, revealing the frightening features of a hardened criminal, while his shirt comes off his Herculean torso. With an ebony bat, and in the company of the prison doctor, Camusot strikes Collin's back and shoulder:

> Seventeen holes thus appeared, distributed at random; but despite the care with which they examined his back, they didn't make out the shape of any letters. The clerk pointed out that the horizontal bar of a T might be represented by two holes as wide apart as the two serifs of the bar of that letter, and that another hole marked the foot of the vertical bar.
>
> "That's nonetheless quite vague," said Camusot, seeing doubt expressed on the face of the doctor of the Conciergerie.
>
> (P 359/P 6:751)

Collin, we learn, has peppered himself with buckshot to efface the "fatal letters," the TF of *Travaux Forcés*. The effaced script of his convict identity, covered over like a palimpsest, prevents Camusot from making a positive identification. (Balzac here expresses a wide-spread anxiety following the abolition of *la marque* by legislative vote in 1832 that repeat offenders would escape detection.)

Even Bibi-Lupin, eager to lay hands on his old adversary, hesitates, so much has Collin changed himself. The prisoner's voice nonetheless convinces him that it is indeed Collin. Mlle Michonneau, from the Pension Vauquer, now Madame Poiret, having been summoned identifies him by the hair on his chest. She mentions Bianchon and Rastignac as other possible witnesses from the pension, and Collin seizes on Rastignac as a character witness. Camusot, still wavering, replies that a favorable report by the likes of Rastignac and Bianchon—"persons of such high standing in society"—would be sufficient to set the suspect free.

Now, a coup de théâtre: the concierge from the apartment on the Quai Malaquais shows up with a letter addressed to Lucien from Esther (Lucien, off pursuing Clotilde, never saw it) dated "My last day, at 10 in the morning": it becomes wholly clear that Lucien had nothing to do with her death, and nothing to do with the theft of the 750,000 francs from under her pillow. The letter rebukes Lucien for his weakness and his willingness to profit from her love and, before that, Coralie's, but legally it exonerates him and makes him the legal possessor of her legacy. Collin may be on his way to escaping from the hands of justice.

Lucien, however, has yet to be interrogated. Camusot hands him Esther's letter, and Lucien bursts into tears upon reading it. Camusot gives him hope of immediate release but demands that he serve as witness to Collin's identity. The depressed Lucien is all too ready to make a general confession, and when it comes to his patron, he at once spills the beans about his true name and status, something, he affirms, he just found out. Collin, Camusot then informs him, claims to be his father, and Lucien collapses completely. "He! My father!... Oh, Monsieur!...he said that?" He seems momentarily to believe this accursed identity: "A man like Jacques Collin my father?...Oh! My poor mother..." (P 380/P 6:772–73) Too late, he realizes that he has doomed not only Collin but himself by admitting to being the knowing accomplice of an escaped convict.

"The infamous lie that roused his indignation screened a still more infamous truth." (P 382/P 6:773) The novel speaks guardedly here. Is that "more infamous truth" the love that dare not speak its name, has Lucien at last recognized the erotic charge of Collin's interest in him? He realizes in any event that in breaking "the law of solidarity" he has destroyed himself. Camusot returns him to his cell, only to find himself again caught in the crossfire. He receives a note from both Diane de Maufrigneuse and Léontine de Sérizy, noble ladies and rivals now united in requesting that he refrain from interrogating Lucien, and claiming that they have proof of his innocence. His superior, Attorney General Granville, reviews the transcript of the interrogations and tells Camusot that the *juge d'instruction* can look forward to remaining a *juge d'instruction* forever: no promotion. Granville happens to be protégé and friend of the Comte de Sérizy, who adores his wife in spite of her infidelities with Lucien and others. And then Léontine de Sérizy herself appears, protesting that Lucien cannot be guilty. While leaving the room, Granville lets slip that Lucien's confession is recorded in Camusot's papers. So Léontine grabs the papers from Camusot and throws them in the fire. When Granville returns, he completes the subornation of justice by ordering Lucien's release. He also provides for an unthreatening confrontation of Collin, with Rastignac and Bianchon, that he knows will release him as well, though he will secretly keep him under police surveillance in case political winds shift and Collin needs to be returned to prison.

But Lucien has other plans. Back in his cell, he asks for pen and paper and sets to work. He makes his will: he pays off debts to Herrera and to Nucingen; settles his remaining possessions on the children of Eve and David Séchard; provides 750,000 francs to found a home for repentant prostitutes; and orders a white marble tomb for Esther and himself in Père-Lachaise. He writes a retraction of his confession during the interrogation, describing Herrera as merely his spiritual father and denying any identity with Collin. And he writes a letter bidding farewell to his mentor, a gigantic figure, he says, "gifted with an immense power over tender souls, which are drawn to him and ground to pieces. That is grand and beautiful in its way. It's like the venomous plant, rich in color, that fascinates children in the woods. It's the poetry of evil." (P 398/P 6:790) That *poésie du mal* would be developed by Balzac's admirer, Charles Baudelaire. Lucien concludes his letter: "Don't mourn for me: my contempt for you was equal to my admiration." And then he hangs himself, using his cravat, from the bars of the window in his cell. ("One of the greatest tragedies of my life," Oscar Wilde called Lucien's suicide.[3]) Madame de Sérizy, sweeping jailers out of her way, will find his body, embrace it, and fall senseless to the floor. In an official report, Lucien is recorded as having died at home from a cerebral aneurysm.

Prostitution, Theft, and the Third Sex

The fourth and final part of the novel begins with Collin alone in his cell. He paces the room, anxious about what Lucien will say

145

under interrogation, doubtful that he can outwit Camusot and resist solitary confinement. The prison doctor enters with the news of Lucien's suicide. Collin collapses, crying "Oh my son!" When he returns to consciousness, he explains that no one can understand the depth of his emotion since he is not only father but also mother to Lucien. He feels himself going mad.

Part four is called "The Last Incarnation of Vautrin." With Lucien and Esther gone, he alone commands the stage. From now on, we are told, he will be called by his true name, Jacques Collin. But the question remains: What finally is his true identity? Conducted to Lucien's cell, he reads his protégé's farewell letter while holding the inanimate hand that wrote it. We thus read the letter twice, and the repetition is crucial. "If we read Lucien's letter again with Jacques Collin," the narrator tells us, "this supreme document will appear to us what it was for him, a poisoned cup." (P 431/P 6:819) Lucien's betrayals leave Collin immobile and speechless next to the corpse. As Balzac puts it, in the language of ironworkers, "*le fer était roui*": it has succumbed to metal fatigue, it has lost its resistance. "Napoleon knew just this dissolution of all his human powers on the battlefield at Waterloo!" (P 434/P 6:822) Here and elsewhere in Balzac, heroism is always tested against the figure whom the French never can forget. Collin has reached the end of the line. What is he to become?

What he must do first is ordained by Bibi-Lupin, who still hopes to unmask him. Bibi-Lupin, an ex-con himself, consigns Collin to the prison courtyard, which is to say to the criminal underworld of his past, where people know him and have scores to settle with him. Collin's entry into the courtyard is fraught with danger, especially his encounter with a certain Fil-de-Soie ("Silk Thread"), whom he has, from the time of *Père Goriot*, suspected of having betrayed him. Collin, still in the guise of Herrera, suspects a trap, but quickly, expertly, he will reassert his authority as "*dab*," slang for the chief of convict society.

Once again following in Sue's footsteps (and anticipating Hugo's *Les Misérables*), Balzac launches into a digression on criminal argot, the slang of convict society with its "frightful poetry," the language of the "subterranean world" that, like the "third underground" of the theater, is the place where special effects are created. (P 441/P 6:828) Balzac is fascinated by the imagistic force of this argot, which renews a longstanding French tradition of linguistic invention exemplified, for instance, in Rabelais. Slang invigorates language, much as "prostitution and theft are two vital forms of protest, male and female, on the part of the state of nature against the social order." (P 443/P 6:830) Like Collin's protest against the perversions of the social contract.

In the crowded prison courtyard, Collin maneuvers skillfully to avoid detection and obtain what it turns out he has in view: saving his former and, with the death of Lucien, newly important protégé, Théodore Calvi, from the guillotine. Collin's old accomplices at once fall in under his command again—just like Napoleon's soldiers upon his return from the isle of Elba—because they not only recognize but submit to him. Bibi-Lupin's scheme is foiled, allowing Collin to go forward with a plan to save Calvi, who has been sentenced to death for the robbery and murder of an old widow in Nanterre who had just inherited a large sum of money. But here Balzac digresses once more, reflecting on the roots of crime in passion, which is to say, "amatory excess" or "unregulated physical love." Autopsies of executed criminals provide "striking, palpable" evidence of this, and also account for the total adoration and loyalty of their mistresses. So it appears that a large penis lies at the root of crime, which maybe offers an ultimate explanation—to be taken literally or metaphorically?—of Collin's dominance among his peers. His imperviousness to women merely increases his power over men. Fil-de-Soie identifies him as a member of the "third sex," and Calvi as his "queen," destined for execution. Balzac's underworld is paralleled by a homosexual world of ties far more binding, it appears, than those of proper society.

Balzac in turn continues his exploration of the sexual dynamics of social life, both high and low. Leaving the prison, the story returns to the outside world to accompany Amélie Camusot, hell-bent on salvaging her bumbling husband's career. She is making the rounds of Lucien's lovers and also his enemy, the Marquise d'Espard. The Duchesse de Maufrigneuse possesses a collection of Lucien's letters containing "hyperbolical eulogies upon what was least duchesslike about her," and there is also a hidden stash of her replies to him, "celebrating the poetry of the male just as he hymned the glories of womanhood." In the exchange of love letters, the Duchesse says to Amélie, "everything bursts into flame, and caution is thrown to the wind." (P 494/P 6:880) Were the letters to fall into the wrong hands, she would claim they were the beginning of a novel. There is also, it turns out, a compromising correspondence between Clotilde and Lucien somewhere out there. The Duchesse de Grandlieu denies that Clotilde could have written anything improper, but Diane de Maufrigneuse refutes her, saying that she and Clotilde and Léontine de Sérizy "are three daughters of Eve, caught up by the serpent of correspondence." (P 497/P 6:883) The great ladies of the noble Faubourg are fully as passionate as the convicts' molls. Recovering the letters, notes the Duc de Grandlieu, is an action on behalf of the monarchy itself: high society must not be implicated in sexual scandal. Amélie's actions in finding the missing correspondence will be rewarded by Camusot's promotion.

Back at the Palais de Justice, Granville and Camusot are discussing what is to be done about the letters. Footsteps approach, a knock on the door, and Reverend Carlos Herrera enters. In another great theatrical moment, he declares to Granville: "Monsieur le Comte, I am Jacques Collin, and I surrender!" Discarding his disguise, he names himself as the convict he is. (P 511/P 6:895) His announcement resonates as something entirely new in the novel, and in his life. Camusot is sent away; Collin and Granville, "Crime and Justice," confront each other alone. Collin bargains for the life of Théodore Calvi, noting that he holds in his hand the honor of three great families since he knows where to find the incendiary missing letters. "When whores write they get stylish and offer fine sentiments, well then! noble ladies who are stylish and have fine sentiments all day long, write the way whores act. . . . Woman is an inferior being, she obeys too much her organs," Collin summarizes in an act of accusation addressed to the social order as a whole. (P 518/P 6:902) Granville matches Collin's surrender with his own act of generosity, freeing the convict to go retrieve the letters; and Granville in turn is congratulated by the secretary general of the cabinet, who tells him: "We are on the eve of great things and the King doesn't want, at this point, to see the peerage and the great families gossiped about, sullied. . . . This is no longer a sordid criminal action but an affair of state." (P 520/P 6:904)

Collin, with the help of his faithful team, his aunt Jacqueline (aka Asie) among others, will retrieve the letters that link not only the society ladies but himself in love of Lucien, whose cherished ghost hovers over the actions of all four. Jacqueline perceives a change in her nephew: "The death of that boy has turned your head!" And Collin in reply gives a sense of what his final transformation means:

> "Lucien took away my soul, all my happy life; I could live another thirty years in boredom, and I don't have the heart for it. Instead of being the boss of the underworld, I'll be the Figaro of Justice and I'll avenge Lucien. It's only in the skin of the cops that I can properly demolish Corentin. To have a man to eat will give me life again. The estates we create in the world are only appearances; reality is the idea!" he added striking his forehead.
>
> (P 529/P 6:912)

What is the idea that constitutes reality? Collin's words have a Platonic ring, yet that "idea" seems largely to reside in the interchangeability of social roles. Outlaw and police are just two positions on the social chessboard that can easily be swapped. "We were the hunted, now we become the hunters, that's all," he says to Jacqueline. That's all, and that sums up a novel which has demonstrated their essential moral equivalence.

To Granville and Camusot, he explains himself a bit differently: "Last night, holding in my hand the cold hand of the dead young man, I promised myself to give up the senseless struggle I have waged for twenty years against the whole of society... for twenty years I have seen the world in reverse, in its underground, and I recognize that there is in the march of events a force which you call Providence and which I called chance and which my pals call luck." (P 540/P

6:922) Lucien suffered from bad luck, a combination of circumstances surrounding Esther's death. And who was responsible? Collin blames Nucingen: "a man covered with secret infamies, a monster who in the world of tangled interests has committed such crimes that every penny of his fortune is soaked in the tears of some family, a Nucingen who was a legal Jacques Collin in the world of money. You know as well as I do the frauds for which he deserves to hang." (P 541/P 6:923)

With Collin's words, Balzac rounds out the critique of modern society that runs throughout *The Human Comedy*. Lucien the poet, the high aristocratic ladies who under the Restoration have failed to set an example to the nation, Rastignac the social climber, Collin the criminal mastermind, all are the victims—and the accomplices—of the new inhuman reign of capital represented by Nucingen. What is to be done? Balzac's delight in the twists and turns of plots and plottings converges with his clear-sighted recognition of social structure: join the game. In his last incarnation, Collin sees only one position for himself: to serve the power that weighs on us all. He proposes to replace Bibi-Lupin as head of the Sûreté. "I have no other ambition than to be an instrument of law and repression instead of corruption. . . . I am the general of the underworld and I surrender." (P 543/ P 6:925)

An Instrument of Law and Repression

Who finally is Jacques Collin? After he switches from criminal to cop, after he weeps over Lucien's grave, after he secures Calvi's release and retrieves the letters (and reads a passionate unsent letter from Lucien to Madame de Sérizy, saving her from despair and madness),

Granville finds him standing in his drawing room, "somber, erect, lost in the dream of those who have made an 18 Brumaire in their lives." (P 553/P 6:934) The 18th Brumaire An VIII marks the date in the revolutionary calendar when Napoleon Bonaparte seized power. Collin's accession to power parallels Napoleon's. Collin himself will be for six months Bibi-Lupin's lieutenant, then his successor. We learn in the last sentence of the novel that Collin serves in that position for about fifteen years—so under the July Monarchy as well as the Restoration—and retires around 1845.

What the reign of Collin as police chief was like is left to the reader's imagination. But we must recognize finally that the forces of crime and the forces of "repression" are interdependent and possibly indistinguishable. Collin is broadly modeled on Eugène François Vidocq, a serial criminal turned police detective, the founder of the Sûreté Nationale (the undercover investigative arm of the police), who revolutionized detective work. Vidocq was a friend of Balzac's, an extraordinary figure in his own right, and an inspiration for many a literary character, including both Jean Valjean and Inspector Javert in Hugo's *Les Misérables*. But Collin voices a more trenchant critique of the social order, claiming allegiance to Rousseau's vision of a social contract that he thinks has been made a sham in a society where law exists mainly to protect the fraudulent enrichment of a Nucingen. Through all his transformations, Collin demonstrates his fidelity to those he treasures, all men of course: Rastignac, Franchessini, Lucien, Calvi. His eros appears to be largely sublimated into the nurturing of his protégés and vicarious pleasure in their social existence. He projects himself into the world through his creatures, like Balzac the novelist who invests his eros in his created characters.[4]

Collin is the most powerful of a number of demiurgic figures in *The Human Comedy*, men who devote themselves to strategies of utter domination in different fields of endeavor. Men they mostly are, not women, with a few exceptions, notably the formidable manipulative couple Valérie Marneffe and Cousin Bette, in *Cousin Bette* (*La Cousine Bette*). There is the monomaniacal scientist Balthasar Claës in *The Search for the Absolute* (*La Recherche de l'Absolu*), which recounts literally that; the similarly motivated musician Gambara, who invents the "panharmonicon"; and the possessed painter Frenhofer of *The Unknown Masterpiece* (*Le Chef-d'oeuvre inconnu*), who pushes the art of representation beyond its limits, producing a canvas that is illegible. Then there is the philosopher Louis Lambert, who goes mad and tries to castrate himself on the eve of his marriage. Balzac clearly is haunted by these Faustian figures, who seek to go beyond what is permitted to ordinary humans, only to reach an impasse where their very medium of expression is blocked or destroyed. What sets Collin apart from them, and Balzac too, is his firmly rooted realism, even when he dreams of retiring to live the life of a planter in Virginia—and what provides a more realistic image of the true nature of social power than that? Collin is always ready to accommodate his dreams to reality. His final incarnation as a police detective may be read as social mockery, Nietzschean in its demonstration of the equivalence or, better, the indifference of crime and policing.

It's not just that Collin, like later detectives, including Sherlock Holmes, has a certain sympathy or complicity with the devil; it's that he refuses distinctions between good and evil altogether: they are simply positions in the struggle. Whether from the stance of revolt or that of social repression, society muddles indifferently on.

What is truly diabolical about Collin is that he puts in question the very idea of social order. Balzac called himself the "secretary" of society, recording its happenings. Collin, the man who cannot be killed off, whose identity is both branded on him and rendered illegible, challenges, or defies, the very coherence of such an entity, suggesting the possibility that the very subject of *The Human Comedy*, human society itself, is at bottom an illusion if not a fraud.

7. Henriette de Mortsauf
(1785–1820)

Kisses and Flowers

"No young man was ever better prepared than I to feel and to love," says Félix de Vandenesse, and after a childhood spent exiled from an unfeeling mother, all that is lacking is an opportunity and an object. He is twenty, it is 1814, the first year of the Restoration, and his native Tours is throwing a fête for the Duc d'Angoulême, on his way back from exile. The Vandenesses are members of the nobility and fervent supporters of the restored Bourbon monarchy, so Félix is sent to represent them at the reception given in the Duc's honor. He sits alone and forlorn on the sidelines of the ball, when a woman takes the chair next to him. First he notices her intoxicating perfume. Then he turns to look at her. He is dazzled by her bare white slightly blushing shoulders: shoulders with a soul, with a satiny skin, like silk. He sits up straight, and now he can see the swell of her bosom under a chaste veil of tulle: two perfectly round azure globes, "cozily sleeping in clouds of lace."[1] The stuff of adolescent fantasy so far. But then Félix acts on his fantasy: he throws himself onto the woman's back, kissing her shoulders everywhere. "Monsieur?" she exclaims (at least she takes him as a man, not a child), and her face goes purple with offended modesty. Félix leaves, ashamed, but without regret for his experience, ineffaceably marked by the moment. So, we will discover much later, is she.

She is Blanche Henriette de Mortsauf, and *The Lily of the Valley* (*Le Lys dans la vallée*) gives her excruciating story of desire awakened and repressed that Félix—her frustrated would-be lover—recounts but can barely understand. In this novel of baffled eros, arousal will always be followed by censure, denial, frustration. The repressed will return with a vengeance at the end, but without giving us full knowledge of the inner life of a woman who remains as enigmatic to us as to the man who tells her story, and his own. How can a woman live her life? This is a question that Balzac poses in different forms throughout *The Human Comedy*. How is the man who desires her to know and to write her story?

In *The Lily of the Valley*, Balzac apparently sets out to enter a woman's mind yet at the same time tells us how impossible a project that is. What can you know of a woman's life through a male's vision? In *The Duchesse de Langeais*, Balzac presented Antoinette's life in chronologically dislocated form, as if to dramatize the difficulty of knowing as well as possessing her. In the case of Henriette de Mortsauf, apart from two long letters that she writes, the second of them of crucial importance, we don't hear her version of her experience, nor do we have an account given by an objective narrator. It is always Félix we hear, and he is not even addressing us, his readers, directly. Instead, he is writing a confessional letter to his new love interest, Natalie de Manerville, who has said she wants to understand him, his silences, his moodiness, his past. The very first words of his letter to Natalie—"I yield to your desire" ("*Je cede à ton désir*")—characterize his telling of his story as a somewhat unwilling concession to his new love, whose prying he appears to resent, though he consents to it to advance their romance. (CG 1/P 9:969)

He confesses to Natalie that his life is dominated by a ghost, and that he has "imposing memories buried within his soul, like those sea plants that can be glimpsed in calm weather, and that the breakers of the tempest throw up in fragments onto the beach." An effective image for the unconscious and its fragmentary emergence in psychic life. There may be "outbursts" in his long confession, he may wound her, he tells Natalie, but she is the one who has asked for it. "So do not punish me for having obeyed you." All this in the prefatory note introducing the long confessional letter that follows, a note he signs off with the words: "Till this evening." He expects a lover's rendez-vous after she has read the letter. Yet in asking her for understanding, it's as if he is asking for trouble.

Félix describes his deeply unhappy childhood and adolescence, isolated in boarding schools, deprived of money and of maternal affection: very much Balzac's memory of his own childhood. His erotic outburst at the fête at Tours has no immediate sequel—but then he is formally introduced to Henriette by a family friend who is her neighbor, Monsieur de Chessel. Henriette is married to a much older man, the Comte de Mortsauf, and they live in the château of Clochegourde, on the banks of the Indre River in the rich landscape of Touraine. The Comte spent many years in exile as an "émigré," attached to the royal armies leagued against Republican and Napo-leonic France, before returning penniless to attempt to restore his property and fortune. In exile, Félix learns, the Comte indulged in "low-life loves"; his two children, Jacques and Madeleine, show the hereditary effects of syphilis. Their care is their mother's constant worry, while the Comte treats them capriciously and irrationally, adding to her martyrdom. In this painful marital situation, Félix might offer some consolation—but of what kind? On their meeting at Clochegourde, it is clear that the Comtesse recognizes him and remembers: "We were linked by that terrible kiss, a kind of secret that inspired us both with a mutual shame," claims Félix (CG 35–36/P 9:1005). When they are first alone, she recalls the scene—but with the stern admonition that it must never be mentioned. They will be friends. Any sentiment of love, and certainly any thought of sex, is forbidden.

And yet these feelings, these thoughts, are there constantly. Félix puts up with the Comte's abuse and the children's bad tempers because of his utter devotion to his beloved, and all the while his desire is written everywhere, as indeed more subtly is hers. His description of her on his first visit invests her with an intense sensuality held in a state of latency, something like a wildflower yet to blossom or a still-unfolded new leaf. The rich, fertile landscape of the valley of the Indre River expresses something of what she ought to be, something that life with the choleric Comte and two needy children has prevented her from being, while the question of what her own desires may be, and what she knows of them, will be crucial in the novel.

Félix and Henriette are joined by memories of their unhappy childhoods; rejected by their mothers, both feel a deep sense of guilt at their very existence. Félix's sympathetic understanding is such that Henriette is moved to ask him how he has come by his subtle knowledge of the suffering soul. "Were you once a woman?" she asks him.[2] (CG 49/P 9:1020) It is a telling question. Félix has won her over by showing an ability to place himself in her position. Like the androgynous novelist, he tries to look within her to understand her needs and wants. Yet he cannot see her fully, and his drive to possess her body and soul, that epistemophilia characteristic of Balzacian love stories, remains frustrated.

Here begins one of the strangest platonic relationships ever, a series of trials that both provoke and repress a growing passion. Madame de Mortsauf gives only to withhold. Félix begs her to provide him with a special name for her that he alone may use, and since her husband calls her Blanche, she offers Félix her other given name, Henriette. The Comte has a temper tantrum, and Henriette asks Félix to absent himself for a few days; he objects, and she scolds him, ordering him to leave. He wishes to kiss her hand. She hesitates, then accepts, while admonishing him: "Take it only when I offer it. Leave me my free will, otherwise I will become a thing belonging to you and that must not be." (CG 66/P 9:1037) He departs, closing the garden door behind him; she reopens it and offers her hand anew. "In truth, you have been very good this evening, you have consoled me for the future. Take it, my friend, take it!" Félix covers it with multiple kisses. The endless games of trictrac Félix is obligated to play with the Comte present a symbolic parallel to his relationship with Henriette. Félix has never played the game before, and the Comte at first wins easily. Losing more money than he can afford, Félix studies the strategy of the game and begins to win. But this puts the Comte in such a bad temper that he knocks over the game board and rages. Félix learns instead to allow the Comte to win early in their matches, leaving himself to win later, so by the end of evening they come out even. Love with the Comtesse also is a zero-sum game.

With the advent of the Restoration, Henriette's mother, the grand Duchesse de Lenoncourt, expects her daughter will come to

Paris and participate in the revived life of the court. But Henriette will have none of it. She remains in the provinces to look after her husband and children; her rootedness in the landscape is part of her very definition, as a lily nourished in the valley of the Indre. The mellow days of autumn bring the grape harvest, and Clochegourde in its happy moments echoes the Clarens of Rousseau's *New Heloise*: a community of beautiful souls who communicate their emotions without even having to speak, in a kind of ecstatic mutual transparency. Passion is held under a weight of repression: a mere hand kissing is invested with all that mustn't be. It is a paradise that Henriette has willed into being as an image of who she is, her utter devotion to husband and children, her delight in Félix whom she designates as another "child" in the family, including him by imposing on him an anodyne emotional role. Yet it is a paradise with fragile foundations, undermined by what it will not recognize.

The Comte's outbursts of bad temper and vituperation against his wife increase. Henriette tells Félix that she was about to collapse under the weight of her domestic burdens until he appeared in her life. Félix proposes love as the solution, and he is met with a clear refusal. She is willing to sacrifice him if he can't remain content in the role she has assigned him. Silenced, Félix turns to the language of flowers, attempting to "paint an emotion" in the bouquets he gathers from garden and field. "Love has its blazon, and the Comtesse deciphered it secretly. She gave me one of those incisive glances that resemble the cry of a patient probed in his wound: she was at once embarrassed and delighted." (CG 83/P 9:1053) The bouquets, which can take him hours to assemble, speak a language of (nearly) repressed passion. To take just one example of many, at the end of a long paragraph describing the background he creates in his vase:

From the bosom of this torrent of love rises the scarlet poppy, its tassels about to open, spreading its flaming flakes above the starry jessamine, dominating the rain of pollen—that soft mist fluttering in the air and reflecting the light of its myriad particles. What woman intoxicated with the odor of the vernal grasses would fail to understand this wealth of offered thoughts, these ardent desires of a love demanding the happiness refused in a hundred struggles which passion still renews, continuous, unwearying, eternal!

(CG 86/P 9:1057)

Such a passage—and it is much abbreviated—may remind us of how much for nineteenth-century writers (and as late as Proust, for instance) the natural world remains familiar and recognizably symbolic.[3] But Félix also mentions the *selam*, a Persian tradition of floral arrangements designed to convey a specific message. (CG 177/P 9:1148) It is like the secret codes used by prisoners to elude their jailers. For Félix and Henriette, the language of flowers provides a "neuter pleasure," that cheats "nature irritated by long contemplations of the beloved." (CG 87/P 9:1057) For Félix the bouquets afford a mechanism of relief, "like these fissures through which spurt waters held in by an unbreachable dam, and which often prevent a disaster by acknowledging necessity," and Henriette too contemplates the bouquets with heaving breast. They are contented like slaves who have found a way to outwit their master. The master in this case is not so much the Comte as eros itself.

Not the Comte, since Henriette, we come to learn, is denying herself to him as well—he is diseased, and he has made himself distasteful. Yet another version of trictrac goes on. He accuses her of being a "virgin at his expense," of starving him, and this accusation, accompanied by a menacing gesture, makes Henriette faint. Félix carries her into her bedroom—a sanctuary he never has seen before—and she confides in him about her husband: "Oh, that unhappy man. If you only knew...." Is the Comte impotent as well as desirous? (CG 102/P 9:1073) Eros is in bad shape all around.

Love and Politics

At this juncture, Félix's stay as the guest of M. de Chessel is up: his father recalls him to Paris. It is time to embark on a career in the new political order. Henriette writes a long letter to her "man-child," not to be read until he reaches Paris. Like Lord Chesterfield's letters to his son, it is all about how to present himself in society and succeed in a political career; it is largely conventional and conservative in outlook; noblesse oblige is the leitmotif. Cultivate women of fifty, beware of women of twenty: advice that may at once be wise and self-interested. Some readers have taken this hardheaded letter to be a curious product from a woman of sentiment, but I think we can see it as another form of repressed discourse: her passion is now sublimated into social and political terms.

Her advice is politically savvy enough, and Félix is introduced at court. Then, in another of those theatrical thunderclaps of nineteenth-century French history, Napoleon escapes from his island prison on Elba, lands on the south coast of France, and rallies his armies for a last campaign. Louis XVIII goes again into exile, in Belgium, and Félix decides to accompany him. The King rewards his loyalty by entrusting him with a top-secret mission back in France—the Napoleonic adventure is about to collapse at Waterloo—which gives him a chance to take a protracted leave at

Clochegourde. It turns out Félix has made a good career move. Once the Restoration is reestablished, he will become *maître des requêtes* at the Conseil d'État, a post of considerable prestige and responsibility.

But his return to Clochegourde is not easy for Henriette. "When Henriette saw a young man where before she had only seen a child, she lowered her gaze earthward, slowly, tragically. She let her hand be taken and kissed without giving sign of that intimate pleasure which was part of her sensibility, and when she raised her head again her face was pale." (CG 139–40/P 9:1111) Félix, older, now a court functionary, well-dressed, well-mannered, and newly empowered by success, a man, is a threat. To control the situation, she imposes a kind of catechism, a liturgy of her own devising to which he takes exception while reciting after her:

"Tell me, tell me! Will you always love me worshipfully?"
"Worshipfully."
"Forever?"
"Forever."
"Like a virgin Mary, who must always wear her veils and her white crown?"
"Like a visible virgin Mary."
"Like a sister?"
"Like a sister loved too well."
"Like a mother?"
"Like a mother secretly desired."
"Chivalrously, without hope?"
"Chivalrously, but with hope."

(CG 141/P 9:1112)

163

Here the mechanisms of repression are almost too patently visible: Félix is pressed into a role that both he and Henriette realize is unnatural, a poor fiction to which they pledge allegiance. Henriette says to Félix a moment later: if it is politic for you to be a man with the King, "understand, Sir, that here it is politic to remain a child. As a child, you will be loved! I will always resist the force of the man; but what could I refuse to the child? Nothing; he can wish nothing that I cannot grant." (CG 141/P 9:1113)

Henriette here may be as cunning as she is confused. Félix is not a child but a man, and as a man will want sex. She knows that. For that very reason, she must treat him even more as a child, which is to say devoid of sexual knowledge, even though that well-established trade in scarlet poppies was always sexually charged. Henriette is not unaware of the claims of desire, but she has decreed Clochegourde to be a place where time is arrested, and normal human development along with it, an ideal world that she claims to maintain in spite of her maniac husband, debilitated children, and insurgent lover.

The hypochondriac Comte now falls seriously ill; in Henriette's mind it's because he caught a chill in the shade of the walnut tree while she was off complaining to Félix about her unhappiness. Félix joins her in looking after the difficult invalid. And now Henriette's punishing sense of guilt forces her into an imprudent vow. She watches her husband's agitated hands attempting to pull up the bedcovers:

"They claim those are gestures of a dying man," she said. "Oh, if he should die from this illness that we have caused, I will never marry again. I swear it," she added, extending her hand over the Comte's head in a solemn gesture.

(CG 156/P 9:1127–28)

Freud notes that the superego becomes ever harsher and more unforgiving the more concessions one makes to it. Its demands eventually exceed all reason; they represent self-punishment for its own sake. Henriette affirms her impossible bind by promising never to be happy.

And the Comte is not about to die. Henriette and Félix, partners in a kind of "ephemeral marriage," nurse him back to life. As nurses, they are unconstrained and happy; the return of the Comte to health poses a new crisis. Félix tells her he would sacrifice everything for her, whereas she...

"Me," she replied, "of which me are you speaking? I sense several selves in me! These two children," she added, pointing to Madeleine and Jacques, "are selves. Félix," she said in a tone of despair, "do you think me an egotist? Do you think I could sacrifice all eternity to make the happiness of the person who has sacrificed his life to me? That thought is horrible, it goes against all religious teachings. Can a woman thus fallen ever redeem herself? Can her happiness absolve her? You would have me make an early decision on all those questions!"

(CG 164/P 9:1136)

Sometimes, Henriette appears to be blind to the impossible passion in which she is enmeshed; at others, she comes off as preternaturally aware. When Félix, chastised, promises to complain no more, she replies: "Your generosity is killing me." How to take her words?

A royal messenger arrives at Clochegourde: Félix is needed in Paris. Henriette summons him to her bedroom, seats him on the canapé, and gives him a lock of her hair as a present. (The gift of hair was a common love offering in the nineteenth century.) Is she ready to give herself?

> I bent my head slowly toward her forehead, she did not lower it to avoid my lips. I kissed her chastely, without guilty intoxication, without exciting pleasure, but rather with a solemn tenderness. Did she wish to sacrifice everything? Was she only, like me, going to the edge of the precipice? If love had brought her to the point of giving herself, she would not have had such a deep calm, such a religious gaze, and would not have said to me with pure voice: "You are no longer angry with me?"
>
> (CG 167/P 9:1138)

Félix's attempt to reassure himself that he has correctly interpreted Henriette's desires here—that she has not invited further sexual advance—seems unsatisfactory. What does she want? Before, it has seemed that Henriette has willed a world according to her fantasies; now it strikes us that Félix cannot offer a clear understanding of what she thinks and feels.

In Paris, rumors of Félix's devotion to the lady of Clochegourde ironically make him all the more attractive to other women, and Lady Arabella Dudley, the beautiful and somewhat wild wife of an elderly English lord, takes up with him. Arabella is one of Balzac's sexually liberated women, a delicate blond and accomplished equestrienne hunter, something of an Amazon. She makes the most of Félix's pent-up desires. Back in Clochegourde, he discovers that Henriette knows all about this infidelity (her ever-punishing mother has told her the news). Giving off "an odor of flowers cut forever," she greets him coldly. Henriette, she tells him, no longer exists. Félix attempts to make amends by severing the fleshly and the spiritual: "To you all my thought, pure love, youth and old age; to her the desires and pleasures of a fugitive passion; to you my remembrance in all its extent, to her the fullest forgetfulness." (CG 187/P 9:1159) Henriette, however, persists in the outlandish plan she has devised: that Félix must marry her daughter, Madeleine, who has survived puberty and will live, whereas her brother, Jacques, is headed to a premature death. By the end of their conversation, Henriette confesses: "I no longer know what virtue is, and I have no consciousness of my own." (CG 189/P 9:1161) Is Arabella—who has sacrificed husband and children for passion—right, and Henriette, in her insistence on virtue, wrong?

Arabella has made a point of accompanying Félix on this trip to Touraine and is lodged in Tours while he is at Clochegourde. Henriette demands a nighttime carriage ride with Félix, fully aware that they may encounter Arabella during one of her wild horseback rides across the moors. As ever, Henriette's masochism is put to work in her claim that Arabella has "saved" her from falling to Félix's carnal demands: "to her the soils, I don't envy her them at all. To me the glorious love of the angels." (CG 196/P 9:1168) But what she says to Félix is full of confusion: purity loved and purity regretted. The libidinal life of Arabella Dudley puts her own value system into question. They encounter Arabella and her dog racing across their path, and Henriette responds: "What a pleasure to be able to wait for one's lover when one can do it without crime!" (CG 138/P 9:1172) Félix is both the faithful brother who has brought her the greatest happiness she has known and the man who has destroyed her by awakening illicit desire. She ends the evening by sending Félix back to Arabella, her magnanimity and claim to female solidarity inextricable from self-punishment.

The next morning Arabella sends Félix back to Henriette. It is, as Arabella may guess, too late; Henriette claims to be dying. Félix, who has deprived her children of their mother, must take care of them after her death. And yet she pardons him. She blesses his love for the other woman. The sexual impasse has, by this time, become murderous.

The Return of the Repressed

And so the denouement approaches. Some weeks after his return to Paris, Félix learns that Henriette is mortally ill. He rushes to Clochegourde, where he is met by the doctor, who tells him that the Comtesse is dying of an unknown hurt. She has neither eaten nor slept for forty-two days; her digestion is ruined and she is starving to death. At the château, he finds the children and the Abbé de Dominis in prayer; the abbé tells him that while the sainted Madame de Mortsauf had seemed to accept her death, now she is full of envy for the living. She suffers from "vertigo," he says, intoxicated by "the withered flowers of her youth that are fermenting as they fall." (CG 223/P 9:1195) This extraordinary image takes us back to Félix's bouquets, and to Henriette's identity as the lily of the valley of the Indre. Balzac approximates a line from a Shakespeare sonnet: "lilies that fester smell far worse than weeds"; the festering of the dying lily produces a kind of moral fermentation that Félix discovers entering Henriette's bedroom, which she has decorated with bouquets of flowers, while dressing herself all in bridal white. He thinks that the figure on the canapé cannot be his beloved Henriette, nor the Comtesse de Mortsauf, but that "something without a name" described in a sermon of the famous baroque churchman Bossuet as "fighting against nothingness," urged on by "thwarted desires . . . to the egoist's combat of life against death." (CG 228/P 9:1200) Now she speaks: "I am barely thirty-five years old," she says to Félix, "I can have good years to come. Happiness makes one youthful and I want to know happiness. I have made delectable plans, we'll leave Clochegourde behind and go travel in Italy." (CG 228–29/P 9:1201). It is now she who attempts to seduce him, addressing him with a lover's *tu*, caressing him because, she says, she is sick from unrealized desire.

> "They think that my worst pain is thirst. Oh yes, I am thirsty, my friend. It pains me to look at the water of the Indre, but my heart feels a more ardent thirst. I had a thirst for you," she said lowering her voice and taking my hands in her burning hands and pulling me close to speak these words in my ear. "My agony was not seeing you! Didn't you tell me to live? I want to live. I want to ride horseback myself. I want to know everything, Paris, its parties, pleasure."
>
> (CG 229–30/P 9:1202)

To Félix it is a scene of nightmare, as she continues: "Yes, live. Live in realities and not lies! Everything in my life has been a lie." And: "Is it possible that I die, I who have never lived? I who never went to meet a lover on the moor?"[4]

From outside comes the sound of the harvesters at their work in the vineyards—it is autumn—and she cries out: "'Félix! The harvest girls are going to dine, and I,' she said in a child's voice, 'I, their mistress, I am hungry. Thus it is with love. They know happiness, they do!'" The priest falls to his knees chanting the kyrie eleison, and Henriette throws her arms around Félix in a violent embrace. "You won't escape me again! I want to be loved. I'll commit follies like Lady Dudley." Feeling faint, she asks Félix to carry her to the bed. "She was light, but especially she was burning," he reports. Her body is enacting a hysterical vengeance for the impossible life of denial that she has lived even as she warmed herself with Félix's desire and the desire that Félix awoke in her. With this return of the repressed, we witness the final pathos of her passion.

The doctor, with the approval of the priest, intervenes to dose Henriette with opium to ease her agony, and removes all the flowers from her room: their odor and fecundity are seen to cause her profane outbursts. When Henriette comes to, she is ready to make an edifying death, surrounded by family, weeping servants, and clergy. She demands forgiveness for her sins, and tells Félix that she may have wronged him by giving him hopes that as a wife and mother she could only refuse him. Evening falls, and two nightingales are heard singing in the garden as she expires.

But as so often in Balzac, this is not the end: there is another long letter from Henriette to Félix, written before her final illness. If the earlier letter was full of worldly advice, this one is entirely different, a confession that rewrites the story of her life, now for the first time seen fully from her own perspective. This testamentary letter is a curious document. It begins in an accusatory manner, naming Félix as the cause of all her ills, and arguing that he is under a solemn obligation to take care of her children—and the Comte!—after her death, including marrying Madeleine. It is the latest stroke he has given her—presumably his affair with Arabella Dudley—that she claims has killed her. And yet she feels great pleasure in being wounded by the one she loves, she declares, before becoming more self-analytical, and describing how despite marriage and the birth of two children, she had remained at heart a virgin until the reception in Tours:

> Do you still today remember your kisses? They have dominated my life. They cut a furrow through my soul. The ardor of your blood awakened the ardor of mine; your youth penetrated mine, your desires entered into my heart. When I rose up so proudly, I felt a sensation for which there is no word in any language. . . . I understood there existed something unknown to me in the world, a force more beautiful than thought, it was all thoughts, all force, all the future in a shared emotion. . . . If you have forgotten these terrible kisses, I have never been able to wipe them from my memory: I am dying because of them! Yes, each time I saw you after that, it reawakened their imprint; I was shaken from head to toe by the sight of you, by simple anticipation of your coming. Neither time nor my firm will have been able to tame this imperious desire. I couldn't stop asking myself: What must pleasure be like?
>
> (CG 242–43/ P 9:1215–16)

Henriette describes the creation of a memory trace from this moment of trauma. Her unexpected flood of pleasure had to be tamed and diverted into refusal and pain, resulting in a forbidden fascination. For Henriette, every bit as much as for Félix, the kisses of Tours stand as the primal scene. She attempts to repress it, yet it returns, and it will always come back whenever Félix (happiness inscribed in his name) reappears. As Freud liked to quote from Horace, you can drive nature out with a forked stick (like a snake), but it is sure to return, and return precisely by way of your attempt to repress it.[5]

Henriette's letter is remarkably lucid in understanding her predicament, while at the same time continuing to impose a willful blindness on the erotic self she has discovered. Was her lucidity always there, hidden from Félix, or has it been acquired in retrospect at the moment of writing? In acknowledging the effect of Félix's kisses on her psychic—and bodily—life, she demonstrates that her drama is not a simple story of conventional virtue warding off a sexual predator. As in the case of the Duchesse de Langeais, it becomes instead a story about acknowledgment: Can you see what you want and, even if it is forbidden, assume the consequences of that knowledge? Freud's question—What does woman want?—so often faulted for its obtuseness, has at least a limited application to a woman like Henriette for whom sexuality is a realm half discovered and then foreclosed, put under erasure. Before the kisses, she didn't know it was there. After the kisses, it is constantly there but inaccessible. To go there, she believes, would be to destroy her world or—this is the killing confusion—her understanding of the world.

The chaste touchings Félix exchanged with her, she says, clouded her eyes; and her ears echoed with the sound of the senses in revolt. "Oh, if in these moments where I redoubled my coldness toward you you had taken me in your arms I would have died from happiness. Sometimes I wanted you to exercise violence, but prayer quickly banished this sinful thought." This is perhaps less a rape fantasy than a wish that Félix himself understand the desires he has unleashed between them, that he practice the transparency of soul that he values. It is her confessor, it turns out, who has dictated that she love Félix maternally, treating him as a son and the future husband of Madeleine, a perverse idea that makes Madeleine, later Duchesse de Lenoncourt-Chaulieu and friend to Clotilde de Grandlieu, end up hating Félix, and gives her mother another dose of unsustainable masochistic pleasure. She now confesses that the sufferings of love were cruelly equal for Félix and for her. Arabella Dudley, she says, cannot claim superiority to her: "I too was one of these daughters of a fallen race whom men love so much." (CG 245/ P 9:1218)

When she found out about Arabella and Félix, she discovered things about herself that she had never imagined. She was jealous, furious, her life out of control; she had murder in her soul and wanted to rush to Paris. But instead, jealousy opened a "large breech" in her, and death has entered. Death is the only solution. This is not Isolde dying from love, or the Roman Lucretia dying to save her honor. It is something distinctly modern: dying from an inability to reconcile the conflicting drives that make her who she is. She now understands what triggered the problem, and Félix's role, but she cannot think or feel her way out of the impasse of desire. Back to those floral arrangements as messages, back to those games of trictrac with a null result.

Henriette's dilemma takes its place within a long tradition of stories about female "virtue" undergoing the trials of male desire: for instance, Clarissa Harlowe, at the very start of the modern novel. How is *The Lily of the Valley* different? Félix is no Lovelace, as Henriette, looking back and wishing at times he'd been more forceful, almost ruefully acknowledges. Félix is phallic but not a true Don Juan, and she finds it easy enough to defend her virtue against his pressures. Nor can she in confronting him fall back on the naiveté of the young girl. Before Félix's kisses, she may have been unaware of erotic arousal, but her response to her new experience is fully politic. She and her confessor may carry on about the religious duties of virtue and chastity, but Henriette's choice of chastity is of a piece with the advice for getting on in the political world she gives Félix when he goes Paris. That represents the policy she adopts for herself as well, though when Arabella enters the story, all policy is thrown into question.

And so we come back to the question that Balzac poses again and again: How can a woman live her life? He addressed it satirically, but also analytically and with some empathy, in his essays *Physiology of Marriage* and *Petty Troubles of Married Life* (*Petits misères de la vie conjugale*), and also in his novels *The Duchesse de Langeais*, *A Woman of Thirty*, and *The Abandoned Woman*. There is also *The Memoirs of Two Young Wives* (*Mémoires de deux jeunes mariées*), an epistolary novel about two young women just finishing convent school, one of whom enters into an arranged marriage to an older man she doesn't love though he loves her, while the other goes to Paris and falls romantically in love with a Spaniard. The issues debated in the novel touch on the daily challenges of living as women in a society that wants them to be at once virtuous and seductive, as well as competent managers of households and producers of well-behaved children. One of the young women has two children, preaches birth control to keep families affluent, and seeks modest contentment; the other thirsts after intense emotion and romantic fulfillment. In *The Memoirs of Two Young Wives*, unlike *The Lily of the Valley*, Balzac has his women speak in their own voices, asking himself, it seems, what it must mean to be a woman, to negotiate that identity in society. It is not surprising that his novels appealed so to a female readership. That Sainte-Beuve found this appeal unhealthy suggests Sainte-Beuve's failure to think as a woman, which in fact was in part the occasion for *The Lily of the Valley*: Balzac wrote it as a riposte of sorts to Sainte-Beuve's novel *Volupté*, all about a young man's attachment to a virtuous older woman. The book was detestably false, Balzac judged, smelling of the sacristy, and he vowed to skewer Sainte-Beuve with his pen.

What sets Henriette de Mortsauf apart from the stereotype of the besieged virtuous woman is her acute awareness of how the primal scene of Félix's kisses has affected her. She doesn't understand her sensations, but she feels what they do to her. She is to that extent not the traditional "pure woman," and Balzac dissents from the novelistic stereotype. Yes, Henriette will remain chaste, faithful to her husband and her children. But at an enormous cost: the novel is as much or more about the ravages of repression as it is a tale of virtue rewarded. For all his rhetoric of sublime renunciation surrounding Henriette, Balzac at the last shows himself to be almost cynical. He takes apart Henriette's claim to virtue, not quite invalidating it, since on its own terms it is perfectly coherent, but showing it as the result of psychic compromises that take a devastating toll.

Punished for Telling

What about Félix? Henriette dies, and he is left to "sift through a pile of ashes." The whole story, we recall, has been told in a letter, a "love letter," to Natalie de Manerville, yet he appears to take pleasure in displaying the extent of his passion for Henriette and the depth of his mourning and melancholia. This is a mistake. The novel ends with Natalie's reply. Allow me, she says, to complete the education begun by Madame de Mortsauf. She renounces the task of loving him, and says she feels sorry for the next woman he takes up with. He should in the future keep his confessions to himself: "No woman, believe me, will want to rub elbows with the dead woman you keep in your heart." (CG 254/P 9:1127) Félix, she understands, cannot detach himself from the dead Henriette. And also from himself: she accuses him of an incurable egotism. If he continues to unburden himself to other women as he has to her, they will perceive "the aridity of your heart, and you will always be unhappy." (CG 256/P 9:1229)

"I yield to your desire," *The Lily of the Valley* began, as Félix sought to oblige Natalie's wish to know his past, but his narrative will prove to provoke the end of desire, and the end of any affair between them. Describing Henriette's deathbed cries of frustrated passion, Félix says that detaching himself from his love for her was like undergoing a punishment meted out by the Tartars, who "punished adultery by imprisoning a member of the guilty person in the stocks and then giving him a knife to cut it off if he did not wish to die of starvation." (CG 231/P 9:1204) I find it tempting to read "a member" as "the member": Félix experiences something like castration in his romance with Henriette; he emerges from it seemingly diminished—as Natalie senses from his account. When we see him again in *A Daughter of Eve* (*Une Fille d'Ève*), he is a grave and composed diplomat who skillfully negotiates to bring his wife, Marie-Angélique de Granville, back into the marriage bond from her nascent affair with the writer Raoul Nathan. His young wife, we understand, finds him boring.

Natalie de Manerville reappears in *The Marriage Contract* (*Le Contrat de mariage*)—though it's not quite clear, as often in *The Human Comedy*, that she's fully the "same" person in this novel—

which is about how Natalie's spendthrift Spanish mother snookers Comte Paul de Manerville into giving up her daughter's dowry. Natalie and her mother, Madame Evangelista, make Paul's life a misery, and when they have bankrupted him, he sails off to India to attempt to restore his fortunes—and is never heard of again, so far as I can figure out. He learns too late, in a letter from Henri de Marsay, of the machinations of his wife and mother-in-law. Is Félix's love object this same charming, sexy, but cold and scheming deceiver? Once again, it is hard to say. Certainly *The Lily of the Valley* casts her in a more sympathetic light, astute indeed as a reader of Félix's memoir. The different lighting and emphasis is characteristic of Balzac's use of reappearing characters: they don't quite fit the outlines established for them in a single novel; they exceed and blur the lines; character is not reducible to a single description; the individual is multiple. As readers we may at times find it frustrating not to be able to reconcile all the traits of a character. Raoul Nathan in *Lost Illusions* is a truly great novelist, at least Lucien sees him as such, but in *A Daughter of Eve* he has become something of a hack playwright. Time will do that, we might say—and as Henry James said, giving a sense of the passage of time is central to Balzac's artistry.[6] Life goes on, refusing to be pinned down.

The poet Baudelaire commands us to get drunk "On wine, on poetry, on virtue, at your choice."[7] Henriette de Mortsauf at times appears drunk on virtue in lieu of love. Detoxication is painful. Her contradictions make her something more than the simple lily of the valley the title announces. Her relatively brief autobiographical moment—her testamentary letter to Félix—only begins to suggest how problematic his biography of her may have been. In a story that is all about desire, its repression and distortion, its underground existence and twisted manifestations, authorship by the would-be lover raises all sorts of questions. Can a man ever truly write a woman's biography?

Félix, appalled at Henriette's death agony, asks himself whether maybe he belongs "to the race of tigers" (CG 222/P 9:1194), a human predator. The tiger may remind us of the panther in that strange and wonderful story of Balzac's, *A Passion in the Desert*. A French soldier becomes lost in the desert during Napoleon's campaign in Egypt, then shares an oasis with a panther—who becomes something of a love partner, but whom he at the last stabs to death from a misunderstanding. The tale, I suggested, turns on woman as panther, and panther as woman, in a male discourse on female sexuality as alluring and dangerous. It's told by a man who has lost a leg, in a kind of symbolic castration possibly attributable to the panther. It may stand as something of a cautionary tale about the discourse of men on women's wants.

It almost seems as if women should be allowed to tell their own stories. But that happens rarely in *The Human Comedy*: *The Memoirs of Two Young Wives* is the clearest exception, and there are other fleeting moments when women narrate throughout Balzac's work. The vast majority of narrators are male. When they attempt to speak on behalf of a woman, as in *The Lily of the Valley*, they approach, but only unwittingly, the vicarious existence exercised in full awareness by Jacques Collin. What we are left with is complex and indeterminate, the attempt to speak on behalf of. That suggests the novelist's very motive, his interest in creating fictional lives. We need novels in order to enter the minds of others. But that project can run up against the opacities of other minds and spirits. When a man tells us of a woman's desiring, we should beware of blindness.

8. Colonel Chabert
(1765–after 1840)

Death to Life

OF ALL THE STIRRING TALES in *The Human Comedy*, none is quite so amazing in its telling as that of Colonel Hyacinthe Chabert. He is dead. He died heroically at the Battle of Eylau in 1807, felled by a head wound while leading a successful cavalry charge against the Prussians, was buried in the common grave on the battlefield, and his death was recorded in *Victoires et Conquêtes*, the official chronicle of Napoleon's Grande Armée. Yet here he is, or claims to be, some eleven years later, in Derville's law office, asking to reclaim his identity. Who is this crazy old man? Even when he gains Derville's help, his quest appears quixotic. The new regime is determined to bury the Napoleonic past: Why should it recognize the rights of this revenant? What can a lawyer do to recover his identity? What will that mean? Chabert's nonrecognition is at once personal, social, and political. Throughout his tale, the legal formalities of the emerging modern world, as well as the fictions on which its own identity is founded, are pitted against the claims of a heroic past. In this short novel, Chabert opens an abyss in ongoing history.

Colonel Chabert (*Le Colonel Chabert*) begins with a wretched, cadaverous figure making his way across the courtyard outside Derville's law office, one of those "dens of chicanery." Inside, the clerks are already laughing at him and thinking up tricks to play on him, while they are ostensibly busy copying a legal document that the head clerk is reading aloud.[1] This is a decree that we have seen before in *The Human Comedy*'s chronicle of the Restoration: it restores lands confiscated from the nobility during the Revolution to their previous owners. It is clearly significant for Chabert's claim: the Restoration of the Bourbon monarchy marks the end of the Napoleonic adventure that capped the revolutionary era, during which Chabert played out his heroic life and death. History itself has buried him.

Chabert began his life in the public orphanage, the Enfants Trouvés. As a soldier under Napoleon's command, he rose swiftly through the ranks: the horrendous death toll of officers meant that advancement could come swiftly. Napoleon's generals and marshals were mostly young men. Chabert served in the Egyptian campaign and in all the European theaters of the Napoleonic Wars; when the Emperor revived the titles abolished by the Revolution to create his own loyal nobility, he was dubbed Comte Chabert. He married Rose Chapotel, making her Comtesse Chabert, who then, after his death, remarried Comte Ferraud, a member of the old aristocracy. This satisfied Napoleon's desire to realize a fusion of the old nobility and his own creation.

The old man who shows up in Derville's office, his clerks say, "*a l'air d'un déterré*," as if he hadn't slept all night or had just staggered back from a binge: he looks like someone dug up from the grave. (ND 9/P 3:316) But the metaphorical expression in this case turns out to be literally true. When the clerks ask his name, he tells them: "Chabert." The one who died at Eylau? "The same," Chabert replies, with simple dignity. Balzac underlines his incredible situation: he is a living oxymoron. He comes to the lawyer in an attempt to recover his right to call himself alive. His first accomplishment must be winning Derville's willingness simply to hear his tale, which the lawyer agrees to do during the private time when he prepares his court cases—one o'clock in the morning. "Speak," he says—tell me your story. Chabert has finally found the interlocutor he has been looking for, and needs.

Chabert tells of the ultimate Gothic horror, burial alive. Recovering consciousness, he finds himself under a pile of corpses, buried alive by the dead, in the true silence of the grave. He makes use of a severed arm to heave himself up through the heaped bodies, his head finally emerging through the snow covering the battlefield, and is rescued by German peasants. Bodies were stripped of their uniforms and possessions following battle, so he emerges from the earth naked as a babe, with nothing to prove his identity. Wounded by a saber blow to his head, he is suffering from temporary amnesia; it will take him some six months to remember that he is Colonel Chabert, a claim that is documented by both the doctor who cares for him and a notary to whom he later makes a declaration. The fortunes of war then drive him from one German town to another; he becomes a beggar, is incarcerated as a madman. Released and on his way back to France, he meets an old comrade-in-arms, Boutin. Thanks to a long-ago shared adventure in an Italian brothel, Boutin can vouch for Chabert's identity, about which Chabert himself still remains uncertain. Boutin is to seek out Chabert's wife in Paris, but then, after Napoleon's escape from captivity on the isle of Elba, Boutin rallies to the Grande Armée and is killed at the Battle of Waterloo. So Chabert enters Paris alone, at the same time as the Cossacks in the avant-garde of the forces come to restore the French monarchy. In Derville's office, he looks like "a Rembrandt without the frame": no gilded border for this devastated old man.

The tale Chabert recounts to Derville is impossible yet convincing. Derville does listen to him—Chabert is so moved by his polite attention that he grasps Derville's hand—and he thinks he believes him. Nonetheless, Derville judges that any litigation will have a doubtful outcome. "We may have to compromise," he says: "*Il faudra peut-être transiger.*" (ND 34/P 3:333) Chabert understands all too well that he belongs to an era now past. "Our sun has set, we are all cold now." (ND 11/P 3:331) But at Derville's proposal, he reacts with outrage: "'Compromise,' repeated Colonel Chabert. 'Am I alive or am I dead?'" Here Balzac dramatizes yet another difference of perspective between the old and the new orders. In Chabert's world questions of existence and identity are straight up or down. The new era in which Deville operates conceives that the self is not solitary but rather, as the psychologist Jerome Bruner describes it, "transactional," forged in interaction with others—including, in this case, the social class structure enforced by the Restoration.[2] And indeed, *transaction* is the word the lawyer uses in proposing his legal negotiation.

Derville looks into what happened to Chabert's fortune and pension following his "death"; the case, he reports, is "excessively complicated," to which the old soldier replies that no, it is "perfectly simple." (ND 47/P 3:340) His wife by no means sees it that way. She and Chabert had no children; she has two with her new husband. Her situation sets Derville thinking. The Comtesse Ferraud

is now very rich, her inheritance from Chabert having been aug-
mented by a special tax indemnity she received as the widow of a
war hero. Delbecq, a sometime lawyer without much scruple, has
further increased her fortune through investments, while her new
husband has had his family lands, now very valuable, restored (see
the decree the clerks are copying at the outset of the story). He is
rising fast in the royal administration. A wealthy and fortunate couple then, secure in their new life.

And yet Derville figures out that the Comtesse lives with a "moral
cancer." (ND 60/P 3:349) Her husband now regrets having married
her. He would be so much better off married to a daughter of the
Faubourg Saint-Germain, who would bring him greater social distinction, perhaps even that peerage that Rastignac will attain. So
Derville arranges to visit the Comtesse, armed with sticks as well as
carrots.

Transacting Identities

Derville explains to the Comtesse that her first husband is alive. She
denies this, but Derville traps her into admitting she has in fact
received a letter from Chabert, which she burned. She haughtily
claims that the courts will find for her; she proposes to get rid of the
plaintiff with a modest sum. Not so fast, says Derville: if you go to
court, you might encounter an unexpected enemy. Who might that
be? she inquires. Your husband, replies Derville.

> "He would defend me, Monsieur!"
> "No, Madame."
> "What reason would he have to abandon me, Monsieur?"

"Why, to marry the only daughter of a Peer of France, whose peerage would then be transmitted to him by royal decree."

(ND 66–67/P 3:353–54)

Derville has hit home: "The Comtesse went pale." Now the Comtesse needs his help: What should she do? He tells her what he told Chabert: "Compromise"—*transiger*.

Balzac's first title for *Colonel Chabert* was in fact *The Transaction* (*La Transaction*), and that transaction is what most of the rest of the narrative will recount. Derville goes to work writing a settlement by which the Comtesse will recognize Chabert's identity, while he will renounce any marital rights and join her in pursuing a judgment annulling both his death decree and their marriage. She will also pay Chabert an annuity of 24,000 francs. Derville separates the two principals in different rooms of his office, and explains the terms of the settlement to the Comtesse. She balks at the proposed the annuity: "That's much too much. . . . We'll go to court." (ND 73/P 3:357) Chabert, who has been listening from the next room, bursts in, his hand thrust in his waistcoat in Napoleonic posture. The Comtesse recognizes him. And yet she recognizes at the same moment that no one but herself would be able to identify the old colonel, so utterly changed is his appearance. So she denies his existence.

"But Monsieur is not Colonel Chabert," exclaimed the Comtesse, feigning surprise.

"Ah!" said the old man in a bitterly ironic tone of voice, "Do you want proof? I picked you up at the Palais-Royal . . ."

The Comtesse blanched.

(ND 74/P 3:357)

The Palais-Royal was the center of prostitution in Paris. As Chabert will explain to Derville, during the Napoleonic Wars men took their wives wherever they found them. By insulting the Comtesse, however, he has undermined his case. After observing the Comtesse's reactions, Derville tells Chabert he now is sure that he is telling the truth, but he will have to try to repair his blundering intrusion.

When Chabert leaves Derville's office, he finds the Comtesse waiting for him at the foot of the staircase. She still knows how to seduce. She invites him into her carriage, and they set off together for her country house in Groslay. She admits to Chabert that she has recognized him—the sole balm, he says, that can make him forget his misfortunes—but that she cannot expose her situation in public. She throws herself upon the goodness of his character; she speaks of her new role as mother. "The dead are then so wrong to return to life?" responds Chabert. (ND 79/P 3:360) The countess of the Empire, he discovers, is now a countess of the Restoration—not only higher in rank but also more polished, more diplomatic, and more skilled at intrigue. Chabert agrees to sacrifice himself to her happiness, renouncing all marital rights, and now she pushes for more: "Understand in that case that you must renounce your identity and do so in legal form." (ND 84/P 3:363) This raises Chabert's hackles: "What, my word isn't good enough?"

Now the Comtesse plays her trump card, producing her two children. Who will get them in a court judgment? she laments. And Chabert resolves to join the dead again. But Delbecq, the Comtesse's lawyer, has prepared a document so crude—Chabert is to declare himself an impostor—that he refuses to sign. In the Comtesse's garden, he overhears her conversation with Delbecq: "the old horse shied away," he says, and she replies that they will have to put him in the madhouse at Charenton. (ND 88/P 3:366) Chabert, ever impulsive, leaps from hiding and slaps Delbecq in the face. But once his anger has passed, he feels nothing but disgust with the prospect of a "hateful battle" in the courts. He will not, he tells the Comtesse, seek to regain the name that he made famous. And the Comtesse, "with the profound lucidity that comes from great wickedness or the fierce egotism of society," decides that his verbal promise is enough. Legal documents are no longer at issue, only a soldier's honor.

And so Chabert disappears; what happens to him is unclear. Derville wants his fee—he has staked 2,000 francs he won at the gambling tables on the equally chancy outcome of Chabert's case— but Delbecq in response tells him the lie that Chabert has admitted to being an impostor. So Derville has lost 2,000 francs in the misadventure. Later, conducting business at the Palais de Justice, Derville is witness to a sentencing: a certain Hyacinthe, a vagabond, is remanded to the workhouse in Saint-Denis for two months—as good as a life sentence since once in the workhouse there was no way out. Derville recognizes this Hyacinthe as the "false" Colonel Chabert, and follows him along with the other convicted men into the waiting room of the Records Office, a sad and sinister place that for the convicted is "a mere preface to the dramas of the morgue or the guillotine." (ND 94/P 3:369) Derville complains about the nonpayment of his bills, and Chabert asks permission to write a note to the Comtesse Ferraud that he promises will result in reimbursement. And in fact, when Derville sends it to the Comtesse he receives immediate payment. We never learn what the note says. Why, Derville asks Chabert, hasn't he demanded an annuity for himself in return for renouncing his identity? To which the Colonel replies:

"Don't speak of it.... You cannot know how much I scorn this outward life that most men hold dear. I was suddenly taken with an illness, disgust for humankind. When I think that Napoleon is imprisoned on Saint-Helena, nothing on earth matters to me. I can no longer be a soldier—there's my real misfortune." (ND 95/P 3:370)

Here Chabert reattaches his personal history to that of the nation. France without Napoleon holds no meaning for him. The final defeat of Napoleon, held prisoner by the British on the remote island of Saint-Helena (until his death, some three years in the future), represents to Chabert the end of everything he lived for, and indeed his very identity as a military hero. With Chabert's story, Balzac in fact addresses a pressing social problem of the Restoration years: the presence of a large population of former Napoleonic officers and soldiers, living on very modest pensions if on anything at all, who would be a source of political unrest throughout the Restoration and after. In 1840 the parliamentary monarchy would seek to appease this group by bringing back the Emperor's body for ceremonial entombment in the Invalides. This merely furthered the Napoleonic myth and created fertile ground for the return of the nephew, Louis-Napoléon Bonaparte, to political life. Following the Revolution of 1848, he would ascend to the presidency; then his coup d'état made him Emperor Napoleon III and ushered in the Second Empire.

A Life in History

The story of Chabert's reappearance in Paris dates to 1818. Now the novel leaps forward to 1840. Derville and one of his former clerks, Godeschal, now a lawyer himself, are on their way out of Paris when they walk past the Hospice de la Vieillesse, an old age home, in the suburb of Bicêtre. Godeschal notices an old man seated on a mile-stone drying his handkerchief in the sun, looking like a grotesque caricature of a statue. Derville peers through his monocle; he recognizes the man. "This old man," he says to Godeschal, "is a whole poem, or as the Romantics say, a drama. Have you ever met the Comtesse Ferraud?" (ND 97–98/P 3:371) If Chabert is in the Hospice, that must be the Comtesse's doing: she could never forgive him for reminding her that he picked her up on the street like a hackney cab. "I still remember the tiger's glance she gave him at that moment." This is a simplification of the complex story we have followed, true enough in the one detail but ignoring the historical sweep and significance of Chabert's destiny. Now we learn that Derville "told Godeschal the preceding story," which seems to claim that Derville has been the narrator of all that we have read so far.[3]

The story arouses Godeschal's curiosity, so when he and Derville are on the way back to Paris two days later, they pause at Bicêtre to see Chabert again. But when Derville addresses him by his name and rank, the old soldier demurs: "Not Chabert! Not Chabert! My name is Hyacinthe. . . . I'm no longer a man, I'm number 164, room 7." (ND 198/P 3:372) Such is the outcome of his quest to recover his identity. They offer him a twenty-franc piece. He thanks them with a "stupid look," calling out: "Brave troopers!" He then pretends to shoulder a gun and take aim, shouting with a smile: "Fire both barrels! Long live Napoleon!" And then: "He waved his cane in the air in an imaginary arabesque."

An imaginary arabesque, like the epigraph to *The Fatal Skin*, the squiggled line from *Tristram Shandy*, showing how Corporal Trim waved his cane in the air to describe the unfettered life of the bachelor. The reference here is bitterly ironic: Chabert is anything but unfettered, a bachelor only because his wife has renounced him and stripped him of his identity. Derville wonders if he is senile, and another inmate says that Chabert has been in the Hospice since 1820, and that once a passing Prussian officer joked that he seemed so old he might have been at the Battle of Rossbach (in 1757, Prussian victory over the French). "I was too young for that," Chabert replied, "but I was old enough to fight at Jena"—where Napoleon defeated the Prussians in 1806. The Prussian officer decamps quickly.

Now Derville sums his story up in epic terms:

> "What a destiny!" exclaimed Derville. "Coming out of the Enfants Trouvés, he returns to die in the Hospice, having in the meantime helped Napoleon conquer Egypt and Europe."
>
> (ND 99–100/P 3:373)

But then Derville turns from Chabert's exemplary life to his own.

> "Do you know, my friend," Derville resumed after a pause, "that there are in our society three men, the Priest, the Doctor, and the Lawyer, who cannot think well of the world? They all are clothed in black, perhaps because they are in mourning for all virtues and all illusions. The unhappiest of the three is the lawyer. When a man seeks out the priest, he comes motivated by repentance, by remorse, by beliefs that make him interesting, that elevate him and elevate the soul of the confessor, whose task is not without a certain joy: he purifies, heals, reconciles. But we lawyers witness repeatedly the same bad emotions, nothing corrects them. Our offices are like sewers that cannot be cleaned out."
>
> (ND 100/P 3:373)

189

Derville now gives a list of horrors he has witnessed as a lawyer:

> I have seen a father die in a garret without a penny or possessions, abandoned by two daughters to whom he had given 40,000 pounds income! I have seen wills burned; I have seen mothers stripping their children of their fortunes, husbands robbing their wives, wives killing their husbands by using the love they aroused to make them mad or imbecile, in order to live in peace with a lover. . . .
>
> (ND 109/P 3:373)

The list continues, and we recognize the allusions to *Père Goriot* and *Gobseck*, as to other novels of *The Human Comedy*: *Ursule Mirouët* (the plot centers on a stolen will) and *Cousin Pons* (ditto) and *The Black Sheep* (*La Rabouilleuse*; killing a husband).

This inventory of domestic crimes—Balzac's own creations—adds resonance to Derville's following remark: "In the end, all the horrors novelists think they have invented always fall short of the truth." "All is true," we read on page one of *Père Goriot*. The novelist, like the black-robed priest, the doctor, and the lawyer, possesses a knowledge of humankind that condemns him to perpetual mourning for the loss of ideals—including those Chabert once lived for. That's what "realism" means.

"You're going to experience such lovely matters yourself," Derville tells Godeschal. "As for me, I am going to take up life in the country with my wife. Paris revolts me." Derville's longings for retirement echo Vautrin's, and throughout *The Human Comedy* the pastoral dream stands in contrast to urban existence, which is conceived to be both horrifying and seductive, a world of heightened emotion and pleasure as well as pain. Whereas provincial life appears narrow and benighted, a place for the defeated and disabused. Godeschal offers his disabused reply to Derville: "I've already seen plenty in Desroches' office."

The lawyer's office is a sewer that cannot be cleaned out, just passed on or rather sold (as, we learn in another novel, Derville sells out to Godeschal). What then is the place of Chabert's story in the novelist's study? Colonel Chabert's "destiny" unfurls the historical backdrop to the whole of *The Human Comedy*: an era of extraordinary change, of revolution, civil strife, conquest, empire, restoration, and reaction. It is a story that the present order seeks to bury in the past, or obscure with legalisms, but as the history of Colonel Chabert shows in exemplary form, this can't wholly succeed. The law may fail to reestablish his identity and his very right to exist, but as a kind of ghost he lives on, a haunting conscience to the present. Like Raphaël de Valentin, recounted in his brief, flaming trajectory between desire and death, Chabert, the specter of the suppressed past, is one of the key mythic presences in *The Human Comedy*. His life story represents more than itself.

Law, Identity, and the Nation

Balzac is supposed to have placed a statuette of Napoleon in his study, exclaiming: "What he began by the sword, I will finish with the pen!" The story may be apocryphal, but its grandiose rhetoric is apt. The military conquests of Napoleon didn't quite succeed in defining a lasting modern nation, so it is up to the novelist to complete the task, to be "the secretary of society," to bring it all into focus. The organizing principle advanced in the "Avant-Propos," or "Author's Introduction" to *The Human Comedy* is zoological: the human world is to be classified on the same principles as the animal world. "There have been, and will always be, Social Species just as there are Zoological Species," Balzac writes.[4] But there are differences: male and female animals match up easily; male and female humans are often mismatched, the wife of a merchant failing to find the prince she deserves—and so forth. Here is a large source of Balzacian drama. This mismatch of the sexes, together with the human passion for things, furnishings, accessories, those objects that define who we are, means that his social accounting will have three categories: "men, women, and things, that is to say persons and the material representation that they give to their thought: in brief, man and life." (AS liv–lv/P 1:9)

The "Author's Introduction" praises Walter Scott as the first novelist to reach for social inclusivity: to give a total portrait of the historical moment in which his various novels take place. Balzac can be said to bring the historical novel up to date: to give a total picture of the modern world. "Walter Scott raised the novel to the philosophical value of history," he writes. That judgment is important. If the story of men, women, and things is supposed to recount the social history of nineteenth-century France in the same way that Scott evokes twelfth-century England or seventeenth-century Scotland, it must go further than the historical trappings. "Philosophical" means that the novel must not just describe but understand the historical moment, and maybe history itself. Here the Philosophical Studies in *The Human Comedy* are crucial: Balzac wants to get back to the first causes of secondary effects.

Colonel Chabert's need to hire a lawyer to establish who he is, and Derville's insistence on the transactional, negotiated nature of modern identity, marks the end of an era and the beginning of a new one: a man's deeds matter less than his social reception. The novelist of the modern world, likewise, can make his way only by delving into the forces propelling the new society, in order to show both its face and its deep structure. The "Author's Introduction," written when Balzac was already well advanced in his monumental work, displays his growing consciousness of what his novels have been all about.

There are characters in *The Human Comedy* who seek to remake the social world by their individual genius, or to rise above it: Rabourdin in *The Employees* (*Les Employés*), who would completely reform the state bureaucracy, is one example, and the alchemist Balthasar Claës, the musician Gambara, and the painter Frenhofer. Then of course there is Collin, who exercises occult power over the lives of others, who aspires to the status of superman. But even he surrenders in the end. Perhaps Balzac's crazed philosopher Louis Lambert, another loner, identifies a corresponding vulnerability of the social world when he posits what he calls the "law of disorganization," according to which the more complex a society becomes, the more differentiated in role and function, the more it loses cohesion. Lambert states: "When the effect produced is no longer related to its cause, there is disorganization." That disorganization calls for heroic gestures in response, but they are doomed to succumb to social inertia.

All of modern France lies implicated in Chabert's unsuccessful struggle to say who he is. He claims a common history with his compatriots, but they now reject it. The setting sun of the Napoleonic epic leads us into a heartless modernity, a conflicted and litigious era where the lawyer is key to negotiating just about everything, including personal identity. Comes the triumph of the banal bourgeois, eternally dressed in black, though not without nostalgic reference to the glorious past. You don't want that past—the "abyss of revolutions," as King Louis XVIII called it, must be shut down—but it is nonetheless there, knocking at the door of modernity. In scarcely over a hundred pages—this is one of Balzac's most spare and effective works—*Colonel Chabert* gives a biography, marked by the pathos of history, that stands for far more than the single life story.

9. Marco Facino Cane
(1738–1820) *and Friend*

Hidden Dramas

To enter into the lives of others: in some deep sense that must be the very motive for writing novels. Balzac's tale *Facino Cane* puts that motive front and center. Facino Cane's story, like Henriette de Mortsauf's, is told to us by another person, though the way the narrator comes by the story and the demands it makes on the reader are quite different. The narrator is as central to the story as Facino himself. What's more, he is a writer, who lived as an impoverished young man on the rue de Lesdiguières, an obscure street near the Bastille (as did the young Balzac), in the working-class district of Paris known as the Faubourg Saint-Antoine, a neighborhood that has been a "seedbed of revolutions."[1] "A passion for knowledge had thrown me into a garret room where I worked nights, and I would spend the day in a nearby library established by Monsieur, the King's brother," he tells us of those early years. (NY 3/P 6:1019) But his studies at the library, whatever they may have been, were not the true focus of his attention. Instead, "I would walk about observing the customs of the neighborhood, its inhabitants and their character," and this practice of observation is by no means casual: "observation had already become an intuitive habit; it would penetrate into the soul without neglecting the body, or rather, so thoroughly did it grasp the external details that it moved immediately beyond. It allowed me to live a person's life, let me put myself in his place, the way a dervish in *The Arabian Nights* would take over a person's body and soul by pronouncing certain words over him."

In Balzac, *The Arabian Nights* is always a touchstone for something extraordinary, magical, beyond the banal real, and at the start of *Facino Cane* we sense that the novelist is telling of his very novelistic practice. We see his faculty of observation doing its visionary work. The narrator follows a couple on their way back from the Théâtre de l'Ambigu-Comique, which specialized in melodrama and vaudeville. They speak of the play they have seen, of work, of difficult bosses, of the long winter and the high cost of potatoes and peat; they argue heatedly about their debt to the baker. The narrator zooms in: "I could join in their lives: I would feel their rags on my back, I would be walking in their tattered shoes; their longings, their needs would all move through my soul, or my soul through theirs." (NY 4/P 6:1020)

The young writer demonstrates powers that are comparable to Jacques Collin's, if less sinister. Living through others takes on a metaphysical quality: "Dropping my own habits, becoming another person through a kind of intoxication of my imaginative faculties, and playing the game at will—that was my delight. To what do I owe this gift? Is it some second sight? One of those talents whose overuse could lead to madness? I have never looked into the sources of this capacity—I have it and I use it, that's all."

Balzac was haunted by the notion that his powers of penetration and of creation encroached on those of God; that they constituted an "abuse" that could lead to madness, and as we've seen, *The Human Comedy* is full of monomaniacs—the philosopher Louis Lambert, the painter Frenhofer, the chemist-alchemist Balthasar Claës, the baffled musician Gambara—who go over the edge of madness. But the young impecunious student of *Facino Cane* was still testing his powers, fascinated by the "hidden dramas" of his working-class neighbors, "tragic and comic, masterpieces born of chance." (NY 5/P 6:1020) The man he has become now offers to pull one of those stories out of "the sack of memory," a story that starts with his revisiting that old neighborhood (he's moved out and up, we assume) to attend the wedding of his sometime maid's sister. The festivities take place in a wine warehouse, a shabby hall where the poor but animated crowd is being entertained by three blind musicians from the Quinze-Vingts hospice.

It is the clarinetist who impresses him: "My curiosity was roused to the highest pitch, my soul crossed over into the body of the clarinetist." (NY 6/P 6:1022) His face resembles "Dante's plaster death mask," its magnificence heightened by the dead eyes that are none-theless "alive with the mind's energy." It is the face of an "old Homer who harbored within himself an Odyssey consigned to oblivion," the young man decides, and during a pause in the music he approaches the clarinetist to ask where he comes from. (NY 7/P 6:1023) Venice, he learns, and further that the old man is eighty-two and has been blind for fifty of those years. His companions jokingly refer to him as "the doge," and in response he proudly names himself as "Marco Facino Cane, Prince of Varese"—a Venetian patrician, eligible for election as doge, descended from the famous condottiere, soldier of fortune, Facino Cane, who fled the wrath of the Visconti in Milan and settled in the Republic of Venice, since extinguished by Napoleon's conquest. "He made a frightening gesture—of patriotism long dead and of disgust for human affairs," as it is interpreted by this preternaturally perceptive narrator. (NY 9/P 6:1024). Sniffing out the narrator's interest, Facino Cane stops playing. "Let's leave," he says, his words "like an electric shower" to the narrator. Outside, sitting by the moats next to the Bastille, he urgently demands that the young man take him to Venice, where he will make him "richer than the ten richest houses in Amsterdam or London, richer than the Rothschilds, yes, rich as in *The Thousand and One Nights*."

Facino's Golden Vision

Facino tells his life story. It is a picaresque tale of love, combat, prison and escape, riches, then blindness and destitution. He courts eighteen-year-old Bianca, who is married to a rich senator, strangles her husband, flees to Milan (with a few diamonds and five rolled-up Titians to pay his way), before returning to Bianca, now the inamorata of a state official, the provveditore, who, on surprising the couple, summons his sidekicks to escort Facino to a dungeon, one of the underground *pozzi*, originally cisterns, beneath the ducal palace. What next? Facino has a special power, he has explained: he can smell gold. Even now that he is blind, a jeweler's shop will stop him in his tracks. In the dungeon, he discovers an Arabic inscription directing him to a tunnel that an earlier inmate had begun but did not finish. Facino begins to dig with the hilt of his sword, works at extending the tunnel, sensing, seeing even, that gold lies ahead. And indeed, when he finally penetrates a wooden wall at the far end of the tunnel, he discovers that he has found his way into the secret treasury of the Republic; the doge himself is there, with a member of the Council of Ten, inspecting the vault's contents. He bribes his jailer with promises of unimaginable riches—together they will load them on a ship bound for Smyrna—and there Bianca will join him.

> In a single night, the hole was cut larger, and we descended into the secret treasury. What a night! I saw four full bins of gold; in the anteroom, silver was stacked in two great piles, with a pathway between for crossing the room, and the coins stood five feet high against the walls.... In his joy, [the jailer] failed at first to notice a table piled with diamonds. I threw myself on them nimbly enough to load up my sailor's smock and my trouser pockets. Good Lord! And I didn't even take a third of what was there....
>
> (NY 13/P 6:1029)

After transporting a mere two thousand pounds of gold to the waiting gondola, they are off. In Smyrna they transfer to a new ship, bound for France, and the jailer falls overboard and is drowned, leaving Facino in full possession of the loot, though without the accomplice who could later have led him back to the treasury. He sells his diamonds and converts his ingots into coin, lies low in Madrid, leads a "dazzling" existence in Paris—and is stricken blind. He tells his listener (that is, the narrator): "I am convinced that the affliction is the consequence of my time in the dungeon, my work digging the tunnel—unless my capacity to see gold somehow was

an abuse of the visual faculty that predestined me to lose my sight."
(NY 15/P 6:1030)

Here we sense a parallel: Facino's conviction that his power to
"see" gold has blinded him sounds very much like the narrator's fear
that his preternatural insight into the lives of others, allowing him
passage into their very bodies and souls, may be an abuse of his
mental faculties—the word "*abus*" is used in both these instances.
Blindness and madness punish the hubris of the man who possesses
and employs a faculty for knowledge not given to other men.

Facino now has a French mistress who takes him to see a famous
oculist in London—each episode in his tale involves a geographical
dislocation—but then strips him of his riches and abandons him in
Hyde Park. With the coming of the French Revolution, he is committed to the hospice in which he lives still, pining to return to
Venice, believing that now the Republic of Venice is no more, he
may be pardoned and free to return again to the secret treasury. Of
course, without his accomplice the jailer he doesn't know which was
his cell. But no matter, he tells his listener, come with me to Venice,
I will see the gold through the prison walls, I will sense it beneath
the waters of the canal. He earlier had tried to persuade Napoleon
to help him, the Austrian Emperor as well. Both dismissed him as
a madman. So he ends his narration with a renewed plea to his listener: "Come now, let us leave for Venice. We leave as beggars and
we'll return as princes! We'll buy back my properties and you will
be my heir, the Prince of Varese!" (NY 15/P 6:1031)

The narrator of Balzac's story, having listened to Facino's story,
is confronted with a demand for action. As in *Gobseck* and *The Fatal
Skin* and *The Lily of the Valley* and a number of other novels, Balzac
embeds tales within tales in a way that highlights the listener as well

as the teller. How the listener responds makes all the difference: that is the test of the truth and power of the tale. Here, the result is unclear. The listener, the narrator, is "dazzled" by what Facino has recounted. "I gazed at the sight of his white head, and there before the dark water of the Bastille moats, water as still as that in the Venice canals, I had no answer." The image juxtaposes the moats around the ruins of the Bastille fortress and the canals of Venice, their dark waters reflecting the different fortunes of two different political realms, two possible realities that are never resolved. Facino responds to the narrator's silence with a "gesture that evoked all the philosophy of despair"—like that frightening gesture that attracted the young man's attention earlier, and so many other gestures in Balzac that carry a freight of meaning far beyond what gesture can actually perform. Facino picks up his clarinet and plays a Venetian barcarolle, "ultimate prayer of the exile, the last longing for a lost name." The narrator's eyes fill with tears. Facino speaks again:

> "That treasure-house," he whispered. "I can still see it, bright as a dream. I'm strolling through it, the diamonds sparkle, I am not so blind as you think: gold and diamonds light my night, the night of the last Facino Cane—for my title will pass to the Memmi clan. Ah Lord! The murderer's punishment has begun so very early! Ave Maria…"
>
> (NY 16/P 6:1031)

"We'll go to Venice!" the narrator now cries. "'So I have found a man!' Facino exclaims, his face aflame." The narrator leads him back to the entrance of the Quinze-Vingts; Facino wants to know if they will leave tomorrow. "As soon as we put together some money," the narrator tells him. But we can beg along the way, Facino replies. "I am robust, and you're young when you see gold ahead." And then the story ends: "Facino Cane died during the winter, after a two-month illness. The poor man had suffered a bad cold." (NY 16/P 6:1031)

Are we to believe the narrator really meant to go to Venice? Is he speaking in good faith, or is he merely humoring the old man? Has he been overpowered by Facino's dazzling tale—or perhaps his own power to enter into others' ways of seeing? Is he himself like the gold that lights up Facino's darkness? Without giving any indication of what the narrator's response means, the tale ends, leaving us in suspense. It is an ambiguous conclusion that puts the reader on the spot: What are we to believe about this story, these storytellers? How does the tale and its telling matter to us? Balzac dramatizes forcefully the question intrinsic to any storytelling: Do we believe it? What's its point? What are we supposed to do with it? What kind of action does it call for?

Balzac is always concerned with the power of storytelling and the outcomes it can produce. So many of his tales and novels are about people telling stories to each other, as much about that social exchange as they are about the stories told. Listeners are spurred to real-life action in response to fictions. Stories may be used to seduce, as in the novella *Sarrasine*, as also in *The Lily of the Valley*, though that attempt can often backfire. Yet Balzac himself succeeded in a kind of seduction by writing of the elusive Evelina Hanska. When it came to his readership, persuasion through storytelling was also crucial to success, and at the same time a problem that he dramatizes repeatedly.

Social Pathology

But Balzac's ambitions did not stop at the seductions of storytelling. He wanted not only to hold his readers in thrall but also to explain pretty much the whole world. He claims in his 1842 "Author's Introduction" to *The Human Comedy* to be a mere "secretary," that the true author of the work is French society itself. And then he lays out the three large categories of *The Human Comedy*, the Studies of Manners, the Philosophical Studies, and the Analytic Studies, claiming that in a series they will move from social effects to their underlying causes. He sets out to

> discover the meaning hidden in this immense assemblage of figures, passions, and events. Finally, after searching, if not finding, this reason, this social motor, didn't I need to reflect on natural principles to see how societies fall away from or come close to the eternal principle of the true and the beautiful? Despite the extent of these premises, which could have constituted a book of their own, for my work to be complete it needed a conclusion. Thus represented, Society should carry within it the reason of its movement.[2]

I don't find this wholly coherent, and the *Études analytiques* are the least realized, most fragmentary part of *The Human Comedy*. It is clear, however, that above and beyond the social dramas that are the stuff of most novels, Balzac wanted to arrive at a theory of social life. And his stories about storytelling, and reactions to the story told, are part of the endeavor to get at motivations, rounded out by Analytic Studies of how social institutions function: *Physiology of Marriage*, *Little Miseries of Conjugal Life*, and, most important, *Pathology of Social Life* (*Pathologie de la vie sociale*). The title may remind us of Freud's *Psychopathology of Everyday Life*, in which he set out to study the psychic meanings of slips of the tongue and other "parapraxes." Freud's famous lines from his case history of his patient "Dora" might, for instance, be uttered by the young narrator of *Facino Cane*, or by his creator: "He that has eyes to see and ears to hear may convince himself that no mortal can keep a secret. If his lips are silent, he chatters with his fingertips; betrayal oozes out of him at every pore. And thus the task of making conscious the most hidden recesses of the mind is one which it is quite possible to accomplish."[3] Facino's vision of vast riches and the novelist's vision of the motives of human behavior are both attuned to the hidden, the dramatic, that, like Freud's analyses, suggest an erotic charge that animates the world. They may speak also of a power beyond what is permitted to humankind.

Balzac's theory of social life is at heart a semiotics of social life. His *Pathology of Social Life* survives in three fragments: *Treatise on Elegant Living* (*Traité de la vie élégante*), *Theory of Movement* (*Théorie de la démarche*), and *Treatise of Modern Stimulants* (*Traité des excitants modernes*). There are also several very interesting short journalistic pieces, written around 1830, that seem to belong to the project of the *Pathology*, though it's not always clear whether these are by Balzac or someone else, or possibly collaborations.[4] The problem, as he often states it, is that in the boring, bourgeois nineteenth century, everyone looks alike. Destroying traditional privileges and distinctions, the Revolution democratized appearances. Everyone wears black and carries a top hat (not true for workingmen of course, but Balzac is primarily interested in gentility and the upwardly mobile). So what then can serve as a sign of individual distinction? Balzac's "Author's Introduction" describes his great work as a history of men, women, and things, and things are crucial: the knot in one's cravat, the knob of a cane, the buttons of cuff links, the cut of a coat, the shine on one's boots, the whole world of "necessary superfluities" that Lucien de Rubempré discovers during his first promenade in the Tuileries Garden, after his arrival from Angoulême.[5] It is in acquiring things that a person fashions a necessary self for himself and the world at large. This is why Rastignac's and Lucien's tailor thinks of himself as a "hyphen" between a young man's present and his future. Given the right outfit, a young man may be able to make a marriage that will put a reality behind his social appearance. This transactional reality explains why Henri de Marsay, who spends hours at his morning toilette, is a dominant presence throughout *The Human Comedy*. He seeks and achieves distinction.

The dandy's self-presentation is the height of deliberation; other people reveal themselves less artfully or more unwittingly. How people reveal themselves is the central concern of Balzac's social pathology. I noted earlier that he described his *Treatise on Elegant Living* as "the metaphysics of things," metaphysics because things are always signs of something beyond their physical presence.[6] I mentioned the pre–Sherlock Holmes premises of *A Study of Manners by Way of Gloves* (possibly not by Balzac himself though thoroughly like him in thought and style), where late one evening the Countess examines the gloves of all the men in her circle and tells each what he has been doing over the past hours. Balzac's semiotics is all about detection, the need to discover who people really are.[7]

In a similar spirit, his printshop produced *Petit Dictionnaire critique et anecdotique des enseignes de Paris* (Little Critical and Anecdotic Dictionary of the Shopsigns of Paris), to which he probably contributed as writer, which attempts to read the cityscape in an intelligible, organized way. There is a similar endeavor at the start of *Ferragus*, the first novella of *Story of the Thirteen*, which the narrator begins with a moral "physiognomy" of Parisian streets, as I mentioned in chapter one. Balzac writes that there are:

> streets that are dishonored as much as a man branded with infamy; then there are also noble streets, then those that are simply honest, then young streets on whose morality the public hasn't yet formed an opinion; then murderous streets, streets older than old dowagers are old, estimable streets, streets that are always clean, streets that are always dirty, working-class streets, busy streets, mercantile streets. That's to say that the streets of Paris have human qualities and impress on us by their physiognomy certain ideas that we cannot resist. . . .[8]

And so the passage goes on. In such Balzacian "physiognomies," often published as sketches in periodicals and then slotted into his fiction, we move from a simple naming of characteristics to something that verges on allegory: appearances conceal, or reveal to the trained eye, a world of "ideas." The *Pathology of Social Life* meant to provide a key to appearances, to the look of things—particularly city things, streets and houses and passersby—to the affect and idea that they create in the eye of the observer. Objects become signs to be read. But the Balzacian observer is rarely content with a simple or literal reading: he needs to see behind the surface, where there is always something more to be found. Balzac's world, like Freud's, is one where everything is symptomatic and interpretation is endless.

Central to the *Pathology of Social Life* is the curious *Theory of Movement*. Much of this text presents a satiric account of precisely how contemporary men and women walk and move, an analysis of the human gait (a term in English more often applied to horses), a kind of "physiognomy of the body," but then it goes beyond that, seeking to comprehend the overall meaning in human movement. Movement becomes the outward projection of an inner force:

> For me, from then on, MOVEMENT included Thought, the purest action of human beings; the Word, translation of their thoughts; and then Gait and Gesture, the more or less impassioned accomplishment of the Word.... From the transformations of thought in the voice, which is the touch by which the soul acts most spontaneously, derive the miracles of eloquence, the heavenly enrichments of vocal music. Is not the word in some manner the gait of the Heart and the brain!
>
> Thus, Gait being understood as the expression of corporal movements, and voice as that of intellectual movements, it seemed to me impossible for movement to lie. In this respect, the deep understanding of Gait became a complete science.[9]

Like some of Freud's interpretations, this appears close to sheer madness. In Balzac, the psychological and the sociological, along with his very peculiar sense of the spiritual, interpenetrate each other in a way that offers a comprehensive, if always only suggestive, theory of everything, tempting us with a visionary solution, while equally— because everything is fluid and in question—leaving everything, all final meanings, in suspense.

The *Theory of Movement* belongs to Balzac's repertory of pseudosciences, to be sure, but one that is integral to his work as a novelist. The writer is always busy reading his characters' movements and gestures, from Facino Cane's "frightening gesture of extinguished patriotism and disgust for human affairs" to the elegant woman in *Another Study of Womankind*, who "lets her hand droop, hanging over the arm of a chair, like dewdrops on the rim of a flower, and with this everything has been said, she has pronounced an unappealable judgment...."[10] Or to give another example, also from *Another Study of Womankind*: "an indescribable gesture escaped the young woman, expressing at once her evident irritation at seeing her dependence so openly displayed, with no trace of respect for her autonomy, and the offense done to her womanly dignity or to her husband. But there was also, in her clenched features, in her darkened brow, a sort of foreboding. Perhaps she had foreseen her fate." (NY 52/P 3:707) In that observed but "indescribable gesture" lies rich semiotic potential, opening to the novelist the whole story of a life and the problem of "destiny." And here again Balzac is close to Freud.

The Lives of Others

Questions of the type that the young narrator of *Facino Cane* poses to the old blind musician—essentially: Who are you?—get their answer in the form of an individual's life story. The narrator saves Facino's story from oblivion, passing it on to us that we may grasp its ambitions and feel its pathos. And yet that narrator, alert to the stories buried within people, ends with a dead Facino. It's as if the power of entering the lives of others in order to tell their stories might be not only an "abuse" for the storyteller but also mortal for its subject. Telling stories may, in the manner of the fatal skin, both fulfill and deplete you. One more tale calls for comment since it addresses the power and the impotence of storytelling directly: the novella *Adieu*.

Two men, Colonel Philippe de Sucy and his friend the Marquis d'Albon, are hunting in the woods when they are surprised to discover a ruined abbey, like the castle of Sleeping Beauty (in French, *La Belle au bois dormant*). They are even more astonished to find two feral women running around outdoors, half naked and unable to speak, in one of whom Philippe recognizes his long-lost love, the Comtesse Stéphanie de Vandières. Philippe faints, falling stricken to the ground; his life is thought to be in danger. When he recovers, however, he dispatches the Marquis to find out how it is that his cherished Stéphanie has been reduced to the state she is in.

The Marquis returns to the abbey, where he encounters Stéphanie's uncle, a doctor, who cares for her but cannot cure her, and the uncle now tells him the story that explains not only her condition but also Philippe's shock. Napoleon's retreat from Moscow in 1812 reached a tragic denouement in the disastrous crossing the Berezina River. Philippe was there, as was Stéphanie, evidently his mistress, and her husband, the Comte, among the freezing remnants of the French army. The French set the bridge over the river afire to prevent the passage of the Cossacks, so Philippe labors heroically to build a raft to make the crossing. But the raft is soon overloaded; Philippe must remain behind. "Adieu," his lover bids him. As the raft makes shuddering contact with the far bank, the Comte is thrown overboard; an ice floe decapitates him. Philippe hears Stéphanie calling "Adieu!" Then he falls to his knees, frozen with horror, exhausted, defeated; he is captured and sent to Siberia. Stéphanie has gone mad, she becomes the degraded "plaything" of the retreating French army.

Once her uncle has told the horrendous story of Stéphanie's traumatic experience, Philippe decides he will cure her, hoping not only to restore her to her senses but also to resume the course of their love, picking up where it left off. He is determined that she shall recognize him—we sense the narcissism in this project—but he fails over and over again. So he conceives a truly radical therapy. Leaving Stéphanie with her uncle, he retreats to his estate outside of Paris and goes to work to re-create the scene of the Berezina crossing, in order to restage the original traumatic moment. He ravages the grounds of his estate, builds and then burns a bridge over a river, creates a ruined army camp, hires peasants whom he dresses as French soldiers and Cossacks. One day it snows, and looking at his work he "recognizes" the Berezina, faithfully reproduced. Stéphanie is drugged with opium, dressed in the clothes she wore during the Russian campaign, put into a carriage, and brought to the riverbank as the Cossacks unleash their war cry and descend on the remnants of the French army. Now memory and intelligence flare up like a living flame within her. She recognizes the scene; she recognizes Philippe. She falls into his arms, she speaks: "Adieu, Philippe. I love you. Adieu!"—and then she dies.[11] The therapy has been all too successful: it has reanimated the spiritually dead Stéphanie and in the process killed her. The attempt to restore Stéphanie's "reason," to reattach her life to her past biography and continue that life as Philippe's partner, fails dramatically. Before the attempted cure she was not unhappy, her uncle points out: she simply did not conform to Philippe's desire that she behave as a conventional woman and lover. The radical reformation of another's life appears another of those attempts to usurp a kind of divine power. It's possibly, in the manner of *Facino Cane*, one more allegory of the novelist: the abuse of the power to enter others' lives, to animate them and tell their stories, leads to disaster. Humans have to be accorded a greater freedom, perhaps, even when that freedom means nonconformity to human definitions of reason and relationship.

Balzac may in *Adieu* have been inspired by the "dramaturgical" therapies of the remarkable contemporary psychiatrist Philippe Pinel—who tried to bring his patients back to the scene of trauma in order to cure them—but the outcome imagined by Balzac is dire.[12] Is this what happens when the "intoxication" of the imaginative faculties described by the narrator of *Facino Cane* leads to more than an imaginative interference in the lives of others? The intervention of the narrator in Facino's life seems benign in comparison with Philippe's in Stéphanie's: he promises a cure but that costs her life. That's too high a price to pay for the rewriting of someone's life plot. And if Philippe sees his intentions as noble and disinterested, we may suspect that his need to restore Stéphanie responds to selfish and possessive motives as well: to his need for recognition and response from "his" woman.

Stéphanie's revival at the end of *Adieu* has always reminded me of the ending of Shakespeare's *Winter's Tale*, where Hermione, thought to have died as the result of her husband Leontes's insane jealous rage, reappears as a statue that then is brought to life by Paulina as Leontes watches. As she descends from her pedestal and enters his embrace, Leontes cries out: "O, she's warm! / If this be magic, let it be an art / Lawful as eating." Hermione's restoration, then, is white magic, lawful magic, and in fact no magic at all but the result of Paulina's scheme to protect, preserve, and then restore her to a Leontes who himself has undergone a long and painful cure of his madness. Stéphanie's case is less benign and Philippe's motives less pure. Unlike the redemption staged at the end of *The Winter's Tale* and other Shakespearean romances, the climax of *Adieu* gives us an intervention in the order of things that brings retribution: a dramatic and indeed theatrical success that costs too much. The tale ends by recounting Philippe's suicide.

In *Adieu*, in *Facino Cane*, as in *Colonel Chabert*, *The Duchesse de Langeais*, *The Lily of the Valley*, and *The Fatal Skin*, there are personal stories that others need to hear, to understand, to react to. With Stéphanie, as with Chabert and Antoinette de Langeais and Henriette de Mortsauf, principal characters have in differing degrees been deprived of speech; they cannot speak for themselves publicly; their identities have been obscured. Narrators and the novelist must attempt to uncover or disinter their identities through telling their stories. The lives of others demand our attention. We come back to Balzac's obsession with vicarious life, living by or delegation through another, given its fullest exposition by Collin, when as Carlos Herrera he cruises Lucien at the end of *Lost Illusions*. Collin's attempts at shaping the lives of his protégés, and eventually the very history of his time, points both to the joy of narrative creation and the absence of any governing story in the lives of Balzac's time. Following the fall of Napoleon, there is no one story that binds everyone together; there is not even a single nation but a conflict to say to whom France belongs. The Restoration failed to produce a principle of authority, and provoked another revolution instead. The collective life of France lacks cohesion, and for Balzac that's the story to be told: the proliferation of individuals struggling to impose themselves, like those spiders in a jar evoked by Vautrin in counseling Rastignac. Justice, love, literature, political mastery—all are up for grabs in a struggle with uncertain outcomes. Louis Lambert's "law of disorganization" calls for an organizing gesture in response. The only place you find it is in writing a book that competes with the civil registry, a book that memorializes a chaotic society by bringing together its diverse narratives. And by attempting to explain everything, even as it recognizes that this is impossible since the very principles of explanation are themselves obscure. Balzac necessarily ends up like Scheherazade, telling stories night after night to stave off the silence of the end.

Like Collin, Balzac wants to recognize the realities of his moment; also like Collin, he wants to create a new reality. In Collin's final capitulation to the world as it is, Balzac may recognize the impossibility of his own totalizing project, a *Human Comedy* destined to remain always incomplete but nonetheless compelling for that. He goes on making up characters and stories without end, stories very often about the telling of stories and their effect on others. In "the long prison of his labor," as Henry James described it, Balzac lived through those lives he created. Fulfillment lies in experiencing life and riches and love through your imaginary beings. Each of these beings of any importance (and even many of very little importance) must be endowed with a biography, a life story that explains how he or she happens to be there where they are at the present moment. The crossing of paths in Balzac's fictions may appear to be a matter of coincidence but usually is deeply motivated, as Georg Lukács maintained.[13] A certain life history has brought you to a place—on the banks of the Charente River, at the gates of Sleeping Beauty's castle —where another life history has brought someone else. The intersection of the two lives then carries a sense of shock and destiny.

In his *Theory of Movement* Balzac quotes Virgil: "*Et vera incessu patuit dea*"—"the goddess reveals herself by her gait," we might translate. (OD 1:263) That revelation of character in its movement and action is what narrative fiction is all about, and at the heart of Balzac's understanding of humans as interactive social beings. Henry

James in "The Lesson of Balzac" praised his precursor for giving his characters "the long rope," for acting themselves out. That grant of freedom to his created life was for James crucial to Balzac's success in representation of persons in the world. James saw Balzac's creation of character as ultimately motivated by love: "The love, as we call it, the joy in their communicated and exhibited movement, in their standing on their feet and going of themselves and acting out their characters.... He at all events robustly loved the sense of another explored, assumed, assimilated identity...."[14] James concludes this discussion by claiming: "It all comes back, in fine, to that respect for the liberty of the subject which I should be willing to name as the great sign of the painter of the first order."

Facino Cane and *Adieu*, like *Colonel Chabert* and *The Lily of the Valley* and *The Duchesse de Langeais* in radically different ways, speak to the question of the "liberty of the subject," the respect accorded— or not—to the lives of others. They suggest both the joy of entering into other lives and the possibly dire consequences of assuming responsibility for another life. Perhaps most of all they point to the exuberance of Balzac's creation of fictive persons along with his acute self-consciousness about such acts of creation. There is nothing simple, nothing given about creating the lives of others. An abuse of the capacity to do so may lead you to madness. Your attempt to restore the inert to life may be death-dealing as well as life-giving. The creator of fictional lives needs to account for what he is doing.

10. Living in Fictional Lives

The only real people are the people who never existed.
—OSCAR WILDE

Other Eyes

THERE IS A MOMENT in Marcel Proust's *In Search of Lost Time* when the narrator, listening to the triumphal septet of his fictional composer Vinteuil, unfolds a lyric passage in praise of Vinteuil and also the fictional painter Elstir:

> A pair of wings, a different respiratory system, that enabled us to travel through space, wouldn't help us at all. For if we visited Mars or Venus while keeping the same senses, they would clothe everything we could see in the same aspect as the things of Earth. The only true voyage, the only bath in the Fountain of Youth, would be not to visit strange lands but to possess other eyes, to see the universe through the eyes of another, of a hundred others, to see the hundred universes that each of them sees, that each of them is; and this we can do with an Elstir, a Vinteuil; with such as them we do really fly from star to star.[1]

To possess other eyes, to see the universe through the eyes of another, of a hundred others: this I think captures our love of and our need for novels, for fictional accounts of the world that let us experience it beyond the limits of our own pair of eyes, to imagine it, provisionally, as it is seen and felt by someone else, however different that person may be. Balzac seems to have felt this love and this need more than most, and surely he is the novelist who invented the greatest number and variety of other eyes.

What does it mean to have imagined and created so many lives and ways of seeing life? Madness, as we have seen, threatens some of Balzac's visionaries, as if the act of creation were inseparable from transgression, a usurpation of divine power that must and will be punished. Facino Cane is stricken blind; Frenhofer completes a canvas that is completely illegible to anyone else; Claës dies ruined and in despair. Collin, in contrast, succeeds in living vicariously through the lives of others, his protégés and proxies, Rastignac and Lucien de Rubempré, at least for a time. Rastignac, having learned from him, pursues a compromise path of his own, and *Père Goriot* sends Vautrin/Collin to prison. But Balzac brings him back for the finale of *Lost Illusions*, and provides him with a new pupil, Lucien, with whom his relationship is one of both mastery and surrender. Lucien is beautiful; he appears in society and makes good in its upper echelons, he has sex with women, all subject to Collin's will. There is something sadomasochistic about the relation between creature and creator, most obvious in the way the pleasure Lucien takes in the adoring and submissive Esther is matched by Collin's pleasure in taking her away from him. We are never told that actual sex takes place between Collin and Lucien, but a sexual dynamic is always present. Yet sex in Balzac, as I've suggested, is a zero-sum game that uses a man up, just as Raphaël's magic skin shrinks and shrinks. If pleasure is not to result in blindness, exhaustion, or death, it must be like Gobseck's, like the antiques dealer's who gave Raphaël the skin, like Collin's, vicarious and voyeuristic. Collin's ultimate position as the chief of the investigative police makes of him society's chief voyeur, analogous to Raphaël hiding in Fœdora's bedroom to see her undress. Desire in Balzac can be brutal: Rastignac wants to devour the world. Montriveau can imagine his relation to the Duchesse de Langeais only in terms of domination and submission, which in the end marks a failure of what might have been true love. Everywhere in Balzac desire is an urge to find out, to know (Freud's epistemophilia), which is to say that the drive to know is itself sexualized. The novelist, the man who sees through other eyes, may know the deepest pleasure of all—but knows it as fictional.

Balzac, like a number of the characters in *Lost Illusions* and other novels, was of course a professional writer determined to make a living by his pen in a world where literature was becoming a commodity and its production something of an industry, and his vast production of fictions was a response to the market, an effort to climb out of debt and attain a life of luxury. But still. Other novelists who met the demands of the emerging mass market—Alexandre Dumas, Eugène Sue, George Sand—are not so profligate in the creation of characters. The only contemporary analogue is Charles Dickens, who will likewise be able to pull new characters out of a hat as needed for his stories, though Dickens's minor characters, known through their repeated tics, are more caricatural than Balzac's. The least of Balzac's characters is given a whole life.

Was Balzac's profligate creation a compensation for his "real life," a fantasy world in which he escaped from, or triumphed over, a cash-strapped and love-deprived existence? Maybe, and yet we know if only from our daydreams that we are all creatures of fantasy and fiction, poets and novelists of our own lives, coping with the restrictions and limitations of our brief time on earth through made-up stories of all sorts. As Wallace Stevens writes in his "Notes Toward a Supreme Fiction:"

> From this the poem springs, that we live in a world
> That is not our own, and, much more, not ourselves
> And hard it is in spite of blazoned days.

Through fictions, we accommodate ourselves to a world that is not ours, much less ourselves. As psychoanalysts and child psychologists confirm, we cannot cope with reality without made-up stories.

Fictional Characters

I have talked about Balzac's characters as though they were real people, substantial enough to be points of reference in our understanding of the world. That's how traditional novels work, at least when they are successful. Lucien or Gobseck mean something to us as possible people, and there are many anecdotes that show Balzac understood his characters as alive. At the same time, we know that these characters are "really" just printed words on a page, conjuring up a human perspective and voice, the simulacrum of a human being. How do we get from the book to this illusion of a person?

I find myself led back to Proust again, to a moment where the young Marcel is reading in the garden at Combray, and the narrator speaks of the nature of character in fiction. Real people, he claims, are opaque to us; in order to think, feel, see through others, we instead need an *image* of the real:

> all the feelings we are made to experience by the joy or the misfortune of a real person are produced in us only through the intermediary of an image of that joy or that misfortune; the ingeniousness of the first novelist consisted in understanding that in the apparatus of our emotions, the image being the only essential element, the simplification that would consist in purely and simply abolishing real people would be a decisive improvement. A real human being, however profoundly we sympathize with him, is in large part perceived by our senses, that is to say, remains opaque, presents a dead weight which our sensibility cannot lift....

That putative "first novelist" understood that real human beings offer a diminished sense of reality because they are known by way of the senses; only through the fictional being—what Proust calls the "image"—can we grasp the real. He continues:

> The novelist's happy discovery was to have the idea of replacing these parts [of real persons], impenetrable to the soul, by an equal quantity of immaterial parts, that is to say, parts which our soul can assimilate. What does it matter thenceforth if the actions, and the emotions, of this new order of creatures seem to us true, since we have made them ours, since it is within us that they occur, that they hold within their control, as we feverishly turn the pages of the book, the rapidity of our breathing and the intensity of our gaze.[2]

Once these fictions inhabit us, the narrator goes on to say, they trouble us like dreams, but are more lucid than dreams; by virtue of them, we will learn in a couple of hours what might otherwise take many years—or we might never learn, since the profound changes of life take place too slowly for us to perceive them. The heart changes in life; that brings our worst sorrow; but it is only through reading that we understand the processes of change. Experience is transformed into knowledge.

Proust gives here an apologia for the fictional person as cognitive instrument, an optics that lets us read the meanings of temporal change in ways that are closed to us in life. Walter Benjamin in his great essay "The Storyteller" claims that we seek in fiction the knowledge of the meaning of life that is foreclosed to the living because it is completed only in death.[3] Proust goes further in claiming that the fictional person is an essential instrument in this process of acquiring knowledge. The critic Catherine Gallagher makes a similar argument: that the very fictionality of the novelistic person is a necessary correlate of that person's capacity to represent the real for us.[4] It's that "representation" that counts, that provides a kind of mental knowledge of the real that real people don't give us. Proust's imagined "first novelist" enables us to see the world around us transformed through a vision by way of other eyes. Once these other eyes have taken over, they are in control, and our ordinary selves become merely virtual. Proust's concern with seeing the world through the eyes of others leads him in the late pages of *Time Regained* to state: "In reality, each reader is when he reads the very reader of himself. The work of the writer is only a kind of optical instrument that he offers the reader in order to allow him to discern what, without this book, he might not have seen in himself."[5]

Balzac knew intuitively the need for invented persons to represent life for us, with an enhanced sense of the odds and stakes of life. Representation for Balzac always touched on the theatrical, offering life bathed in starker, more revealing light. We see better our represented than our real selves. Rastignac, Lucien, all the characters whose stories I've told here represent in full, dramatic fashion what it might mean to live, love, gamble, and die in ways that we cannot experience for ourselves. Their lives are exemplary ways of being. Fictional characters give us as-if experiments in knowing the world.

Character in fiction is very much a part of Proust's "optical instrument." Recently, some literary critics, drawing on cognitive neuroscience, have suggested that fictional characters, by enhancing our skill at mind reading, or "theory of mind," contribute to social survival by allowing us to understand what others are thinking.[6] Learning to read what's going on in *Pride and Prejudice* or *Middlemarch* both mimics and enhances our real-life social skills, as some research has suggested. Readers of novels have long known that in engaging with fictional characters we improve our ability to scrutinize and decipher other people, their motives, intentions, self-deceptions, false hopes, secret ambitions, and hidden desires. Balzac's characters offer rich material for such investigations, but their dimensions are larger than (to use the favorite example in English literature) Jane Austen's, not least because they are so engaged in the life of their time, learning the skills to survive in a new and troubled social space, defining their identity within historical realities. Deciphering character in Balzac may involve less subtle social inferences than in Austen. But it demands greater historical and sociological context and vision.

Talking about characters in fiction as if they had "real" biographies isn't in good critical repute, and hasn't been for a long time. It seems naive, even delusive, and the work of formalists, starting with the remarkable critics known as the Russian formalists, and then the American New Critics and French structuralists, has taught us to think of literary characters as literary devices and formal codes. For Roland Barthes, character was a kind of semantic illusion, a crossroads where different narrative codes, literary and cultural and perhaps historical, came together and were baptized with a proper name. Yet this formalist notion of character as coded really matches the account of social anthropologists such as Erving Goffman, who understand society as coded.[7] To read Austen or George Eliot or Balzac with this in mind is to discern how the great novelists of the nineteenth and twentieth centuries have taught us to understand other minds and their social interactions. Cognitive psychologists have confirmed what we already knew: that readers of complex novels show a greater capacity for understanding the complexities of human interaction.[8]

The Outer and Inner Lives

Still, what is it about Balzac that drove him to invent so many characters, that made him project himself into so many other selves and stories? Henry James says that of all novelists, Balzac "pretended hardest," his men and women "standing on their feet and going of themselves and acting out their characters."[9] What must it have been like to be in the mind of the creator of so many fictional lives? Journals and letters, those informal and intimate writings where one often looks for answers to such questions, don't offer much help in Balzac's case. He didn't keep a journal, and the correspondence, even the passionate letters to Evelina Hanska, often turn to financial affairs and business, including the business of writing. Though artists figure among his key characters, he doesn't speak much about the secrets of creativity.

The external facts of Balzac's life are well known, and I have already touched on some of them. His father, the ambitious Bernard François Balzac—originally Balssa, from a peasant family in the Tarn—married his mother, Laure Sallambier, from a family of haberdashers, when he was fifty and she eighteen. Their first child, Honoré, was born in 1799; two sisters, Laure and Laurence, followed; then a second boy, Henry, whose father was Jean de Margonne, later, curiously, a friend to Honoré. His mother lavished affection on this love child, whereas Honoré, who always described his mother as cold and unloving, was abandoned to boarding schools and rarely visited. Honoré remained close to his sister Laure. His family moved to Paris in 1814, when his father became a director in a company that furnished supplies to the army, and Honoré began his studies in the law. He served briefly as lawyer's clerk, but obtained his family's permission to take two years off in order to try his hand as a writer, living in a rented room (in the rue de Lesdiguières, like the narrator of *Facino Cane*). He set out to compose a tragedy, and failed miserably. But he continued writing. In the 1820s he wrote Gothic and adventure novels, which he published under pseudonyms; in 1829, he signed his name to *The Chouans*, originally *The Last of the Chouans*, in imitation of James Fenimore Cooper, about the royalist revolt in Brittany during the Revolution. Soon he began to affect that unwarranted pseudo-aristocratic *de*. He went into business as a publisher, a printer, and a type founder: enterprises that only led to debt, though the foundry later flourished under other management. He gained attention with his *Physiology of Marriage*, and then the series of short novels he called *Scenes of Private Life*, then in 1831 *The Fatal Skin*, a rousing success. He was launched on a literary career, though not without many further vicissitudes.

His loves began with a long liaison with Laure de Berny, some twenty-two years older than he, and the Duchesse d'Abrantès, fifteen years his senior, and both contributed much to his education in the ways of the social world. He had a passing romance with the famous courtesan Olympe Pelissier, and a long-standing liaison with Maria du Fresnay, with whom he had a daughter—he assumed she was his—in 1834. There was also a long intermittent relationship with the spirited Countess Sarah Guidoboni-Visconti, who aided him financially and whose son, born in 1836, may have been his child. Between 1834 and 1836, Jules Sandeau, the former lover of Aurore Dudevant aka George Sand, lived with Balzac as his secretary, and there was speculation that they were lovers as well as friends. In 1832, he received a letter from Odessa, signed: "The Stranger." He replied by a classified ad in the *Gazette de France*—read all over Europe— and thus began his passionate correspondence with the Polish Countess Evelina Hanska. They met for the first time in Neuchâtel a year later, and on infrequent occasions thereafter, until, following the death of her husband in 1841, they became engaged. They were finally married in Berdichev, in the Ukraine, in 1850. Balzac was already ill. They returned to the house in Paris that he had lavishly furnished for her, where he took to his bed and died.

Balzac's travels were strenuous and exhausting: all over France, much in Italy, to Austria where he met Prince Metternich, to the Ukraine, on visits to Madame Hanska, to St. Petersburg, to Berlin and other German cities. In 1838 a get-rich-quick scheme led him to Sardinia, where he hoped to reopen abandoned Roman silver mines. It turned out that a company from Marseille had been there first and had already taken over the mines. On at least two occasions he considered running as Legitimist candidate for a seat in the National Assembly. He was passionate about politics, as his novels demonstrate, though often disillusioned. The July Revolution of 1830 merely confirmed the distasteful rise of the bourgeoisie. The more radical Revolution of 1848 should have appeared more threatening to him—but he was absent in Touraine during the violence of the June Days that spring, and then in the autumn off to Evelina in the Ukraine, to remain until his marriage. He presided for a time over the Société des Gens de Lettres, founded, as mentioned earlier, in part at his instigation, and never ceased from militating for authors' rights. He made attempts to enter the Académie Française but was defeated by far lesser writers. Always and above all, and throughout his travels and loves, there was that "long prison of his labor" needed to produce those ninety-some novels and tales, not to mention a few plays and innumerable journalistic pieces—no one in fact has done a complete inventory of them. The image of Balzac dressed in his monk's robe writing all night, sustained by innumerable cups of black coffee, is accurate. He would often sleep briefly in the early evening, then rise toward nine o'clock to begin the night's labors. He had Louis Boulanger paint his portrait wearing the monk's robe, to commemorate and perhaps parody his renunciation of the world in favor of his art. He was physically unprepossessing—short, and as he aged rotund, with poor teeth and generally messy in appearance. But his eyes were deemed magnetic, his conversation brilliant, and his storytelling unforgettable.

His biography doesn't tell us much about what we most wish to know: what drove him to create those 2,472 characters. What do all these invented lives tell us about Balzac's inner life? I am not a partisan of using fictional works to attempt a psychoanalysis of the author: art and life are not continuous, the writing self is not the same as the living self, and such an attempt is at best tautological, rediscovering in the author's psyche what he has already dramatized in his works. This is, as I warned, an antibiography. I do think, though, that certain obsessive patterns return in the work and speak of a consciousness haunted by certain experiences. Over and over again, boys are unloved and abandoned by their mothers, confined to boarding schools or student boardinghouses, deprived of comfort, food, adequate clothing, and always of love. When love comes, throughout *The Human Comedy* it is with electric intensity, and sex unsettles like an earthquake. In *The Girl with the Golden Eyes*, for instance, the dandy Henri de Marsay is blindfolded, whisked through Paris in a coach, and led through labyrinthine passages to a rendezvous in a shell-shaped room decorated in white, crimson, and gold with the mysterious Paquita Valdès. Paquita, though a virgin, is expert in sex, and Henri experiences ecstasy with her until in the midst of orgasm she cries out "Maraquita." This insult to his masculinity must be avenged, but when Henri returns to Paquita to exact his punishment, he discovers the Marquise de San-Réal, Paquita's lover, has beat him to it, and stabbed Paquita to death. As they face each other over Paquita's bloody corpse, recognition dawns. They speak as one: "Lord Dudley must be your father?"[10] These half-siblings have been brought into incestuous proximity—Paquita, moreover, they realize, was at least "faithful to the blood" merely substituting the phallic sibling for the non-phallic. The potential of more than this mediated incest hangs over the final scene, until the Marquise cuts short any thought of their union, abruptly announcing that she is entering a convent: nothing can console her for the loss of what seemed to her the infinite. Love as infinite and absolute, and largely unattainable, is well evoked by the words the soldier at the center of *A Passion in the Desert* uses to describe the strange and dangerous love that developed, when he was lost in the desert and sheltering in a cave, between him and the panther. It was, he tells his listener, like the desert solitude: "God without man."

Theories of sex are everywhere in *The Human Comedy*, however fragmentary or inchoate. Sex is for Balzac the riddle of the sphinx, its very resistance to solution setting basic terms of existence. "Desire sets us afire and Power destroys us," says the antiques dealer of *The Fatal Skin*, in the paradox that governs life subject to both the pleasure principle and the death drive. Recall the scene from that novel where Raphaël watches Fœdora undress, suspecting she has a fatal flaw that prevents her from loving—and finds nothing. Raphaël's infinite desire slowly reduces him, and his magic skin, to nothing. Even the "savers," those who refuse sexual expenditure, such as the antiques dealer and Gobseck, attempting to escape the ineluctable by transforming all their pleasures into orgies within the mind, are doomed. By contrast, the unquenchable desires of Baron Hulot, in Balzac's late novel *Cousin Bette* (1846), preserve him even as they wreak destruction in his family. The story of his multiple amours and their disastrous outcome for all around him appears to end with him reunited with his wife, Adeline, who has rescued him from poverty and reformed him. To no avail. Odd sounds emerge from the maids' quarters on the top floor, and Adeline investigates: the Baron is making promises of marriage to the kitchen maid. Adeline collapses and dies; the septuagenarian Baron marries the maid.

Maybe his monomaniacal eros saves him from the diffuse sexuality of the profligate spenders of *The Human Comedy*. He's a unique case.

In contrast to the irresolvable mystery of sex stands the no less intractable mystery of knowledge pursued by Balzac's monomaniac thinkers, though perhaps these obsessive neurotics have simply converted one problem into the other. That's what Freud would say: they have sexualized thought processes themselves. The purest example in *The Human Comedy* is Balthasar Claës in *The Search for the Absolute*. Claës, the scion of a wealthy Flemish family, married to an adored wife and father of four children, living in a fine old house richly decorated with Flemish art, has a passing conversation with a Polish savant that turns his life around. He takes up chemistry and alchemy, obsessed with finding the minimum particle of living substance—the "absolute" from which everything springs. He locks himself in the laboratory he has built in his house and lays waste to the family fortune, selling off all that art in order to pay for the chemicals and exotic metals he needs. His pursuit of the absolute destroys his wife, and then his favorite daughter strives to resist his depredations. He ends his life reduced to indigence and unhappy unemployment for lack of materials to work with. He dies, raising himself on his deathbed to cry "Eureka," as if the last breath of life had brought him revelation.

Claës is like a Hulot whose sexuality has instead been invested in vain alchemical research. More ambiguous is the person of the painter, Frenhofer, who devotes himself to composing the masterpiece he calls "La Belle Noiseuse." This fictional artist in *The Unknown Masterpiece* spends much of the story in dialogue with two real artists known to history: Frans Porbus and Nicolas Poussin.

He gives them lessons in color and design. Meanwhile, he works in solitude on his masterpiece. When finally he admits the two disciples to his studio, all they discover is a blurred canvas, an apparent overworking of the subject of the painting—they perceive one perfect foot emerge from the cloud of brushwork in one corner of the tableau, but the rest is illegible. "There ends our art upon this earth," Porbus comments.[11] It seems that Frenhofer has indeed had his vision of perfection—the perfect woman's body represented in the perfect painting—but has failed to translate it into the medium of representation. The same problem strikes other artists in *The Human Comedy*: the musician Gambara, for instance, who invents the "panharmonicon," but can play beautifully only when drunk. He too encounters failure on the level of expression—a failure to put his vision into a comprehensible musical idiom. Frenhofer tells his fellow artists: "The mission of art is not to copy nature, but to express it." (NY 13/P 10:418) This ambitiously expressionist view of art resembles Balzac's own. You need to go beyond describing surfaces of the real; you need to get into its inner being and bring that into the realm of representation. Failure will reduce you to a kind of muteness or opacity: nothing legible on the canvas, nothing comprehensible to speak. Frenhofer will at the end burn all his canvases and die.

Frenhofer of *The Unknown Masterpiece* is the best-known of Balzac's monomaniacs, and the story in which he figures became over the years an object of fascinated attention for artists (Picasso illustrated it) and filmmakers (Jacques Rivette produced a 238-minute film of it), but the most important intellectual to encounter an impasse in Balzac's work is Louis Lambert, whose story touches closely on Balzac's own life and obsessions. The narrator of *Louis*

Lambert meets the title character at the college of the Oratorians in Vendôme, where Balzac himself was a student. Brilliant and isolated from the other students who mock him and nickname him "Pythagoras" (while the narrator is called "the Poet"), Lambert interests himself in metaphysics and reads Emanuel Swedenborg, a mystical thinker dear to Balzac, who coupled *Louis Lambert* with the overtly Swedenborgian novel *Séraphita*. Lambert discovers in dreams another self parallel to the waking self, to be explored, and sets about writing a Theory of the Will—the same project given to Raphaël in *The Fatal Skin*—which he conceives of as a magnetic or electric fluid that certain beings can concentrate and project and so achieve mastery over others. But Lambert's great work is discovered and confiscated by the rector of the college, though the narrator will later spend many pages reconstituting its essential perceptions. Lambert spends some time in Paris, then returns to his native Blois, in the Loire Valley, where he meets Pauline de Villenoix, an heiress who remains unmarried because she is illegitimate and has Jewish ancestors. In Pauline, he finds his spiritual counterpart: her Swedenborgian inner angel has almost been liberated from its corporeal envelope. They are to be married, but on the eve of their wedding Louis suffers a seizure and attempts to castrate himself. His uncle rescues him. Pauline will house him in her château and serve as his guardian. Though he is capable only of fragmentary utterances, she learns to grasp their meaning as parts of a coherent inner speech. The narrator visits Lambert in his half-lit room, and all the self-absorbed philosopher has to say is: "Angels are white." Has he gone mad, or is this, as Pauline maintains, a problem of expression? She believes that Lambert (quite like Frenhofer) has a perfectly coherent system of thought but cannot communicate it other than in seemingly meaningless bits and pieces. The narrator finds some of Lambert's letters about human history and civilization from which he gleans his so-called law of disorganization: "No form of civilization has escaped ruin because none has understood this law: When the effect produced is no longer related to its cause, there is disorganization."[12] This sounds like Balzac's own take on the problems of postrevolutionary France and its difficulty in settling to a fixed form of government and a stable society.

Pauline has forced herself to put a number of Lambert's verbal fragments into writing, and though much of it seems to me pretentious nonsense, some of Lambert's aphorisms point to the core of Balzac's preoccupations and even beliefs. Crucial is Lambert's prediction of a reverse incarnation: "And perhaps one day the reverse meaning of the ET VERBUM CARO FACTUM EST [the word was made flesh] will be the summation of a new scripture that will say: AND THE FLESH SHALL BE MADE THE WORD, IT WILL BECOME THE WORD OF GOD." (RB 38:145/P 11:689)

"All that is solid melts into air," Karl Marx said of modern capitalism. Lambert's vision of disincarnation seems strange in a writer so firmly dedicated to the real as Balzac, but in one form or another this longing for transcendence permeates Balzac's world and shapes the aspiration of many of his characters, even some of the most materialist, such as Gobseck, the antiques dealer, even Collin. They are driven beyond conquest of the material world: in their mind's eye they see something else, some idea of intellectual and spiritual delight. And this of course is what the novelist seeks to do, to see things, the solid, unyielding real world, and at the same time to see through it. That's a project that may lead one to the edge of insanity.

For all his diligence as "secretary" to French society, as he puts it in the "Author's Introduction" to *The Human Comedy*, for all his confidence in the power of the novel to capture and dramatize all social relations, Balzac never lets go of his belief that his Studies of Manners—*Études de moeurs*—are not fully adequate to express the real meanings of the society he depicted. Something is lacking, but it doesn't yield easily to inquiry. In the absence of some underlying law or transcendent power, the whole of modern society might be seen as crazed as the artists and philosophers who pursue such a law and such a power, even as they despair of it.

Madness is never far from the surface because Balzac's whole enterprise is fundamentally mad, a pursuit of a total reckoning with the visible and invisible world. His melodrama speaks to a quest to represent everything, to get all social relations and spiritual states onto the stage, to make them express themselves fully. At climatic moments in his novels there is a kind of breakthrough of repression, showing and speaking the deep subject of the drama. "Desire sets us afire and power destroys us": utterances like this one from the antiques dealer in *The Fatal Skin* remind us of the primal forces in play in life as Balzac conceives it, and these forces are at bottom sexual, expressed as drives to conquer, possess, devour, though capable of sublimation by those who truly master the world. The ambition that animates his young heroes often seems a kind of primitive orality, a wish to devour and ingest reality. Matching that is the wish for power over others. It's no accident that both Louis Lambert and Raphaël de Valentin work on never-completed treatises on the will, the force that, if properly understood, could make you master of all. Reality appears as a force field in which everyone is animated to move, often frenetically. As Baudelaire remarked, even Balzac's concierges have genius; everyone in his world is "stuffed with willpower from head to toe."[13] If *The Human Comedy* refers, audaciously, to Dante's *Divine Comedy*, in it heaven and hell are largely overshadowed by purgatory, the realm Rastignac designated as struggle— struggle not only to get ahead but to understand, to represent, to express.

But there is a story of utopian experiment in one of the novels, *The Country Doctor* (*Le Médecin de campagne*). Fleeing his past life (we will not find out why until later in the novel), Dr. Benassis comes to a small village in the Dauphiné, in the foothills of the Alps, not far from Grenoble. It is set deep in a valley where the sun rarely shines, some of the population suffers from cretinism, and there is scarcely any industry or commerce. Benassis undertakes engineering projects, irrigation especially, moves houses to more salubrious locations, initiates small-scale manufacturing, builds a road connecting the village to Grenoble, and organizes the population in ways that reflect the socialist Charles Fourier's idea of cooperative communities. Benassis's vision is at once socialist and thoroughly totalitarian: everything is subjected to patriarchal rule; all must participate in useful labor; "apathy" is strictly banned; and religion is extolled as a "complete system opposing man's natural depraved tendencies."[14] Healthy exercise and industry are held to cure most ills, including the debilitating excessive masturbation engaged in by Adrien, the son of a visiting friend of the doctor's. Benassis's utopia becomes a complete system of care for a largely debilitated population, as maternal as it is paternally ruled. It is a therapeutic community, a place of respite for the wounded, and indeed the epigraph of the novel reads: "To wounded hearts, shadow and silence" ("*Aux coeurs blessés, l'ombre et le silence*").

Toward the end of the novel, we are told Benassis's story, and we learn how wounding and wounded he has been. He abandoned his first wife and his child, and later his true love rejected him for this past crime. Burdened with remorse, in search of expiation, he visits the Grande Chartreuse monastery in the Alps, still largely deserted (religious orders had been outlawed during the French Revolution), another community seeking to rebuild. In an empty cell, Benassis finds an ancient inscription left by one of the monks: "*Fuge, late, tace*"—"Flee, hide, be silent" (very close to Stephen Dedalus: "Silence, exile, and cunning"). Balzac had read the inscription on the door of a cell when he visited the monastery, and though we scarcely think of Balzac as devoted to silence, fleeing and hiding were very much part of a life harassed throughout by creditors and editors. As for silence: it was in nocturnal quiet, when the social world had fallen silent, that he composed his tumultuous novels—like the exiled Dante that he portrays in the short story *The Proscribed* (*Les Proscrits*), who, back at his writing table late at night, "dedicated himself to the terrible demon of work, calling forth words from silence, and ideas from the night."[15]

To Say Everything

Chief of all Balzac's obsessions of course was writing, telling stories. Everything that he wrote under his own name, some ninety titles, falls essentially within a twenty-year period. He thought he could write his way out of debt, but his corrected proofs, almost always about addition more than deletion, suggest something other than the utilitarian writer. We see instead an inability to write less, a need to develop, to add biographical details and life facts, to carry what he has begun to some utopia of writing where all might be said. Jean-Jacques Rousseau claims in his *Confessions* that his goal is to make himself completely transparent to his reader, and this means he must "say everything"—"*tout dire.*" Balzac evidently feels the same way about his creations. To say everything is of course a mad endeavor, never realizable. But it acts as a spur to make you want to fill up every gap, to produce a nearly infinite text. The writing of *The Human Comedy*—its reading, too—demands always more, especially exploration of all those characters whose stories link different texts into a vast and rich social texture.

What must it have been like to inhabit Balzac's mind? Maybe not so different from our experience of reading his novels, since I have the impression that Balzac himself inhabited his fictions as one of his own invented characters. He was a man of fictions, always seeking to make himself up as he went along, reinvent himself in different costumes and guises, even in different sexes, a figure or figment of his own imagination. Here as elsewhere, the condition of the individual mirrors and is mirrored by the social world, likewise seeking to define itself but without clarity or finality. Louis Lambert articulates the social dimension of the problem of identity; the narrator of *Facino Cane* maybe speaks most directly to experience for the individual: that capacity to enter into the lives of others, to put yourself in their place, to see through their eyes and think with their brains is both wondrous and dangerous. Creating fictional persons, including oneself, brings one to the brink of the unknown, to the realm of dreams and daydreams, fantasies of pleasure and domination, wishes fulfilled. But maybe if you keep on writing, ever more, striving to cover all of society and all potentialites of the individual, you can escape the breakdown of a Lambert or a Frenhofer. There is no resting place; you have to keeping trying to get it all down on the page. Silence threatens: as for Balzac's fictional Dante, writing is a constant skirmish with nothingness.

The vast social world of *The Human Comedy* ultimately derives from the solitary act of writing, finding it all in one's head. Yet the work endures, not only for the readers of fiction but also in the research of social historians and demographers and semioticians, because it is so true. It tells us so much about reading other people and entire societies. Balzac remains the first and still the crucial guide to the modern world.

Acknowledgments

Work on this book began during pleasant and productive weeks at John W. Kluge Center at the Library of Congress, for which I am most grateful. I benefited from the hospitality of the Henry Koerner Center, Yale University, during the final stages of writing. I have been reading, teaching, and thinking about Balzac for many years, and I am in debt to friends and colleagues with whom I've discussed his work and who have published some of my essays on it: D. A. Miller, David Shields, Rachel Bowlby, Maurice Samuels, Martine Reid, Mariolina Bertini, Paolo Tortonese, Francesco Spandri, Brigid Doherty, Arien Mack, among many others. Maureen Chun has long been an acute critical reader of my work as well as friend. Working with Edwin Frank as editor has been an energizing dialogue from which I have learned much, including enormous respect for his responsiveness and critical acumen. I am grateful also to the expertise and good cheer of Sara Kramer, who over many years has proved a wonderful interlocutor on all things literary. I was fortunate to have a copyeditor with a deft touch, Karla Eoff. My thanks also to my children, who have always been cheerful about my long hours at the computer.

Notes

INTRODUCTION

1. See Oscar Wilde, "The Decay of Lying," in *Intentions and Other Writings* (Garden City, NY: Dolphin Books, 1891.), 31.
2. This is the figure established by Fernand Lotte in the most recent census, updated by Pierre Citron and Anne-Marie Meininger, *Index des personnages fictifs de la Comédie humaine*, in *La Comédie humaine*, vol. 12 (Paris: Bibliothèque de la Pléiade, 1981).
3. The term was coined by the critic Tzvetan Todorov in discussing *The Decameron* and similar material. See Todorov, "Narrative Men," in *The Poetics of Prose*, trans. Richard Howard (Ithaca, NY: Cornell University Press, 1977).
4. Henry James, "The Lesson of Balzac," in *Literary Criticism* (New York: Library of America, 1984), 2:131.
5. Among the most helpful biographies of Balzac in English are Stefan Zweig, *Balzac* (New York: Viking, 1946); André Maurois, *Prometheus, or the Life of Balzac* (New York: Harper & Row, 1966); V. S. Pritchett, *Balzac* (New York: Alfred A. Knopf, 1973); and, especially, Graham Robb, *Balzac: A Life* (London: Picador, 1994).
6. See Michel Butor, "Balzac et la réalité," in *Répertoire* (Paris: Editions de Minuit, 1960).
7. See James, "Preface to *The American*," in *Literary Criticism*, 2:1063.

EUGÈNE DE RASTIGNAC

1. Quotations are from *Père Goriot*, trans. Henry Reed (New York: Signet Classics, 2004), 111/in French, *Le Père Goriot*, in *La Comédie humaine* (Paris: Bibliothèque de la Pléiade, 1976), 3:139. I will give page numbers from both the English translation and the French in parentheses in the text from now on. I have at times freely modified the Reed translation (the best I know) in order to give a more literal rendering of the French—a practice that I will follow with translations throughout this book. When no translator is mentioned, translation is my own.

2. See Thomas Piketty, *Capital in the Twenty-First Century*, trans. Arthur Goldhammer (Cambridge, MA: Harvard University Press, 2014), 407ff.

3. The text of this deleted scene is given in the Pléiade edition, 3:1321.

4. *Nucingen and Co., Bankers*, trans. Katharine Prescott Wormeley, in *La Comédie Humaine of Honoré de Balzac* (Boston: Little, Brown, 1901), 15:491–92/in French, *La Maison Nucingen*, in *La Comédie humaine* (Paris: Bibliothèque de la Pléiade, 1977), 6:381.

5. The two volumes of Balzac's *Oeuvres diverses* published by the Bibliothèque de la Pléiade contain only those occasional texts that can with certainty be ascribed to Balzac. A third volume was planned (and might have included some of the texts of less certain attribution) but has apparently been abandoned.

6. Balzac, *Treatise on Elegant Living*, trans. Napoleon Jeffries (Cambridge, MA: Wakefield Press, 2010), 26/in French, *Traité de la vie élégante*, in *La Comédie humaine* (Paris: Bibliothèque de la Pléiade, 1981), 12:226.

7. Pierre Rosanvallon, *Le Peuple introuvable. Histoire de la représentation démocratique en France* (Paris: Gallimard, 1998), 288. See also the large use of Balzac in the classic work by Louis Chevalier, *Laboring Classes and Dangerous Classes*, trans. Frank Jellinek (London: Routledge and Kegan Paul, 1973)/in French, *Classes laborieuses et classes dangereuses* (Paris: Plon, 1958).

8. See the fine article by Judith Lyon-Caen, "Saisir, décrire, déchiffrer: les mises en texte du social sous la monarchie de Juillet," *Revue Historique* 306, no. 2 (2004): 303–31.

9. See Erich Auerbach, *Mimesis: The Representation of Reality in Western Literature*, trans. Willard Trask (Princeton: Princeton University Press, 1953), 470–73.

10. Henry James, preface to *The Princess Casamassima*, in *Literary Criticism* (New York: Library of America, 1984), 2:1102.

11. The quotation comes from Balzac's preface to *Une Fille d'Ève*, in *La Comédie humaine*, 3:265–66.

JEAN-ESTHER VAN GOBSECK

1. Quotations are from *Gobseck*, trans. Linda Asher, in Honoré de Balzac, *The Human Comedy: Selected Stories*, ed. Peter Brooks (New York: New York Review Books, 2014), 249/in French, *Gobseck*, in *La Comédie humaine* (Paris: Bibliothèque de la Pléiade, 1976), 2:983.

2. Originally entitled "The Dangers of Misconduct" ("Les Dangers de l'inconduite").

3. Quotations are from *A Harlot High and Low*, trans. Rayner Heppenstall (London: Penguin, 1970), 29/in French, *Splendeurs et misères des courtisanes*, in *La Comédie humaine* (Paris: Bibliothèque de la Pléiade, 1977), 6:442.

ANTOINETTE DE LANGEAIS

1. The film was made by Jacques Rivette in 2007, and titled in French *Ne touchez pas la hache* (Don't touch the ax), which was Balzac's original working title for the novella. That phrase is cited by Montriveau as spoken by one of the warders at the Tower of London in reference to the ax used for executions. While I found the opening of Rivette's film brilliant, the rest of it seemed to me surprisingly flat and unexciting, given the passion and tension of Balzac's story. So I'll say no more about the film.

2. See Sigmund Freud, "Notes Upon a Case of Obsessional Neurosis" (Rat Man), in *The Standard Edition of the Complete Psychological Works of Sigmund Freud*, 24 vols., trans. and ed. James Strachey (London: The Hogarth Press, 1955), 10:244. *Wisstrieb* becomes "epistemophilic instinct" in Strachey's translation, since he chooses always to make the German *Trieb* "instinct" in English, whereas "drive" would seem a better translation. Though some of Strachey's neologisms via the Greek are unfortunate, epistemophilia strikes me as felicitous.

3. Quotations are from *The Duchesse de Langeais*, trans. Carol Cosman, in *The Human Comedy: Selected Stories*, ed. Peter Brooks (New York: New

York Review Books, 2014), 286/in French, *La Duchesse de Langeais*, in *Histoire des Treize* (Paris: Bibliothèque de la Pléiade, 1977), 5:908. The other two stories in *Story of the Thirteen* (*Histoire des Treize*) are *Ferragus* and *The Girl with the Golden Eyes* (*La Fille aux yeux d'or*).

4. A good case in point is the novel *Béatrix*, which contains an extended deconstruction of romantic love. Balzac wrote it after a long visit to George Sand, and used as material what Sand told him about Marie d'Agoult's tortured affair with Franz Liszt.

5. See Marcel Proust, *Contre Sainte-Beuve*, ed. Pierre Clarac (Paris: Bibliothèque de la Pléiade, 1971), 277.

6. Gustave Flaubert, *Madame Bovary*, trans. Lydia Davis (New York: Viking, 2010), 170/in French, *Madame Bovary*, in *Oeuvres*, 2 vols. (Paris: Bibliothèque de la Pléiade, 1951), 1:469.

7. *A Woman of Thirty*, trans. Ellen Marriage (New York: Macmillan, 1901), 182/in French, *La Femme de trente ans*, in *La Comédie humaine* (Paris: Bibliothèque de la Pléiade, 1976), 2:1189.

8. See Ian Watt, *The Rise of the Novel* (London: Chatto & Windus, 1957).

9. One can trace some of Balzac's effect on his women readers by way of letters that have been preserved and published by Marcel Bouteron, *Lettres de femmes adressées à H. de Balzac (1837–1840)*, Cahiers balzaciens nos. 3 and 5 (Paris: La Cité des Livres, 1924–27). See also David Bellos, "Reconnaissances: Balzac et son public féminin," *Oeuvres et critiques* 9, no. 3 (1985): 253–62; Christiane Mounoud-Anglés, *Balzac et ses lectrices* (Paris: Indigo & Côté Femmes Éditions, 1994). On *Physiology of Marriage*, see Catherine Nesci, *La Femme mode d'emploi* (Lexington, KY: French Forum, 1992).

10. On *Sarrasine*, see the remarkable analysis by Roland Barthes in *S/Z*, trans. Richard Miller (New York: Hill & Wang, 1974)/in French, *S/Z* (Paris: Éditions du Seuil, 1970).

RAPHAËL DE VALENTIN

1. Quotations are from *The Fatal Skin*, trans. Atwood H. Townsend (New York: Signet, 1963), 13/in French, *La Peau de chagrin*, in *La Comédie humaine* (Paris: Bibliothèque de la Pléiade, 1979), 10:63.

2. The inscription should look like a pyramid standing on its head. I used as my basic text here the translation by Graham Robb in his biography,

Balzac (London: Picador, 1994), 177, which seems closer to the original than Townsend's version.

3. See Villiers de l'Isle-Adam, *Axël* (1890). The play provides the title of Edmund Wilson's study of French symbolists and decadents, *Axel's Castle* (New York: Scribner's, 1931).

4. See Geoffrey H. Hartman, "Romanticism and Anti-Self-Consciousness," in *The Fate of Reading and Other Essays* (Chicago: University of Chicago Press, 1975).

5. Balzac to Charles de Montalembert, after September 1, 1831, in *Correspondance*, 3 vols. (Paris: Bibliothèque de la Pléiade, 2006–17), 1:396.

6. See the description of the novel as of "a serpentine movement," by Philarète Chasles in his introduction to *Romans et contes philosophiques de Balzac* (in *La Comédie humaine*, 10:1189), originally published by Charles Gosselin in 1831, an introduction that was certainly as much the work of Balzac himself as of his friend Chasles.

7. Ibid.

8. Max Schur, *Freud Living and Dying* (New York: International Universities Press, 1972), 572.

9. See Sigmund Freud, *Analysis Terminable and Interminable*, in *The Standard Edition of the Complete Psychological Works of Sigmund Freud*, 24 vols., trans. James Strachey (London: The Hogarth Press, 1964), 23:211–54.

LUCIEN CHARDON DE RUBEMPRÉ

1. Quotations are from *Lost Illusions*, trans. Kathleen Raine (New York: Modern Library, 2001), 50/in French, *Illusions perdues* (Paris: Bibliothèque de la Pléiade, 1977), 5:166. I will modify at times Raine's excellent translation to give a more literal rendering. My discussion of *Lost Illusions* focuses on part two of the novel, "A Provincial Celebrity in Paris" ("Un grand homme de province à Paris"), the richest part, perhaps the most significant narrative in all of *The Human Comedy*.

2. See the classic essay by René Guise, "Balzac et le roman-feuilleton," in *Balzac* (Nancy: Presses Universitaires de Nancy, 1994), 57–104; also generally: Marie-Ève Thérenty, *La littérature au quotidien. Poétiques journalistiques au XIXe siècle* (Paris: Éditions du Seuil, 2016); Judith Lyon-Caen, *La Lecture et la vie. Les Usages du roman au temps de Balzac* (Paris: Tallandier,

2006); and Raymond Chollet, *Balzac journaliste. Le tournant de 1830* (Paris: Klincksieck, 1983).

3. See Georg Lukács, "Illusions perdues," in *Balzac et le réalisme français*, trans. Paul Lavau (Paris: Maspéro, 1967).

4. For a succinct and illuminating account of this process, see John Lough, *Writer and Public in France* (Oxford: Clarendon, 1978), 288–89.

5. Henry James, "The Lesson of Balzac," in *Literary Criticism* (New York: Library of America, 1984), 2:131. Another version of the *compte/conte* pun comes when the witty courtesan Suzanne du Val-Noble, showing off her magnificent apartment, comments: *"Voilà les comptes des mille et une nuits"*—"Here are the accounts of a thousand and one nights." (ML 422/P 5:493) Again, *comptes*, accounts, sounds like *contes*, tales, as in the French title of *The Arabian Nights, Les Contes des mille-et-une nuits*.

6. Charles Augustin Sainte-Beuve, "De la littérature industrielle," *La Revue des Deux Mondes*, vol. 19 (1839), 675-91. Note that Sainte-Beuve describes the situation of publishing in the 1830s, whereas Balzac ostensibly is describing that of the 1820s. But in fact Balzac tends to blend the time of Lucien's writing career and the time he is writing about it.

7. Pierre Rosanvallon, *Le peuple introuvable. Histoire de la représentation démocratique en France* (Paris: Gallimard, 1998), 288.

8. Edmond Werdet, *De la librairie française, depuis les temps les plus reculés jusqu'à nos jours* (Paris: E. Dentu, 1860).

9. Hippolyte Taine, "Balzac," in *Nouveaux essais de critique et d'histoire* (Paris: Hachette, 1866), 63.

10. Balzac, "Lettre addressée aux écrivains français du XIXe siècle," *La Revue de Paris*, November 1, 1834; see also Balzac's "De l'état actuel de la librairie," in *Oeuvres diverses* (Paris: Bibliothèque de la Pléiade, 1996), 2:662–70.

11. On Chapuys-Montlaville and his speeches in the assembly, see Lise Dumasy, ed., *La Querelle du roman-feuilleton. Littérature, presse et politique, un débat précurseur (1836–1848)* (Grenoble: ELLUG, Université Stendhal, 1999).

JACQUES COLLIN

1. Quotations are from (the wretchedly titled) *A Harlot High and Low*, trans. Rayner Heppenstall (New York: Penguin, 1970), 19/in French, *Splendeurs et misères des courtisanes* (Paris: Bibliothèque de la Pléiade, 1977), 6:432.

2. See Alain Corbin, *Women for Hire*, trans. Alan Sheridan (Cambridge, MA: Harvard University Press, 1996)/in French, *Les Filles de noces: Misère sexuelle et prostitution (19e et 20e siècles)* (Paris: Aubier Montaigne, 1978), for a thorough discussion of the debates around prostitution, whether it should be abolished or policed, and whether and how a former prostitute should be allowed to reenter "decent" society. In *The Mysteries of Paris*, Fleur-de-Marie, sold into a life of prostitution, is redeemed by Rodolphe de Gérolstein—but when he proposes that she marry a respectable man, she demurs: she claims that her stain can never be washed away. So she dies instead of marrying.

3. See Oscar Wilde, "The Decay of Lying," in *Intentions and Other Writings* (Garden City, NY: Dolphin Books, n.d.), 21. Wilde, or rather his spokesperson Vivian, continues: "It is a grief from which I have never been able completely to rid myself. It haunts me in my moments of pleasure. I remember it when I laugh."

4. A very good discussion of Balzac's representation of same-sex intimacy is to be found in Michael Lucey, *The Misfit of the Family: Balzac and the Social Forms of Sexuality* (Durham, NC: Duke University Press, 2003).

HENRIETTE DE MORTSAUF

1. Blue-veined breasts were for centuries considered a beauty asset. Quotations are from *The Lily of the Valley*, trans. Lucienne Hill (New York: Carrol and Graf, 1989), 15/in French, *Le Lys dans la vallée*, in *La Comédie humaine* (Paris: Bibliothèque de la Pléiade, 1978), 9:984.

2. For some unexplained reason, this important line is dropped in Hill's translation.

3. On the language of flowers, see Jack Goody, *The Culture of Flowers* (Cambridge: Cambridge University Press, 1993).

4. In the second version of the novel published in book form, Henriette's lamentations and accusations go on longer and are more explicit still about her sexual deprivation, Félix's fault in not having overcome her resistances, and her desire for a future erotic life. Balzac pruned the scene in response to the objections of his old friend and sometime lover Laure de Berny, who thought he was compromising Henriette's dignity. But in fact his deletions don't alter at all the sense and the

force of the scene. See the variants recorded in the Pléiade edition, 9:1202–3.

5. *"Naturam expelles furca, tamen usque recurret."* Horace, *Epistles*, I.10.24. Quoted by Sigmund Freud in "Delusions and Dreams in Jensen's *Gradiva*," in *The Standard Edition of the Complete Psychological Works of Sigmund Freud*, 24 vols., trans. James Strachey (London: The Hogarth Press, 1959), 9:35.

6. See Henry James on Balzac's capacity to give the sense of passing time in "The Lesson of Balzac," in *Literary Criticism* (New York: Library of America, 1984), 2:136.

7. "Enivrez-vous, de vin, de poésie, de vertu à votre guise": see Charles Baudelaire, "Enivrez-vous," in *Le Spleen de Paris*, in *Oeuvres completes* (Paris: Bibliothèque de la Pléiade, 1954), 338.

COLONEL CHABERT

1. Quotations are from *Colonel Chabert*, trans. Carol Cosman (New York: New Directions, 1997), 4/in French, *Le Colonel Chabert* (Paris: Bibliothèque de la Pléiade, 1976), 3: 313.

2. See Jerome Bruner, "The Transactional Self," in *Actual Minds, Possible Worlds* (Cambridge, MA: Harvard University Press, 1986), 67.

3. Strangely, the English translation drops this line ("Derville then told Godeschal the preceding story"). By doing so, the translation loses a dimension of the narrative structure: the authority conferred on Derville the lawyer as narrator (his role also, recall, in *Gobseck*).

4. "Author's Introduction," in *The Comedy of Human Life of Honoré de Balzac*, vol. 1, ed. George Saintsbury (London: The Athenian Society, 1901), 23–24/in French, "Avant-Propos," in *La Comédie humaine* (Paris: Bibliothèque de la Pléiade, 1976), 1:8.

MARCO FACINO CANE AND FRIEND

1. Quotations are from *Facino Cane*, trans. Linda Asher, in *The Human Comedy: Selected Stories*, ed. Peter Brooks (New York: New York Review Books, 2014), 4/in French, *Facino Cane*, in *La Comédie humaine* (Paris: Bibliothèque de la Pléiade, 1977), 6:1020.

2. "Author's Introduction," in *The Human Comedy*, 25/in French, "Avant-Propos," in *La Comédie humaine* (Paris: Bibliothèque de la Pléiade, 1976), 1:11–12.

3. See Sigmund Freud, *Fragment of an Analysis of a Case of Hysteria* (better known as "Dora"), in *The Standard Edition of the Complete Psychological Works of Sigmund Freud*, 24 vols., trans. James Strachey (London: The Hogarth Press, 1960), 7:77–78.

4. There is a problem in the Pléiade edition of the *Oeuvres diverses*: the two volumes issued were to have been followed by a third, which probably never will appear. The editor of these volumes, Roland Chollet, following the work of the scholar Bruce Tolley, takes a conservative view of what to admit as authentically by Balzac, excluding the maybes, the possibles, and the probables. Like a number of Balzac scholars, I would preserve more latitude of inclusion. On *Pathology of Social Life*, see the fine introduction by Mariolina Bongiovanni Bertini to the Italian translation, *Patologia della vita sociale*, trans. Paolo Tortonese and Pierfranco Minsenti (Torino: Bollati Boringhieri, 1992).

5. The search for distinction encounters the problem of imitation, which undermines the idiosyncratic style: see Paolo Tortonese, "Le bourgeois de Balzac et la girafe de Lamarck. Distinction, imitation, habitude," in *Balzac, l'Invention de la sociologie*, eds. Andrea Del Lungo and Pierre Glaudes (Paris: Garnier, 2019), 155–175.

6. Balzac, *Treatise on Elegant Living*, trans. Napoleon Jeffries (Cambridge, MA: Wakefield Press, 2010), 26/in French, *Traité de la vie élégante*, in *La Comédie humaine* (Paris: Bibliothèque de la Pléiade, 1981), 12:226.

7. On the paradigm of detection, its use in the sciences of man, the detective story, and Freud, see the rich essay by Carlo Ginzburg, "Clues: Roots of an Evidential Paradigm," in *Clues, Myths, and the Historical Method*, trans. John and Anne C. Tedeschi (Baltimore, MD: Johns Hopkins University Press, 2013).

8. *History of the Thirteen*, trans. Herbert J. Hunt (Harmondsworth: Penguin Books, 1974), 31/in French, *Histoire des Treize* (Paris: Bibliothèque de la Pléiade, 1977) 5:793.

9. Balzac, *Théorie de la démarche*, in *La Comédie humaine* (Paris: Bibliothèque de la Pléiade, 1981), 12:1270. See also the well-annotated edition edited

by Paolo Tortonese, *Théorie de la démarche* (Paris: Fayard, 2015). And compare Freud, "Delusions and Dreams in Jensen's *Gradiva*," on the importance of walking: both Freud and Balzac quote the same line from Virgil: "*et vera incessu patuit dea*"—"in her very gait she was revealed as a goddess."

10. *Another Study of Womankind*, trans. Jordan Stump, in *The Human Comedy: Selected Stories*, ed. Peter Brooks (New York: New York Review Books, 2014), 41/in French, *Autre étude de femme*, in *La Comédie humaine* (Paris: Bibliothèque de la Pléiade, 1976), 3:697.

11. *Adieu*, trans. Jordan Stump, in *The Human Comedy: Selected Stories*, 196/ in French, *Adieu*, in *La Comédie humaine*, 10:1013.

12. Pinel took over the Salpêtrière hospital for insane women during the French Revolution and developed the notion of a "*traitement moral*," a psychological cure that takes the patient back to the traumatic pathological event. On Pinel, see Jan Goldstein, *Console and Classify: The French Psychiatric Profession in the Nineteenth Century* (Chicago: University of Chicago Press, 1989).

13. Georg Lukács, "Illusions perdues," in *Balzac et le réalisme français*, trans. Paul Laveau (Paris: Maspéro, 1967), 57.

14. Henry James, "The Lesson of Balzac," in *Literary Criticism* (New York: Library of America, 1984), 2, 131–32.

LIVING IN FICTIONAL LIVES

1. Marcel Proust, *The Captive*, in *In Search of Lost Time*, trans. C. K. Scott Moncrieff and Terence Kilmartin (New York: Modern Library, 1993), 5:343/in French, *La prisonnière*, in *À la recherche du temps perdu* (Paris: Bibliothèque de la Pléiade, 1988), 3:762.

2. Marcel Proust, *Swann's Way*, trans. Lydia Davis (New York: Viking, 2003), 86–87/in French, *Du Côté de chez Swann*, in *À la recherche du temps perdu*, 1:84–85.

3. See Walter Benjamin, "The Storyteller," in *The Storyteller Essays*, trans. Tess Lewis, ed. Samuel Titan (New York: New York Review Books, 2019), 65–66.

4. See Catherine Gallagher, "The Rise of Fictionality," in *The Novel*, ed. Franco Moretti, 2 vols. (Princeton, NJ: Princeton University Press, 2006), 1:336–63.

5. Marcel Proust, *Time Regained*, in *In Search of Lost Time*, trans. Moncrieff and Kilmartin, 6:322/in French, *Le Temps retrouvé*, in *À la recherche du temps perdu*, 4:489–90.

6. See for example Lisa Zunshine, *Why We Read Fiction: Theory of Mind and the Novel* (Columbus, OH: Ohio State University Press, 2006); Alan Palmer, *Fictional Minds* (Lincoln, NE: University of Nebraska Press, 2008); Blakey Vermeule, *Why Do We Care About Literary Characters?* (Baltimore, MD: Johns Hopkins University Press, 2009); and for a more general conspectus of cognitive studies in relation to literary analysis, Terence Cave, *Thinking with Literature: Towards a Cognitive Criticism* (Oxford: Oxford University Press, 2016).

7. For an essay that attempts a systematic comparison of Balzac and Goffman, see Agathe Novak-Lechevalier, "Microsociologie: Balzac, Goffman et le théâtre du monde," in *Balzac, l'invention de la sociologie*, ed. Andrea Del Lungo and Pierre Glaudes (Paris: Garnier, 2019, 301–16).

8. See, for example, Raymond A. Mar et al., "Bookworms versus nerds: Exposure to fiction versus non-fiction, divergent associations with social ability, and the simulation of fictional social worlds," *Journal of Research in Personality* 40, no. 5 (2006): 694–712. The study of character in fiction is presently undergoing a useful reevaluation after long neglect: key here, as well as the books mentioned above, is the seminal study by Alex Woloch, *The One vs. the Many: Minor Characters and the Space of the Protagonist in the Novel* (Princeton, NJ: Princeton University Press, 2003); see also the issue "Character" of *New Literary History* 42, no. 2 (2011); and Amanda Anderson, Rita Felski, and Toril Moi, *Character: Three Inquiries in Literary Studies* (Chicago: University of Chicago Press, 2019).

9. Henry James, "The Lesson of Balzac," in *Literary Criticism* (New York: Library of America, 1984), 134, 132.

10. *The Girl with the Golden Eyes*, trans. Peter Collier (Oxford: Oxford World's Classics, 2012), 136/in French, *La Fille aux yeux d'or*, in *La Comédie humaine* (Paris: Bibliothèque de la Pléiade, 1977), 5:1108.

11. *The Unknown Masterpiece*, trans. Richard Howard (New York: New York Review Books, 2001), 42/in French, *Le Chef-d'oeuvre inconnu*, in *La Comédie humaine* (Paris: Bibliothèque de la Pléiade, 1979), 10:437.

12. *Louis Lambert*, trans. Katharine Prescott Wormeley, in *The Comédie Humaine of Honoré de Balzac* (Boston: Roberts Brothers, 1896), 38:145/in

French, *Louis Lambert*, in *La Comédie humaine* (Paris: Bibliothèque de la Pléiade, 1979), 11:650.

13. Charles Baudelaire, *Oeuvres complètes* (Paris: Bibliothèque de la Pléiade, 1954), 1037

14. *The Country Doctor*, trans. Ellen Marriage and Clara Bell (London: Macmillan, 1896), 95/in French, *Le Médecin de campagne*, in *La Comédie humaine* (Paris: Bibliothèque de la Pléiade, 1978), 9:503.

15. *The Exiles*, trans. Katharine Prescott Wormeley, in *The Comédie Humaine of Honoré de Balzac*, (Boston: Roberts Brothers, 1896), 38:392/in French, *Les Proscrits*, in *La Comédie humaine* (Paris: Bibliothèque de la Pléiade, 1981), 11:547.

Selected Bibliography

BY BALZAC

La Comédie humaine. 12 vols. Paris: Bibliothèque de la Pléiade, 1976–81. I choose to make my references to this edition for sake of uniformity and because it includes all the titles of *The Human Comedy*, though there are many available paperback editions of most of Balzac's novels. Two supplemental volumes of the Pléiade edition contain the *Oeuvres diverses.* The *Index des personnages fictifs de la Comédie humaine,* compiled by Ferdinand Lotte and updated by Pierre Citron and Anne-Marie Meininger, is to be found in volume 12 of the Pléiade edition.

Principal titles of *The Human Comedy*:

Colonel Chabert. Translated by Carol Cosman. New York: New Directions, 1997.

The Duchesse de Langeais. Translated by Carol Cosman. In *The Human Comedy: Selected Stories,* edited by Peter Brooks. New York: New York Review Books, 2014.

Facino Cane. Translated by Linda Asher. In *The Human Comedy: Selected Stories,* edited by Peter Brooks. New York: New York Review Books, 2014.

The Fatal Skin. Translated by Atwood H. Townsend. New York: Signet, 1963.

Gobseck. Translated by Linda Asher. In *The Human Comedy: Selected Stories,* edited by Peter Brooks. New York: New York Review Books, 2014.

A Harlot High and Low. Translated by Rayner Heppenstall. London: Penguin, 1970.

The Lily of the Valley. Translated by Lucienne Hill. New York: Carroll and Graf, 1989.

Lost Illusions. Translated by Kathleen Raine. New York: Modern Library, 2001.

Père Goriot. Translated by Henry Reed. New York: Signet Classics, 2004.

Correspondance, edited by Roger Pierrot and Hervé Yon. 3 vols. Paris: Bibliothèque de la Pléiade, 2006–2017.

Lettres à Madame Hanska, edited by Roger Pierrot. 2 vols. Paris: Robert Lafont, 1990.

BIOGRAPHIES OF BALZAC

Carter, David A. *Brief Lives: Balzac.* London: Hesperus, 2008.

Gengembre, Gérard. *Balzac: le forçat des lettres.* Paris: Perrin, 2013.

Maurois, André. *Prometheus, or, the Life of Balzac.* New York: Harper & Row, 1966.

Pritchett, V. S. *Balzac.* New York: Alfred A. Knopf, 1973.

Robb, Graham. *Balzac.* London: Picador, 1994.

Zweig, Stefan. *Balzac.* New York: Viking, 1946.

SOME SIGNIFICANT STUDIES OF BALZAC AND HIS WORK

Abraham, Pierre. *Créatures chez Balzac.* Paris: Gallimard, 1931.

Allemand, André. *Unité et structure de l'univers balzacien.* Paris: Plon, 1965.

Barbéris, Pierre. *Balzac et le mal du siècle.* Paris: Gallimard, 1970.

Bardèche, Maurice. *Balzac romancier.* Paris: Plon, 1943.

Barthes, Roland. *S/Z.* Translated by Richard Miller. New York: Hill and Wang, 1975.

Béguin, Albert. *Balzac visionnaire.* Genève: Skira, 1946.

Beizer, Janet L. *Family Plots: Balzac's Narrative Generations.* New Haven, CT: Yale University Press, 1986.

Bory, Jean-Louis. *Pour Balzac et quelques autres.* Paris: Éditions Julliard, 1959.

Bouivier, René, and Edouard Maynial. *De quoi vivait Balzac?* Paris: Les Deux Rives, 1949.

Butor, Michel. "Balzac et la réalité," in *Répertoire.* Paris: Éditions de Minuit, 1960.

Chollet, Raymond. *Balzac journaliste. Le tournant de 1830.* Paris: Klincksieck, 1983.

Curtius, Ernst-Robert. *Balzac.* Paris: Bernard Grasset, 1933.

Descombes, Vincent. "Who's Who in *La Comédie humaine.*" *MLN* 98, no. 4 (1983): 675–701.

Eigeldinger, Marc. *La Philosophie de l'art chez Balzac.* Genève: Pierre Cailler, 1957.

Guise, René. "Balzac et le roman-feuilleton." In *Balzac.* Nancy: Presses Universitaires de Nancy, 1994, 57–104.

Guyon, Bernard. *La Pensée politique et sociale de Balzac*. Paris: A. Colin, 1969.

Heathcote, Owen, and Andrew Watts. *The Cambridge Companion to Balzac*. Cambridge: Cambridge University Press, 2017.

Hemmings, F. W. J. *Balzac: An Interpretation of la Comédie Humaine*. New York: Random House, 1967.

Hunt, H. G. *Balzac's Comédie Humaine*. London: University of London Press, 1964.

James, Henry. "The Lesson of Balzac." In *Literary Criticism*, vol. 2. New York: Library of America, 1984.

Kanes, Martin. *Balzac's Comedy of Words*. Princeton, NJ: Princeton University Press, 1976.

Levin, Harry. "Balzac." In *The Gates of Horn*. New York: Oxford University Press, 1963.

Lucey, Michael. *The Misfit of the Family: Balzac and the Social Forms of Sexuality*. Durham, NC: Duke University Press, 2003.

Lukács, Georg. *Balzac et le réalisme français*. Translated by Paul Laveau. Paris: Maspéro, 1967.

Michon, Pierre. *Trois Auteurs*. Lagrasse: Verdier, 1997.

Proust, Marcel. "Le Balzac de M. de Guermantes." In *Contre Sainte-Beuve*. Paris: Bibliothèque de la Pléiade, 1971.

Pugh, Anthony. *Balzac's Recurring Characters*. Toronto: University of Toronto Press, 1974.

Taine, Hippolyte. "Balzac." In *Nouveaux essais de critique et d'histoire*. Paris: Hachette, 1866.

Tortonese, Paolo. "Le bourgeois de Balzac et la girafe de Lamarck. Distinction, imitation, habitude." In *Balzac, l'Invention de la sociologie*, edited by Andrea Del Lungo and Pierre Glaudes. Paris: Garnier, 2019.

Vachon, Stéphane. *Les Travaux et les jours d'Honoré de Balzac*. Saint-Denis: Presses Universitaires de Vincennes, 1992.

OTHER RELEVANT WORKS

Auerbach, Erich. *Mimesis*. Translated by Willard Trask. Princeton, NJ: Princeton University Press, 1963.

Benjamin, Walter. "The Storyteller," translated by Harry Zohn. In *Selected Writings*, vol. 3 (1935–38), edited by Howard Eiland and Michael W. Jennings. Cambridge, MA: Harvard University Press, 2002, 143–62.

Brooks, Peter. *The Melodramatic Imagination*. New Haven, CT: Yale University Press, 1976.

Chevalier, Louis. *Laboring Classes and Dangerous Classes.* Translated by Frank Jellinek. New York: Howard Fertig, 1975. In French, *Classes laborieuses et classes dangereuses.* Paris: Plon, 1958.

Dumasy, Lise, editor. *La Querelle du roman-feuilleton: Littérature, presse et politique, un débat précurseur (1836–1848).* Grenoble: ELLUG, Université Stendhal, 1999.

Gallagher, Catherine. "The Rise of Fictionality." In *The Novel,* edited by Franco Moretti. 2 vols. Princeton, NJ: Princeton University Press, 2006. 1: 336–63.

Lough, John. *Writer and Public in France.* Oxford: Clarendon, 1978.

Lyon-Caen, Judith. *La Lecture et la vie. Les Usages du roman au temps de Balzac.* Paris: Tallandier, 2006.

———. "Saisir, décrire, déchiffrer: les mises en texte du social sous la monarchie de Juillet." *Revue Historique* 306, no. 2 (2004): 303–31.

Piketty, Thomas. *Capital in the Twenty-First Century.* Translated by Arthur Goldhammer. Cambridge, MA: Harvard University Press, 2014.

Rosanvallon, Pierre. *Le Peuple introuvable. Histoire de la représentation démocratique en France.* Paris: Gallimard, 1998.

Sainte-Beuve, Charles Augustin. "De la littérature industrielle." *La Revue des Deux Mondes* (1839).

Schur, Max. *Freud: Living and Dying.* New York: International Universities Press, 1972.

Stowe, William W. *Balzac, James, and the Realistic Novel.* Princeton, NJ: Princeton University Press, 1983.

Thérenty, Marie-Ève. *La littérature au quotidien. Poétiques journalistiques au XIXe siècle.* Paris: Éditions du Seuil, 2016.

Vermeule, Blakey. *Why Do We Care About Literary Characters?* Baltimore, MD: Johns Hopkins University Press, 2009.

Watt, Ian. *The Rise of the Novel.* London: Chatto and Windus, 1958.

Werdet, Edmond. *De la librairie française, depuis les temps les plus reculés jusqu'à nos jours.* Paris: E. Dentu, 1860.

Zunshine, Lisa. *Why We Read Fiction: Theory of Mind and the Novel.* Columbus, OH: Ohio State University Press, 2006.

Chronology: France from the Revolution to 1850

	France	Balzac
1789	French Revolution begins	
1793	King Louis XVI executed	
1799	November: coup d'état of Napoléon Bonaparte	Born on May 20
1804	Napoleon crowned Emperor	Sent to school at Pension Leguay-Pinel, Tours
1807		Boarder at Collège de Vendôme
1814	April: Napoleon surrenders at Fontainebleau, exiled to Elba; first Restoration: King Louis XVIII grants the Charter (constitution) to his subjects	Autumn: family moves to Paris
1815	February–March: Napoleon escapes from Elba, rallies his armies; June: final defeat at Battle of Waterloo, exile to Saint-Helena; second Restoration: King Louis XVIII	
1816		Begins law studies; clerk to a solicitor

	France	Balzac
1819		Obtains law degree; starts writing tragedy, *Cromwell*
1821	Napoleon dies on Saint-Helena	
1822		Publishes first novels under pseudonyms
1824	King Louis XVIII dies	
1825	King Charles X crowned in the Cathedral of Reims	
1826		Acquires printshop
1828		Forced to liquidate and sell printshop and type foundry
1829		*Le dernier Chouan*, first novel signed as Balzac; *Physiologie du mariage*; *Scènes de la vie privée*
1830	July: French capture Alger and begin occupation of Algeria; Charles X issues "trois ordonnances," sparking July Revolution; Louis-Philippe d'Orléans becomes King; Charles X exiled to England	Active as journalist
1831		*La Peau de chagrin*
1832	Cholera outbreak in Paris; brutally repressed insurrection at funeral of General Lamarque	Receives first letter from "l'Etrangère" (Madame Evelina Hanska)
1833		*Louis Lambert*; *Le Médecin de campagne*; first meeting with Madame Hanska in Neuchâtel
1834		*Eugénie Grandet*; *La femme abandonnée*; *La Recherche de l'Absolu*; *La Femme de trente ans*

France	Balzac
1835	*Le Père Goriot* (publication begun in December 1834); purchases *La Chronique de Paris*
1836	*Le Lys dans la vallée*; in prison for a week for refusal to do National Guard duty; liquidation of *La Chronique de Paris*
1837	*Illusions perdues*, part 1; travels in Italy; *César Birotteau*
1838	Travels to Sardinia to reopen Roman silver mines; acquires Les Jardies, property in Paris suburbs
1839	*Béatrix*; becomes president of Société des Gens de Lettres
1840	*Vautrin* (play) banned by censors after two performances
1841	*Une ténébreuse affaire*; *Ursule Mirouët*; *Mémoires de deux jeunes mariées*
1842	"Avant-Propos" of *La Comédie humaine*
1843 Paris–Orleans and Paris–Rouen railway lines inaugurated	In St. Petersburg with Evelina Hanska
1844	*Modeste Mignon*; *Splendeurs et misères des courtisanes: Esther*
1845	Project for *La Comédie humaine* in 26 volumes, with 137 titles (will complete 91)

	France	Balzac
1846		*La Cousine Bette*
1847		*Le Cousin Pons*; Evelina Hanska in Paris incognito; in September, visits her estate in Wierzchownia, Ukraine
1848	February: revolution in Paris; King Louis-Philippe abdicates; Second Republic declared; June Days insurrection of Paris workers brutally suppressed; December: Louis-Napoléon Bonaparte elected president	Returns from Ukraine in time to witness sack of Tuileries Palace; then in Touraine
1849		Makes two unsuccessful attempts at election to Académie Française
1850		Marries Evelina Hanska in the Ukraine; returns to Paris, ill; dies August 18, buried in Père-Lachaise cemetery, funeral eulogy by Victor Hugo
1851	December coup d'état of Louis-Napoléon Bonaparte	
1852	December proclamation of Second Empire: Emperor Napoléon III	

Index

Abandoned Woman, The (*La femme abandonnée*), 26, 37, 174
Abber, Louise, 75
Abrantès, Duchesse d', 224
Adieu, 208–14
Adrien Genestas (*The Country Doctor*), 233
Aiglemont, Hélène d', 73
Albon, Marquis d', 209
Amélie. *See* Camusot, Amélie
Analytic Studies (*Études analytiques*). See under *Human Comedy, The*
Angoulême, Duc d', 155
Another Study of Womankind (*Autre étude de femme*), 208
Aquilina, 82–83, 89
Arabian Nights, The, 2, 80, 96, 113, 127, 196, 244n5
Archbishop of Paris, 135
Arthez, Daniel d', 110, 116–18, 128
Asie. *See* Collin, Jacqueline
Auberge rouge, L'. See *Red Inn, The*
Auerbach, Erich, 35; *Mimesis*, 35
Austen, Jane, 18, 221, 222
Autre étude de femme. See *Another Study of Womankind*

Balzac, Bernard François, 223
Bargeton, Louise de (née Marie-Louise Anaïs de Négrepelisse), 105–6, 114, 117, 120, 126, 133
Barthes, Roland, 222
Baudelaire, Charles, 87, 145, 177, 232–33
Baudraye, Dinah de la, 75
Beauséant, Vicomtesse Claire de, 13–14, 17, 19, 20, 22–23, 26–27, 29–30, 36, 37, 50, 56, 75
Béatrix, 242n4
Benassis, Dr., 233–34
Bérénice, 118
Berny, Laure de, 224, 245n4
Bette, Cousin (Lisbeth Fischer), 153
Bianca, 198–99
Bianchon, Horace, 6, 24, 30, 36, 37, 39, 93, 95, 143
Bibi-Lupin, 141, 143, 146, 147, 151, 152
Bixiou, Jean-Jacques, 36, 51, 82, 134
Black Sheep, The (*La Rabouilleuse*), 190
Blamont-Chauvry, Princesse de, 67
Blondet, Émile, 36, 108, 112
Blücher, General, 107–8, 109
Bonaparte, Napoleon. *See* Napoleon Bonaparte
Born, Comte de, 40, 49
Boulanger, Louis, 225

Boutin, 181–82
Brandon, Lady, 29–30
Bruner, Jerome, 182
Buloz, François, 125
Buret, Eugène, 35; *La Misère des classes laborieuses en France et en Angleterre*, 35
Butor, Michel, 8

Cabinet des antiques, Le. See *Collection of Antiquities, The*
Cadignan, Princesse de, 1. *See also* Maufrigneuse, Diane de
Calvi, Théodore, 37, 147–48, 149, 151, 152
Camusot (*Lost Illusions*), 111, 118
Camusot, Amélie, 141, 148–49
Camusot de Marville, 140–44, 146, 148, 149, 150
Canalis, Melchior de, 7
Cardot, 89
Castries, Marquise (later Duchesse) de, 8
Chabert, Colonel Hyacinthe, 179–94, 212; wife: Chapotel, Rose (Comtesse Chabert, later Comtesse Ferraud), 180, 181, 182–86, 188, 189
Chapuys-Montlaville, Baron, 128–30
Charles X, King, 3, 115, 118
Chasles, Philarète, 98, 243n6
Châtelet, Sixte du, 133
Chef-d'oeuvre inconnu, Le. See *Unknown Masterpiece, The*
Chessel, Monsieur de, 157, 162
Chouans, The (*Les Chouans*), 223
Chrestien, Michel, 118
Christophe, 30
Cimarosa, 85
Cinq-Cygne, Laurence de, 76

Claës, Balthasar, 153, 193, 197, 216, 228
Cointet Brothers, 119, 120
Collection of Antiquities, The (*Le Cabinet des antiques*), 140–41
Collin, Jacques, 25, 36, 52, 64, 87, 126–27, 130, 131–54, 178, 193, 196, 212–13, 216–17, 231. *See also* Herrera, Carlos; Vautrin
Collin, Jacqueline (Asie), 140, 149
Colonel Chabert (*Le Colonel Chabert*), 179–94, 212, 214
Comte, Auguste, 34
Contenson, 136, 138, 139
Contrat de mariage, Le. See *Marriage Contract, The*
Cooper, James Fenimore, 223
Coralie, 111, 113, 114, 117, 118, 143
Corentin, 136, 138, 150
Country Doctor, The (*Le Médecin de campagne*), 233
Cousin Bette, 153, 227
Cousin Pons, 190
Cursy, Raoul de, 82

Dante Alighieri, 197, 233, 234, 236
Daughter of Eve, A (*Une Fille d'Ève*), 36–37, 177
Dauriat, 111–12
Decameron, The (Boccaccio), 2
Delbecq, 183, 185–86
Dernier des Chouans, Le. See *Chouans, The*
Derville, 37, 39–49, 52–53, 139, 179–92, 246n3
Desroches, 82, 191
Dickens, Charles, 117, 217
Diderot, Denis, 113; *Paradox of the Actor*, 113
Dominis, Abbé de, 168

Duchesse de Langeais, The (*La Duchesse de Langeais*). See under *Story of the Thirteen*
Dudley, Lady Arabella, 166–68, 170, 171, 173, 174
Dudley, Lord, 226
Dumas, Alexandre, 11, 123, 217

Eliot, George, 222
Émile (*The Fatal Skin*), 82–83, 87–90, 99, 101
Empedocles of Agrigentum, 102
Employees, The (*Les Employés*), 193
Esgrignon, Victurnien d', 140
Espard, Marquise Anthénaïs d', 75, 106–7, 114, 115, 141, 148
Étude de moeurs par les gants. See *Study of Manners by Way of Gloves, A*
Euphrasie, 82–83, 89

Facino Cane, 195–214, 223, 235
Facino Cane, Marco, 195, 197–202, 207–8, 211
Fatal Skin, The (*La Peau de chagrin*), 12, 41, 76, 78–103
Femme abandonnée, La. See *Abandoned Woman, The*
Femme de trente ans, La. See *Woman of Thirty, A*
Fendant and Cavalier, 117
Ferdinand VII, King, 57
Ferragus. See under *Story of the Thirteen*
Ferraud, Comte, 180
Fil-de-Soie (Silk Thread), 146, 148
Fille aux yeux d'or, La. See under *Story of the Thirteen*
Fille d'Ève, Une. See *Daughter of Eve, A*
Flaubert, Gustave, 73; *Madame Bovary*, 73

Fœdora, Comtesse, 84–87, 88, 91, 92, 100, 101, 217, 227
Fourier, Charles, 233
Franchessini, Colonel, 30, 132, 152
Frenhofer, 9, 153, 193, 197, 216, 228–29, 230, 235
Fresnay, Maria du, 224
Freud, Sigmund, 34, 44, 46, 56, 78, 84, 85, 86, 102, 165, 172, 204, 206, 207, 208, 217, 228, 247–48n9; *Analysis Terminable and Interminable*, 102; *Beyond the Pleasure Principle*, 78, 102; *Psychopathology of Everyday Life, The*, 34, 204

Gall, Franz Joseph, 35
Gambara, 153, 193, 197, 229
Gigonnet, 42
Girardin, Émile de, 109
Giraud, Léon, 118
Girl with the Golden Eyes, The (*La Fille aux yeux d'or*). See under *Story of the Thirteen*
Girodet, Anne-Louis, 76
Gobseck, 18, 28, 37, 39–51, 190, 200
Gobseck, 15, 16, 18, 28, 37, 38–54, 80, 94, 139, 140, 217, 218, 227, 231; grandniece: Sarah (La Belle Hollandaise), 47; great-grandniece: Esther (La Torpille), 47
Godeschal, 187–88, 190–91
Goffman, Erving, 222
Grandlieu, Clotilde de, 130, 135, 139–40, 143, 148, 173
Grandlieu, Duc de, 49, 135, 138, 149
Grandlieu, Duchesse de, 148
Grandlieu, Vicomtesse de, 39–40, 42, 43, 47, 49–50; daughter:

Camille de Grandlieu, 39–40, 43, 47, 49–50, 53
Granville, Comte de, 141, 144, 149, 150, 152
Granville, Marie-Angélique de, 176
Guidoboni-Visconti, Countess Sarah, 224

Hanska, Evelina, 4, 202, 223, 224–25
Harlot High and Low, A (*Splendeurs et misères des courtisanes*), 25, 37, 47, 51–53, 127, 130, 131–52
Hauteserre, Adrien de, 77
Herrera, Carlos, 51–52, 126–27, 131, 134, 136, 138, 140, 141, 145, 147, 149, 151. *See also* Collin, Jacques; Vautrin
Histoire des Treize. See *Story of the Thirteen*
Homer, 51, 197
Horace, 172
House of Nucingen, The (*La Maison Nucingen*), 32, 36
Hugo, Victor, 111, 147, 152; *Les Misérables*, 147, 152
Hulot, Baron, 227–28; wife: Adeline, 227
Human Comedy, The, 2–9, 12, 18, 28, 32, 37, 38, 39, 50, 53, 69, 74, 77, 82, 97, 105, 113, 124, 131–32, 151, 153, 154, 156, 176, 178, 179, 180, 190–91, 193, 197, 203, 205, 226–29, 232–33, 235–36; Analytic Studies (*Études analytiques*), 97, 203; Philosophical Studies (*Études philosophiques*), 97, 192, 203; Studies of Manners (*Études de moeurs*), 97, 203

Illusions perdues. See *Lost Illusions*

James, Henry, 4–5, 6, 8–9, 35–36, 120, 177, 213–14, 222, 241
James, William, 5
Japhet, 92
Jonathas, 90
Justine, 86

Lamartine, Alphonse de, 7
Lambert, Louis, 8–9, 28, 153, 193, 197, 212, 229–31, 232, 235
Langeais, Duc de, 60
Langeais, Duchesse Antoinette de (Sister Theresa, née Antoinette de Navarreins), 19, 37, 55–77, 156, 172, 212, 217
Last of the Chouans, The (*Le Dernier des Chouans*). See *Chouans, The*
Lavater, Kaspar, 35
Lavrille, 92
Lenoncourt, Duchesse de, 159
Lenoncourt-Chaulieu Duchesse de, 140, 173. *See also* Mortsauf, Madeleine de
Lily of the Valley, The (*Le Lys dans la vallée*), 66, 74–75, 125, 156, 173, 174–75, 176, 177, 178, 200, 202, 212, 214
Little Miseries of Conjugal Life. See *Petty Troubles of Married Life*
Local Muse, The (*La Muse du département*), 75
Lost Illusions (*Illusions perdues*), 22, 37, 59, 82, 104–30, 131, 132, 177, 212, 216–17
Louis XVI, King, 28, 123
Louis XVIII, King, 115, 162, 194
Louis Lambert, 229–31. *See also* Lambert, Louis
Louis-Philippe d'Orléans, King of the French, 3, 23

Lousteau, Etienne, 51, 107, 109,
111–12, 116, 117, 128
Lukács, Georg, 117, 213
Lupeaulx, des, 134
Lydie, 138–39
Lys dans la vallée, Le. See *Lily of the
Valley, The*

Maison Nucingen, La. See *House of
Nucingen, The*
Malvaut, Fanny, 41, 53
Manerville, Comte Paul de, 36,
Manerville, Natalie de, 156–57,
175–77; mother: Madame
Evangelista, 177
Marcillac, 17
Marneffe, Valérie, 153
*Marriage Contract, The (Le Contrat de
mariage),* 176–77
Marsay, Henri de, 23, 36, 62, 69, 72,
106–7, 135, 177, 205, 226
Maufrigneuse, Diane de, 135, 140,
141, 144, 148
Médecin de campagne, Le. See *Country
Doctor, The*
Mémoires de deux jeunes mariées.
See *Memoirs of Two Young
Wives, The*
*Memoirs of Two Young Wives, The
(Mémoires de deux jeunes mariées),*
174–75
Merlin, Hector, 112
Metsu, 40
Metternich, Prince, 224
Michonneau, Mlle (Madame
Poiret), 13, 25, 35, 143
Molière, 49
Montalembert, Comte de, 97
Montriveau, Marquis and General
Armand de, 56–71, 77, 217

Mortsauf, Blanche Henriette de,
155–78, 195, 212
Mortsauf, Comte de, 157–62,
164–65
Mortsauf, Jacques, 157, 165, 167
Mortsauf, Madeleine de, 140, 157,
165, 167, 171, 173
*Murky Business, A (Une ténébreuse
affaire),* 76–77
Muse du département, La. See *Local
Muse, The*

Napoleon Bonaparte, 3, 4, 19, 33, 58,
59, 60, 72, 76, 107, 147, 152, 162, 178,
179, 180, 181, 187, 188, 189, 191, 200,
209, 212
Napoleon III (Louis-Napoléon
Bonaparte), 187
Nathan, Raoul, 36, 109, 111–12, 113,
176, 177
Navarreins, Duc de, 83
*New Theory of the Luncheon (Nouvelle
théorie du déjeuner),* 33
Nouvelle théorie du déjeuner. See *New
Theory of the Luncheon*
Nucingen, Baron de, 18, 19, 26, 31,
52–53, 113, 124, 130, 134–40, 145,
151, 152
Nucingen and Co., Bankers. See *House
of Nucingen, The*
Nucingen, Delphine de, 18, 22–30,
32, 36, 62, 87

O'Flaharty, Major, 89
Old Maid, The (La Vieille Fille), 109
Origen, 90, 103

Pamiers, Vidame de, 67
Parent-Duchatelet, A. B., 35; *De la
prostitution dans la ville de Paris,* 35

Passion dans le désert, Une. See *Passion in the Desert, A*

Passion in the Desert, A (*Une Passion dans le désert*), 8, 72, 178, 227

Pathologie de la vie sociale. See *Pathology of Social Life*

Pathology of Social Life (*Pathologie de la vie sociale*), 34, 204, 206–7

Pauline (*The Fatal Skin*), 84–85, 91–96, 99

Peau de chagrin, La. See *Fatal Skin, The*

Pelissier, Olympe, 224

Père Goriot (*Le Père Goriot*), 11–37, 38–39, 42, 44, 47, 56, 64, 82, 87, 98, 123, 126, 131–32, 141–42, 147, 190, 216

Petit-Claude, 120

Petites misères de la vie conjugale. See *Petty Troubles of Married Life*

Petty Troubles of Married Life (*Petites misères de la vie conjugale*), 174, 203

Peyrade, 136, 138

Philosophical Studies (*Études philosophiques*). See under *Human Comedy, The*

Physiologie du cigare. See *Physiology of the Cigar*

Physiologie du marriage. See *Physiology of Marriage*

Physiology of Marriage (*Physiologie du mariage*), 74, 174, 203, 224

Physiology of the Cigar (*Physiologie du cigare*), 33

Piketty, Thomas, 21

Pinel, Philippe, 211, 248n12

Planchette, 92

Poiret, Madame. *See* Michonneau, Mlle

Poiret, Monsieur, 13, 22, 25, 35

Porbus, Frans, 228–29

Pourriquet, 90

Poussin, Nicolas, 228

Proscribed, The (*Les Proscrits*), 234

Proscrits, Les. See *Proscribed, The*

Proust, Marcel, 5, 7, 72, 87, 126, 161, 215, 218–21

Provincial Muse, The. See *Local Muse, The*

Rabelais, 147

Rabouilleuse, La. See *Black Sheep, The*

Rabourdin, 193

Raphael, 79

Rastignac, Comtesse de Augusta, 23

Rastignac, Eugène de (Massiac), 11–37, 50, 56, 72, 74, 82, 84–85, 87–88, 107, 123, 131, 132, 133–34, 143, 144, 151, 152, 183, 205, 212, 216, 217, 221, 233

Recherche de l'Absolu, La. See *Search for the Absolute, The*

Red Inn, The (*L'Auberge rouge*), 21, 82

Rembrandt, 40

Restaud, Comte de, 19, 31, 39, 43–47

Restaud, Comte Ernest de, 39, 43–47, 49–50, 53

Restaud, Comtesse Anastasie de, 14–18, 20, 27, 29, 36, 38–39, 41–47, 50

Richardson, Samuel, 74

Rivette, Jacques, 229, 241n1

Ronquerolles, Marquis de, 62, 69–71

Rosanvallon, Pierre, 34, 123

Rossini, 85

Rousseau, Jean-Jacques, 24, 25, 84, 93, 129, 132, 152, 160, 235; *Discourse on the Origin of Inequality,*

132; *Julie, or the New Heloise*, 93, 160

Rubempré, Marquis Chardon de (Lucien Chardon), 22, 36, 37, 51, 72, 76, 104–30, 132, 133, 141, 142, 205, 216

Sade, Marquis de, 86

Sainte-Beuve, Charles Augustin, 74, 122–23, 125, 128, 175; "On Industrial Literature," 122–23; *Volupté*, 175

Sallambier, Laure, 223

Sand, George, 111, 217, 224, 242

Sandeau, Jules, 8, 224

San-Réal, Marquise de, 72, 226–27

Sarrasine, 76, 202

Scenes of Private Life (*Scènes de la vie privée*), 224

Schur, Max, 102

Scott, Walter, 192

Search for the Absolute, The (*La Recherche de l'Absolu*), 8, 153, 228

Séchard, David, 52–53, 106, 119–20, 145

Séchard, Eve, 52–53, 145

Séchard, Jérôme-Nicholas, 120, 121

Séraphîta, 230

Sérizy, Comtesse Léontine de, 63, 66, 134, 135, 144, 145, 148, 151

Simeuse, Paul-Marie and Marie-Paul, 76–77

Splendeurs et misères des courtisanes. See *Harlot High and Low, A*

Sterne, Laurence, 97; *Tristram Shandy*, 97

Stevens, Wallace, 218

Story of the Thirteen (*Histoire des Treize*), 34, 62, 72, 206; *Duchesse*

de Langeais, The, 55–73, 86, 115, 156, 172, 174, 212, 214, 217; *Ferragus*, 33–34, 62, 206; *Girl with the Golden Eyes, The* (*La Fille aux yeux d'or*), 62, 72, 76, 226–27

Strachey, James, 56, 241n2

Studies of Manners (*Études de moeurs*). See under *Human Comedy, The*

Study of Manners by Way of Gloves, A (*Étude de moeurs par les gants*), 33, 205

Sucy, Colonel Philippe de, 209

Sue, Eugène, 129, 133, 217; *The Mysteries of Paris* (*Les Mystères de Paris*), 129, 133, 245n2

Swedenborg, Emanuel, 230

Taillefer, Frédéric, 21, 24, 30, 132

Taillefer, Jean-Frédéric, 21, 82

Taillefer, Victorine, 13, 21, 24–26, 82

Taine, Hippolyte, 124

Talleyrand, Charles Maurice, 58

Ténébreuse affaire, Une. See *Murky Business, A*

Théorie de la démarche. See *Theory of Movement*

Theory of Movement (*Théorie de la démarche*), 34, 204, 206–7, 213

Titian, 198

Touches, Félicité des, 2

Trailles, Maxime de, 17, 18, 27, 38–39, 42

Traité de la vie élégante. See *Treatise on Elegant Living*

Traité des excitants modernes. See *Treatise of Modern Stimulants*

Treatise of Modern Stimulants (*Traité des excitants modernes*), 34, 204

Treatise on Elegant Living (*Traité de la vie élégante*), 33, 34, 204, 205

Unknown Masterpiece, The (*Le Chef-d'oeuvre inconnu*), 153, 228–29
Ursule Mirouët, 190

Valdès, Paquita, 72, 226
Valentin, Marquis Raphaël de, 78–103, 107, 191, 217, 227, 230, 232
Val-Noble, Suzanne du, 139, 244n5
Vandenesse, Félix de, 74, 155
Vandières, Comtesse Stéphanie de, 209
Vauquer, Madame, 13, 35
Vautrin, 11–16, 19–27, 29–33, 36–38, 47, 51, 52, 64, 72, 82, 126, 130, 131,

133, 146, 190, 212, 216. *See also* Collin, Jacques; Herrera, Carlos
Vernou, Félicien, 112
Vidocq, Eugène François, 152
Vieille Fille, La. See *Old Maid, The*
Vignon, Claude, 108, 115, 129
Villenoix, Pauline de, 230–31
Villiers de l'Isle-Adam, 93
Virgil, 213, 247–48n9

Warhol, Andy, 122
Watt, Ian, 74
Werbrust, 42
Werdet, Edmond, 124
Wilde, Oscar, 1, 145, 215
Woman of Thirty, A (*La Femme de trente ans*), 73, 74, 174
Wormeley, Katherine Prescott, 5

PETER BROOKS has been teaching and writing about Honoré de Balzac for many years. Among his books are the nonfiction volumes *The Melodramatic Imagination*, *Reading for the Plot*, *Psychoanalysis and Storytelling*, *Troubling Confessions*, *Realist Vision*, *Henry James Goes to Paris*, and *Flaubert in the Ruins of Paris*, as well as two novels, *World Elsewhere* and *The Emperor's Body*. In 2014 Brooks edited a collection of Balzac's stories for New York Review Books, *The Human Comedy: Selected Stories*. He is the Sterling Professor Emeritus of Comparative Literature at Yale.